The Logic of Humanitarian Arms Control and Disarmament

The Logic of Humanitarian Arms Control and Disarmament

A Power-Analytical Approach

Nik Hynek and Anzhelika Solovyeva

ROWMAN & LITTLEFIELD
Lanham • Boulder • New York • London

Published by Rowman & Littlefield
An imprint of The Rowman & Littlefield Publishing Group, Inc.
4501 Forbes Boulevard, Suite 200, Lanham, Maryland 20706
www.rowman.com

6 Tinworth Street, London SE11 5AL, United Kingdom

British Library Cataloguing in Publication Information Available

Library of Congress Cataloging-in-Publication Data

Names: Hynek, Nik, author. | Solovyeva, Anzhelika, 1994- author.
Title: The logic of humanitarian arms control and disarmament : a power-analytical approach / Nik
    Hynek and Anzhelika Solovyeva.
Description: New York : Rowman & Littlefield Publishing Group, 2020. | Includes bibliographical
    references and index. | Summary: "This novel and original book examines and disaggregates,
    theoretically and empirically, operations of power in international security regimes"--Provided
    by publisher.
Identifiers: LCCN 2020033391 (print) | LCCN 2020033392 (ebook) | ISBN 9781786611659 (Cloth :
    acid-free paper) | ISBN 9781786611666 (ePub) | ISBN 9781538149874 (pbk)
Subjects: LCSH: Arms control. | Disarmament. | Security, International. | Diplomacy--History. |
    Nuclear arms control. | Nuclear disarmament.
Classification: LCC JZ5625 .H96 2020 (print) | LCC JZ5625 (ebook) | DDC 327.1/74--dc23
LC record available at https://lccn.loc.gov/2020033391
LC ebook record available at https://lccn.loc.gov/2020033392

Nik Hynek gratefully acknowledges funding for this work from Metropolitan University Prague C4SS VVZ 74-04. Anzhelika Solovyeva gratefully acknowledges funding for this work from Charles University in Prague, UNCE Human-Machine Nexus and Its Implications for International Order (UNCE/HUM/037).

Contents

Acknowledgments

The preparation of this manuscript was undertaken with financial support from two research grants. Nik Hynek gratefully acknowledges funding for this work from Metropolitan University Prague C4SS VVZ 74-04. Anzhelika Solovyeva gratefully acknowledges funding for this work from Charles University in Prague, UNCE Human-Machine Nexus and Its Implications for International Order (UNCE/HUM/037). Also, we would like to express our warmest thanks to Professor Robert Jervis, Professor Keith Krause, and Dr. Mike Bourne for their invaluable comments on earlier versions of elements of this manuscript, as well as their trust in our research. The book would have been poorer without the comments of four anonymous readers whose challenges and insights we gratefully acknowledge too. We owe a special debt to Xing Su for kindly proofreading the entire manuscript. We would also like to acknowledge that chapter 1 builds on Nik Hynek "Theorizing International Security Regimes: A Power-Analytical Approach," *International Politics* 55 (2018): 352–68, and Nik Hynek, "Regime Theory as IR Theory: Reflection on Three Waves of 'Isms,'" *Central European Journal of International and Security Studies* 11, no. 1 (2017): 11–30; and an earlier version of chapter 3 was previously published as Nik Hynek, "Re-visioning Morality and Progress in the Security Domain: Insights from Humanitarian Prohibition Politics," *International Politics* 55 (2018): 421–40. Finally, we wish to thank our families for their long-standing support and encouragement of our academic endeavors.

Introduction

This book examines and disaggregates, theoretically and empirically, operations of power in international security regimes appertaining to humanitarian arms control and disarmament. The goal is to grasp *the logic* underlying the general historical pattern of stigmatization and regulation/proscription of various weapons and weapons-related practices on humanitarian grounds. Such regimes, varying in degree from regulatory to prohibitory, are understood as sets of normative discourses, political structures and dependencies (anarchies, hierarchies, and heterarchies), and agencies through which power operates within a given security issue area with a regulatory effect. In International Relations (IR), regime analysis has been dominated by several generations of regime theory/theorization. As this book makes clear, not only has the IR Regime Theory been of limited utility for the security domain due to its heavy focus on economic and environmental regimes, but it too heuristically suffered from its rigid pegging to general IR Theory. As the initial discussion in the theory chapter shows, it is not surprising then that the evolution of IR Regime Theory has largely been mirroring the evolution of IR Theory in general: from the neorealist/neoliberal institutionalist convergence regime theory through cognitivism to critical constructivist/poststructural regime theorization.

The commitment of this book is to remedy this situation by bringing together robust power analysis and international security regimes. It provides the reader with a theoretically and empirically uncompromising and comprehensive analysis of the selected international security regimes, which goes beyond any one school of IR Regime Theory. In doing so, it completely abandons existing, and piecemeal, analyses of regimes within the intellectual field of IR based on conventional grand/mid-range theorization. Instead it opts for theoretical eclecticism, which is shown to be vital for a comprehensive analysis of security regimes. The role of a theoretically organizing and uniting device is served by what is termed here the *power-analytical approach*. It utilizes four types of powers—productive, structural, institutional, and compulsory—and further expands existing scholarship theoretically. Indeed, advantages of power analysis for the security domain are highlighted and systematically shown. The power-analytical approach allows, inter alia, studying structurationist (that is, not only structural) processes of coconstitution and coproduction in and around those regimes. This is exactly the dynamics that traditional agent-based, regime-theory explanations fail to see and examine. In concrete terms, the power-analytical approach focuses on specific renderings of discourses and heterarchies related to such regimes: it tackles the question of how they establish channels through which sociopolitical and economic privileges get distributed, how they create structural relations among actors with a possibility of their reversal or rearticulation, and finally how they build up, challenge, and relocate walls of legal obligations.

International regulatory/prohibitory regimes and/or their considerations have often been framed in broad, normative terms. This has led many analysts to maintain that "Moral IR" has been on a steady rise. One of the key advantages of the power-analytical approach to humanitarian arms control and disarmament regimes—and one of the key objectives of this book—lies in its cautious analytical and theoretical resistance to progressivism and universalizing liberal thinking. As the book makes clear, manipulation of ethical categories and discourses happens for various purposes, sometimes contradictory ones, and often others than the seeming humanitarianism. For these reasons, we strongly prefer to term such regimes (international) "security regimes" rather than "human security/ humanitarian regimes." At the same time, the book orients itself on "humanitarian disarmament" regimes because it is in this domain where it is most interesting to show the naïve optimism of many commentators on "Moral IR" within their "home turf."

Specifically, this book brings together and transcends three previously discrete subfields: general IR Regime Theory literature (IRRT), Analyses of Security Regimes (ASR), and theoretical literature on power. This is the edifice defining the theoretical originality and novelty of the book. What follows is a brief overview of relevant literature to various parts of this project. In the following chapters, this discussion is further particularized and nuanced. In regards of IRRT, the existing book-length contribution having a particular theoretical utility for this book project is that written by Hasenclever, Mayer, and Rittberger titled *Theories of International Regimes* (1997). It focuses on an intellectual critique of the neorealist/neoliberal institutionalist IRRT and offers what is seen as a stronger alternative, cognitivist/thin constructivist reconstruction of IRRT. This theory-only book concludes with identification of four areas where no version of IRRT (including theirs) has been capable of making a strong contribution: power of legitimacy, narrative structures, identity-related binary separations, and conditions of possibility for emergence and transformations of historical orders. All four areas are made central and tackled by this proposed book. What Hasenclever, Mayer, and Rittberger complained about in 1997 can still be echoed in 2020. Two single–case study exceptions have been Nina Tannenwald's *The Nuclear Taboo* published by Cambridge University Press in 2007 and Richard Price's *Chemical Weapons Taboo* published in 1997 by Cornell University Press. While these have been groundbreaking books, they neither focused on the empirical material proposed here (Tannenwald focuses on domestic US discourses and practices) nor did they claim primary contribution to IRRT. The best article-length piece falling to this body of literature is still Robert Jervis's "Security Regimes" (1982) published in *International Organization*.

When it comes to ASR literature (apart from Jervis, Price, and Tannenwald, who all fall under this category too), there has been an edited volume produced by Harald Müller and Carmen Wunderlich titled *Norm Dynamics in Multilateral Arms Control: Interests, Conflicts and Justice* (2013). This is an interesting contribution that brings together a group of predominantly German scholars with a background in norm dynamics/regime conflicts nexus. Unlike the proposed book, it primarily focuses on agency and specific (types) of actors, so its general approach is different. The second interesting specimen of ASR is Denise Garcia's *Disarmament Diplomacy and Human Security: Regimes, Norms and Moral Progress in International Relations* published by Routledge in 2011. Garcia's previous book was on small arms and light weapons (*Small Arms and Security* published by Routledge in 2008). Her 2011 book broadens the focus from small arms to the Arms Trade Treaty and cluster munitions. While erudite and relevant, we challenge Garcia's vision of "moral international politics," "Moral IR" (as a field), and progressivist reading of humanitarian disarmament in this book. Still more, there has been a cardinal if older contribution by Keith Krause: *Arms and the State: Patterns of Military Production and Trade* (1995) published by Cambridge University Press. While this book is about arms production and transfers, it contextually touches on all three literatures while remaining differently focused (theoretically and empirically) from this book. It features security regimes discussion and theorization (in relation to technological diffusion and its limits), as well as power analysis aimed at uncovering structural asymmetries and dependencies (three qualitative tiers of states). Krause's more recent move (his journal articles) toward critical security analysis and related theorization remains important inspiration for this book too.

The third cluster features books related to power analysis. There has been no existing book that would get close to the power-analytical approach introduced here. It should be noted that this approach has built and further elaborated on the scholarship analyzing the concept of power as introduced by Barnett and Duvall (2005) and Guzzini (1993). In further reinforcement of the power-analytical approach, several books—none of which focused on the issue area under discussion as microscopically as here—are utilized: Foucault's *Power/Knowledge: Selected Interviews and Other Writings 1972–1977* (1980); Deleuze and Guattari's *Anti-Oedipus: Capitalism and Schizophrenia* (1983) and *A Thousand Plateaus: Capitalism and Schizophrenia* (1987); Lukes's *Power: A Radical View* (1974); Clegg, Courpasson, and Phillips's *Power and Organizations* (2006); and Cox's *Production Power and World Order: Social Forces in the Making of History* (1987).

The critical theoretical efforts as performed in this book are to disaggregate the concept of "power," its workings, and make it relevant for and connected to humanitarian arms control and disarmament regimes. In terms of research strategy, the four-dimensional analysis of power is utilized as the key analytical grid for the book. The power matrix allows for standardization and comparability among/across cases and the resulting multifaceted analysis of regime formation, workings, and their effects. Meta-theoretically and methodologically distinct types of power deserve further elaboration and specification. For this reason we focus on a more detailed theoretical elaboration of the four dimensions, to methodology in one direction and to more general metatheory/philosophy in the other. Specifically, we pay attention to theoretical underpinnings of the four: critical constructivism/poststructuralism for productive power, Marxism for structural power, liberalism for institutional power, and realism for compulsory power. We show how each of the four underpinning theoretical schools leaves its footprints in empirical chapters. Also, the notion of the "regime" is properly examined. In addition to a temporal outline of the generations of regime theory, we scrutinize theoretical positions in and methodological approaches to the wider terrain of regime theorization. This research strategy is informed by the interest in finding out how and why the four theoretical positions cohere and interrelate, especially along the lines of poststructuralism/critical constructivism-Marxism (a structural interplay between the production of civilizational/normative narratives and exploitation of structural disparities and loopholes in the international security system) and liberalism-realism (agent-based great power politics interplay with other states, international organizations [IOs], and NGOs). We believe this is crucial to produce a more robust, coherent, and theoretically eclectic power-analysis of humanitarian arms control and disarmament regimes we analyze in this book.

Empirically, we offer five cases where we deploy the power-analytical approach. The chosen research design is comparative and interpretative, whereby we also show how operations of different power configurations may be tightly intertwined in practice and thus jointly analyzed. We are initially interested in analyzing longue durée linkages and historic-structural conditions of possibility for contemporary humanitarian arms control and disarmament regimes. For these reasons, the book begins with a power analysis of the nineteenth-century composite regime. Here, through a joint investigation of structural and compulsory power displays, we illustrate how power hierarchies may be dynamic in the face of military power prevalence and its rampant exercises (arms races, great power wars, colonial warfare, etc.). What follows is a power-analytical reading of four contemporary international security regimes involving humanitarian-disarmament efforts. For starters, we focus on a "dual" case study of two successful bans concerning distinct and well-defined types of conventional weapons, namely antipersonnel landmines (APLs) and cluster munitions (CMs) respectively. As we show, it bears notable traits of the continuation of the nineteenth-century humanitarian arms control and disarmament. This chapter in turn sheds light on how compulsory and institutional power configurations may operate in a strong nexus. The selected analytical strategy is seen as particularly suitable for addressing this case since the creation of both regimes was deeply immersed in coalitions of like-minded countries, exercises of power outside of the United Nations (UN) system, and workings of informal institutions. The next chapter is dedicated to small arms and light weapons (SALW). On balance, this is an important case showing what happens when broader-based stigmatization of an entire composite class within the ambit of conventional weapons has been unsuccessful. We feature it due to these attempts and to show how arms control regulatory efforts have shifted from the focus on the category itself to its flows and trade. Also echoing the nineteenth-century humanitarian arms control and disarmament, it embodies a still rare exemplar of how a weapons-related practice, not a tool, may be ultimately stigmatized. This all is epitomized by the campaign resulting in the Arms Trade Treaty (ATT), which is analyzed here too. Considering the relative dynamism in SALW power hierarchies maintained through regular interactions (commercial and strategic arms deals, licenses and production rights, even coercive force and violence, etc.), a deep convergence between the workings of structural and compulsory power is analytically captured again. The next case put under the microscope represents the "hard case" of humanitarian disarmament efforts. The power-analytical approach is deployed to study the power configuration attempting to establish a formalized nuclear nonuse regime. Here, we pay attention to an ostensible aim of the transnational advocacy network and like-minded states wishing to see complete, and global, nuclear disarmament. This case is also interesting from a comparative perspective because it exemplifies how broad-based stigmatization of an entire weapons category has been successful informally but never put on a sound legal footing and spilled over to disarmament. Finally, we have decided to provide the reader with a detailed perspective on one of the most vibrant issues of contemporary and surely future humanitarian arms control and disarmament: autonomous weapons involving the utilization of Artificial Intelligence. These weapons, usually (and as we show problematically) referred to as Killer Robots, have seen an unprecedented rise of not only the advocacy bloc but especially of scientists. We attempt to provide the reader with a multiperspectival, theoretically informed analysis showing the workings of such activities and counter-practices/interests. This case is interesting to consider also because it clearly depicts how stigmatization, targeting a particular practice in the first place, by definition falls to an entire group of weapons in the conventional realm. Both of the latter cases are addressed through a fully fledged analysis of the four power configurations, each in its own courtyard. This is because both have still relied upon traditional institutional loci, as well as epitomized global structures of relatively invariant distribution of military power regardless of direct interactions (the exclusive nuclear club and well-defined partners in deterrence and autonomous weapons still in development). What follows is the conclusion that features a comparison of the examined cases and highlights main empirical findings. Subsequently, they are taken back to theory considerations and carefully generalized to serve as a benchmark for other empirical material.

The structure of the book is as follows. Chapter 1 is devoted to a thorough explanation of regime theorization in IR as well as to tracing the evolution route of the scholarship. Building on this, it eventually seeks to develop a novel conceptualization of international security regimes through introducing the power-analytical approach and explaining the rationale for theoretical eclecticism and analysis of different operations of power in security regimes. In particular, the chapter opens with a detailed scrutiny of the significance of regime theorization for this project, as well as for the fields of International Relations and International Security. It shows how regime theorization has evolved as an integral part of IR theory, with all its consequences and limits. While this may not be surprising given that regime theory has been a standard occupier of IR theoretical space, not much has been systematically written on both evolutionary qualities of regime theory as such, and its changing yet strong pegging to IR theories and approaches. First, the chapter discusses existing IR theorization of regimes, which has coalesced around three specific "waves" of regimes theorization: the neo-neoconvergence regime theory, cognitivism, and radical constructivism/poststructuralism. Second, it assesses the heuristic utility of the three waves of regime theorization in relation to possible domains of empirical application. Finally, this chapter paves the way for the next one by displaying the limits and blinds spots of existing regime theorization in relation to the key concept of this book: power and its operations. Based on this, it makes a strong case for and seeks to develop a novel conceptualization of international security regimes. It answers a question of how to strike a balance between theoretical eclecticism, which is believed to be vital for a comprehensive analysis of security regimes, and the need to have a uniting device to organize such research. It is for these reasons that a power-analytical approach utilizing four types of powers — productive, structural, institutional, and compulsory — is used and its advantages for regime analysis are flagged. The value added of such an advancement lies in international security regimes being understood more plastically than through conventional lenses. Specifically, they are approached as intertwined sets of normative discourses, political structures (anarchies, hierarchies, and heterarchies), and agencies through which power operates within a given security issue area with a regulatory effect. Specific renderings of discourses and hete-rarchies establish channels through which sociopolitical and economic privileges are distributed, they create structural relations among actors with a possibility of their reversal or rearticulation, and they build up, challenge, and relocate walls of legal obligations.

The five subsequent chapters are devoted to empirical cases, with multiple parallels drawn in a comparative and contrasting manner among the selected cases of weapons security regulation and beyond. Chapter 2 examines operations of power, which enabled the emergence of humanitarian disarmament campaigns, related politics, and the conse-quent establishment of the nineteenth-century humanitarian arms control and disarmament composite regime. It begins by showing the impor-tance of productive power in the constitution of horizons of possibility for humanitarian disarmament, especially through broad, ethically an-chored disarmament discourses. However, it also shows politico-economic interests behind the issue, a feature that will resurface repeat-edly in the consequent chapters. With all of this in mind, the chapter draws a line between a peace-supporting realm and realpolitik, including interstices between the two, in terms of the prevalent developments and motivations by the dominant actors. What is up for scrutiny includes the rise of humanitarianism, the democratization of politics, great power wars, and the emerging practice of humanitarian interventions, arms races, and a growing military gap between technologically leading and inferior countries, emerging and revisionist powers, colonial powers and colonial warfare, as well as the declining role of the Concert of Europe for the organization of European and international security. We elucidate how most of the major powers were caught in between, while also por-traying an exceptional stance progressively taken by Russia. In light of this, three conferences get detailed scrutiny: the 1868 St. Petersburg Con-ference and the 1899 and 1907 Hague Conferences. In regards to these, we show how the consequences and limits of the selected deliberations and their products reflected the aforesaid dominant discourses and practices, including an impetus provided by Russia. With truly remarkable ad-vancements on both diplomatic and legal fronts admitted, a critical anal-ysis is also performed to demonstrate how the original ambitions turned out relatively too large for the prevalent diplomatic potential. The pre-sented inquiry aims to do so particularly by pointing out the exclusive format of the three conferences and the still limited scope of the core outcome documents. To thoroughly account for the special role played by Russia at that time, this study also considers a Russian-based evalua-tion of these developments via incorporating the core longer-standing Russian language literature on the matter. All that said for a starter, the significance of these nineteenth-century precedents and associated prin-ciples for understanding contemporary international security regimes is consistently showcased throughout the book.

Chapter 3 offers a power-analytical reading of two humanitarian disarmament regimes formed during the past two decades to ban the use of APLs and CMs respectively. In doing so, it seeks to provide a novel understanding and theorization of these contemporary global security regimes and their related prohibition politics. The ban of APLs in 1997 marked a significant shift in humanitarian disarmament. Consequently, a humanitarian disarmament model emerged, consisting of bypassing permanent arms-control fora ("The Ottawa Process"). The presented chapter, however, shuns celebratory commentary on the "success" of the APL campaign as there is already abundant and, it will be argued, erroneous literature doing so. The ascent of the APL-related "Ottawa model" to the arena traditionally dominated by power interests of major powers and ossified lowest common denominator consensus was confirmed in 2008 when CMs were prohibited in a very similar fashion ("The Oslo Process"), after the failure of a relevant UN regulatory process to secure their prohibition, and the global public and political outcry against the controversial use of CMs by the Israeli Army in its raids against the Hezbollah. Operations of power in the case of CMs reveal the degree of the emancipation/domination paradox. Structural power linked to the functioning of the Cluster Munition Coalition has seen military utility of those weapons dwindle. Many states—and that has included the past first-tier producers of CMs—have rearticulated their economic interests in this light. They had learned that restructured military utility could have been in fact used to retain the power asymmetry by a shift from weapons production to their destruction both at home and in conflict zones. Two main contributions to the topic are the application of the power-analytical framework specifically developed to suit an analysis of formation and workings of global prohibition regimes (including heterarchy-of-power discussion of the relationship between states and nonstate actors) and the use of multitemporal perspectivism allowing the analyst to interlink humanitarian longue durée, or epochal, time frames marked by contingent ethical transformations in relation to other forces, instant-time frame analysis, and eventalization, that is, an analysis of events. Then, instead of the usual—and flawed at best—heroic discussions of victory of global civil society, rise of moral International Relations, and supposed progressivist teleology, a more complex regime configuration with many contradictions, artefacts, and their layering inside and about those regimes looms large. Finally, the chapter reveals operations of institutional/compulsory power complexes through politics related to remedial provisions on victim assistance.

The following chapter (chapter 4) continues and expands on the discussion presented in the previous one. It traces the workings of power with respect to a broader category of SALW and marginally conventional weapons in general. This case, however, does not readily fit within the traditional understanding of humanitarian disarmament and this inquiry seeks to elucidate the related nuances. First, this study demonstrates how and explains why stigmatization of SALW has principally evolved around a certain related practice rather than this cluster of weapons altogether. Still chiefly defined by its involvement in practices of that sort, the deviant weapons category also gets detailed scrutiny from the perspective of its material aspects. This discussion is crucial because it displays how broader-based stigmatization of compulsory prudent weapons turns out to be unsuccessful. Second, the chapter shows how strong gun lobby advocacy, which features a rather offbeat case of nongovernmental opposition to humanitarian arms control and disarmament, in part accounts for these dynamics. Third, it explicates how all states, besides being variously inclined, quite extraordinarily share powerful incentives in preserving both the disputed weapons and their flows. Fourth, while detailing the power hierarchies, associated interests, and grips of direct mutual influence that define the key stakeholders, it repeatedly showcases a critical and rather case-specific convergence between the involved actors' standing and leverage in the realm of SALW. By virtue of this complex investigation, it considers how humanitarian efforts to regulate SALW and the projected resistance embody categorically identical actors but exhaustively clarifies why a particular regulatory regime with certain powers and limitations has eventually become embedded. In doing so, it also sheds light on how the character of the key outcome documents directly reflects the nature of the pivotal decision-making fora. In regards to this, the chapter reflects on various international and regional regulatory endeavors from the perspective of their cardinal limitations in sustaining an effective SALW regime. The recent crowning achievement in the domain of SALW and conventional weapons more generally, namely the ATT, is inter alia scrutinized and implications of this study for understanding its future prospects are flagged. Keeping in mind the inherent convergence between legally proscribed APLs and a broader cluster of SALW, traits of their security regulation are juxtaposed for a better grasp of the latter. More generally, this study consistently demonstrates how and why the case of SALW has not followed the scenario of humanitarian disarmament, while occasionally echoing the pattern and deeply convergent with its underlying norms.

In chapter 5, the power-analytical approach is deployed to study the power configuration of the "hard core" of security practice: nuclear weapons. In particular, this analysis traces the workings of power related to humanitarian attempts to establish a formalized nuclear nonuse regime, reinforced by an aspiration for complete, and global, nuclear disarmament and the existing resistance to it. In the first place, the notion of the *stigmatization-delegitimization complex*, upon which such humanitarian efforts have consistently built up, is introduced and dissected. In doing so, this chapter shows how various interpretations of the Non-Proliferation Treaty (NPT) and security have originally defined the rift between the respective sides and ultimately led to the Nuclear Weapons Convention. To define and analyze the split in material terms, a detailed power-analytical reading of related direct and diffuse interactions between the key stakeholders is provided. A longue durée perspective is taken to examine such interactions in order to trace the transhistoricity of the nuclear disarmament campaign and the enduring nature of a relatively invariant resistant bloc. Relying on the therein introduced notion of the *antinuclear humanitarian transhistorical bloc*, this study systematically shows how the same, or at least categorically similar, actors who would strive to outlaw atomic weapons in and around the 1950s stand by the same agenda in and around the 1980s and drive the same campaign in the post–Cold War era. In turn, portraying opposition to such endeavors through the prism of a verily exclusive club, we make intelligible how it has withstood these antinuclear sentiments to date. By virtue of this whole scrutiny, the chapter seeks to demonstrate and elucidate how and why there has eventually settled a highly imbalanced nuclear weapons regime with respect to the original goal of nonproliferation versus that of disarmament. It also interprets how nuclear weapons have, despite their considerable structural indispensability, been successfully stigmatized as an entire category (the nonuse tradition) but why this norm has never been properly formalized. Overall, this chapter represents a comprehensive piece of issue-oriented research because it outlines and interprets various international, regional, bilateral, and unilateral efforts at regulating or outlawing the possession, transfer, testing, and use of nuclear (weapons) technology. The case is complemented by drawing crucial parallels, in particular that between the nuclear weapons and commerce regimes as well as that between stigmatization and proscription of atomic weapons and the broader category of weapons of mass destruction (WMD). The Nuclear Weapons Convention, a culmination of regulatory politics in the domain, is also scrutinized, with implications of this inquiry for understanding its future prospects flagged.

Chapter 6 aims to tailor the power-analytical approach to the latest and highly topical endeavor in the area of humanitarian arms control and disarmament, the Campaign to Stop Killer Robots. This one has called for a blanket preventive global ban on the development, production, and use of weapons systems capable of autonomously initiating lethal force. While no issue-oriented legal regulatory/prohibitory framework has emerged to date, two tightly intertwined strands of developments are considered. First, multiple parallels and analogies are drawn between the piecemeal emerging legal regime on cyberweapons and security regulation of this new generation of fully autonomous (lethal) weapons. Second, this chapter traces power configurations related to international regulatory/prohibition politics evolving in particular around the security issue of Killer Robots. In doing so, humanitarian regulatory/prohibitionary efforts and a thrust of skepticism or sometimes even explicit resistance are juxtaposed. For comprehending the prospects of this "confrontation," we consider the dominant narratives, structural and institutional statuses, as well as associated interests and leverage grips of the key stakeholders. Based on this, the chapter reflects on the prospects of a ban on Killer Robots developed within or outside of the traditional deliberation and decision-making fora. The latter scenario cannot be disregarded in light of a serious consideration of the option by campaigners as well as a precedent set by the Ottawa (APLs) and Oslo (CMs) processes. More generally, this case is particularly suitable to showcase and interpret at least four more general issues in the area of (preventive) humanitarian disarmament. First, it features the most vivid illustration of a strong nexus between cultural and sci-fi imaginaries, though also pertinent to a number of other herein studied cases, and global security governance. Second, considering that autonomous (lethal) weapons challenge the distinction between weapons, methods warfare, and warriors, this case epitomizes how a stigma gradually attached to a general weapons-related practice (the removal of human control over the use of lethal force) directly concerns and falls to an entire well-defined category of weapons. Third, this case demonstrates what happens when the lack of a meaningful practical basis for stigmitization politics meets a disproportionally radical and exclusive prohibitionary discourse. Finally, considering that a preventive approach to humanitarian disarmament is not mainstream in the matter of international security regimes, this inquiry is also crucial to elucidate how and under which conditions it can suffer setbacks or be shelved at least.

What follows is the conclusion highlighting main empirical findings, taking them back to theory development and generalizing them for other empirical material. In particular, the concluding section distills a number of important lessons concerning similarities and differences across the selected case studies. Based on a multidimensional comparative interpretation of related nuances, as in part already sketched earlier, it offers a careful generalization concerning the relative prospects, scope, and strength of regulatory/prohibitory frameworks from the perspective of humanitarian arms control and disarmament as well as the dynamics of their institutionalization. Most importantly, it outlines and graphically synthesizes the *logic* of humanitarian arms control and disarmament as the outcome of this study. Finally, the usefulness of the used power-analytical approach is discussed in detail and its significance for further research is highlighted and analyzed. The question is subdivided into three areas: its usefulness for the analyzed case studies in the book, for other international security regimes, and for general IR and Security Studies. For each of these areas, positive heuristics are outlined. Last but not least, the book also concludes by paying attention to how the presented comparative study refines the theorization of different types of power and their complex configurations.

ONE

Theorizing International Security Regimes

From Three Waves of "Isms" to the Power-Analytical Approach

This theoretical chapter seeks to develop alternative ways to conceptually grasp international prohibition/regulatory regimes. It attempts to go beyond existing, and piecemeal, theorization of regimes within the intellectual field of IR. It serves as an introductory piece for a series of following empirical studies. By doing so, it sets up a theoretical agenda and reflects on and outlines perspectives for comparative research. While relying on the means of conceptual analysis rather than definitions, *international security regimes* are understood here as *sets of normative discourses and political structures (anarchies, hierarchies, and heterarchies) through which power operates within a given security issue area with a regulatory effect.* Specific renderings of discourses and heterarchies establish channels through which sociopolitical and economic privileges are distributed; they create structural relations among actors with a possibility of their reversal or rearticulation and they build up, challenge, and relocate walls of legal obligations—all of this within a given security domain, with a systemic quality.

The chapter proceeds as follows. First, it discusses existing IR theorization of regimes. The discussion coalesces around three "waves" of regime theorization: the neo-neoconvergence regime theory, the cognitivism most systematically represented by the Tübingen School, and radical constructivist/poststructuralist understanding. It should be outright noted that they are conceived of heuristically, that is, not entirely mutually exclusive and coexistent in time. Out of each it extracts a series of features that can be harnessed to study security regimes more robustly and in a comparative fashion. The second part of the chapter answers a question of how to strike a balance between theoretical eclecticism, which is believed to be vital for a comprehensive and plastic analysis of security regimes, and the need to have a uniting device to organize such research. It is for these reasons that the most sophisticated existing conceptualization of *power* available, that is, Barnett and Duvall's (2005) typology, is used as the central conceptual vocabulary, interlinking various strands of literature to a single analytical framework usable for this project. For positive heuristic purposes, the framework offered will reverse the usual order of things: rather than going from the material to the ideational, as well as from rational to reflectivist, it outlines the vision where the constitutive power of the discourse, the discourse in its materiality, cannot be sidelined or made of secondary importance.

THEORIZATION OF REGIMES IN IR: THREE "WAVES" OF SCHOLARSHIP

This section begins with a theoretically oriented discussion of regime analysis that can be identified within the discipline of IR. Indeed, such discussion needs to factor in the empirical domain in question, the scope, complexity, and theme of regulation (Keohane and Victor 2010; Alter and Meunier 2009; Drezner 2009), as well as political dynamics and leadership related to their formation and effectiveness (Levy, Young, and Zürn 1995; Young 1991). This takes on importance when considering that the majority of the existing scholarship on theories of regimes came to be articulated from within International Political Economy and Earth Science, rather than Security Studies (for notable exceptions, cf. Müller 1995, 1993; Krause 1990; Nye 1987; Jervis 1982). Geographically, complex interplay between regional and global attempts to regulate specific issue areas (Adler and Greve 2009; Bourne 2007; Duffield 1994). Legally, the range from difficulties to be regulated to regulation measures and/or full prohibition is displayed in the series of case studies offered in this book (also cf. Efrat 2010; Miron 2001; Krause and Latham 1998; Aceves 1997).

The discussion of the three "waves" of theorization of regimes is utilized toward an extraction of some of the criteria embraced by empirical studies in this book. A power-analysis approach is then used to organize this analysis and order thinking. All studied issues contained in this book fall into the category of security regimes (cf. Jervis 1982). With a caveat that not all issues studied here experience that degree of regulation, Ethan Nadelmann (1990; for effectiveness, cf. Getz 2006) delimited global prohibition regimes as institutionalizations of explicit and implicit norms prohibiting certain activities of both state and nonstate actors (through systemic diffusion in the international space, in international public law, as well as domestic criminal law) and processes by which these norms are enforced. The prohibition and regulatory regimes thus conceived are *substantive* (rather than merely procedural) and *global* in scale—or at least they contain a globalizing (or totalizing) ambition in order to eliminate possible "regime leakages" and exploitation of loopholes (Müller and Wunderlich 2013; Garcia 2011, 40–41, 69; Alker and Greenberg 1977). On the other side of the regulatory spectrum, there are international nonregimes, that is, functional and thematic instances of empirical absence concerning the formation of regulating rules and institutions and of "transnational policy arenas characterized by the absence of multilateral agreements for policy coordination among states" (Dimitrov et al. 2007, 231). The whole spectrum of regulation is examined in this book.

Consequentialist Regime Theories

The first generation of regime analysis can be linked to what has been known as the theoretical convergence between neoliberal institutionalism and neorealism (Andreatta and Koenig-Archibugi 2010; Baldwin 1993; Nye 1988; Keohane 1986; Ruggie 1983). It newly emerged as a research venue linked to the complex interdependency theory (Ruggie 1983, 1975; Keohane and Nye 1977; Young 1982), which attempted to balance the focus on state-centric framework and relative capabilities with the importance of international institutions and absolute gains. While not entirely neo-neosynthesis (Waever 1996) as differences on the degree of possible cooperation, role of hegemons, and centrality of international institutions remained (Breitmeier, Young, and Zürn 2006; Keohane and Martin 1995; Grieco 1988), the convergence could be seen in the consequentialist reasoning, reduction of uncertainties, fears, and transaction costs, as well as in the existence of future expectations driven by the conviction that cooperation among states is possible despite the structural logic of anarchy (Oye 1986; Rosenau 1986).

Existing definitions of regimes clearly demonstrate the theoretical link. Stephen Krasner (1982, 186) depicted regimes as "sets of implicit and explicit principles, norms, rules, and decision-making procedures around which actors' expectations converge in a given area of international relations." Further down the denotative line, Haas (1983) argued that "principles" featured beliefs of fact, causation, and rectitude; "norms" could be comprehended as standards of behavior defined in terms of rights and obligations; "rules" then being specific prescriptions and prohibitions concerning actors' behavior; and procedures encompassing dominant practices for making and implementing collective choices. Another influential rationalist scholar, Robert Keohane (1989, 4), specified regimes as "institutions with explicit rules, agreed upon by governments, that pertain to particular sets of issues in international relations," where institutions were understood as "persistent and connected

sets of rules (formal and informal) that prescribe behavioral roles, constrain activity, and shape expectations" (1989, 3). Moreover, Keohane also
pointed to the importance of enforcement mechanisms by way of "injunc-
tions" (Keohane 1984, 57). On the other hand, while sharing rationalist
convictions, Oran Young (1980, 331–32) attempted a broader depiction of
regimes that would circumscribe the problematic area concerning rules,
norms, and principles: "regimes are social institutions governing the actions of those interested in specifiable activities. As such, they are recognized patterns of practice around which expectations converge."

General theoretical contours and two influential specimens in the
form of Krasner and Keohane's definitions of regimes referred to earlier
testify to the multiple limitations of this generation of scholarship. Theoretically, critics pointed out the paucity of linkages between "informal
ordering devices of international regimes with the formal institutional
mechanisms of international organization" (Kratochwil and Ruggie 1986,
754). These authors also questioned the degree of conceptual precision
(hierarchy and relations among components), instrumentalism, and predominantly positivist epistemological and methodological leanings. The
consequences were said to be the lack of attention to actors' interpretations, meaning attachment and intersubjective understanding (1986,
763–70). Moreover, another identified shortcoming of the early generation of regime theorization was said to be its lack of focus on domestic
politics (Haggard and Simmons 1987; for exceptions, cf. Ruggie 1982;
Young 1980). Theoretical underdevelopment of affinities between domestic politics and its international corollaries has also been connected to
reductionism in understanding various facets of sovereignty. While state-
centrism has indeed been one of the edifices in analyzing regimes, state
sovereignty has usually been depicted in a narrow sense. Krasner's (1999)
understanding of sovereignty has become the IR standard: he decouples
sovereignty through the specification of its four types: international legal
(diplomatic recognition, prerogatives, formal position), Westphalian
(noninterference in domestic matters), domestic (national authority structures and their efficiency), and interdependence ("states are losing their
ability to control movements across their own borders" [Krasner 2003]).
Ironically, the last two—domestic sovereignty and interdependence sovereignty, with their focus on state control rather than state authority—
have been largely absent from IR focus generally and theorization of
regimes specifically (Goldsmith 2000, 962).

The most interesting criticism of the first wave of regime analysis was
offered by Strange (1982) and Keeley (1990) who both focused on what
could be termed as the politics of regime theory. In her iconoclastic, and
one could argue time-proven, criticism and refusal of the denotative dynamics supposedly leading to greater robustness of the concept and theory, Susan Strange (1982, 480 and 487–88) maintained that they were articulated in a way that "tends to exclude hidden agendas and to leave

unheard and unheeded complaints, whether they come from the under-privileged, the disenfranchised or the unborn, about the way the system works . . . government, rulership, and authority are the essence of the word 'regime,' not consensus, nor justice, nor efficiency in administration." All of this with a heavy focus on US concerns, issues, and preferences. In a similar vein, Keeley (1990, 83–84) argued that consequentialist regime theory is implicitly skewed toward liberal analysis and the sense of a community among international actors. In an original and witty way, he took Krasner's work and—in his own words—"abused" it to study nonliberal regimes through which historical empires (the Mongols and Athenians) spread and maintained influence, thus putting "more distance between a theory of regimes . . . and prescriptive analyses of or claims made for particular regimes . . . as prescriptions make it a language of apology or justification, a form of special pleading by and for the powerful and satisfied" (1990, 84).

Cognitivism and Theories of Regimes

By the beginning of the 1990s, a new strand of regime theorization came to disciplinary prominence. The ascent of cognitivist, or knowledge-based, theories of regimes rendered the previous assumption of consequentialism and fixed, rationally determined state preferences flawed and out of touch with the empirical domain (Smith 1987). Additionally, it cautiously shifted the debate of regimes from state-centrism to neofunctionally (Haas 1982) and neoinstitutionally (March and Olsen 1998; Powell and DiMaggio 1991, 5–8) inspired research on international organization, their bureaucracies, and involvement of epistemic communities, that is, transnational networks of scientists that stepped frequently into the decision-making process under conditions of political uncertainty and issue complexity, altering previous decisional paths and understanding of problems (Haas 1992). As Peter M. Haas (1989, 377) noted in the theoretical cross-fertilization of the scholarly work on epistemic communities and theorization of regimes, "in addition to providing a form of order in an anarchic international political system, regimes may also contribute to governmental learning and influence patterns of behavior by empowering new groups who are able to direct their governments towards new ends." Last but not least, the rise of cognitivist research programs on regimes could be seen as a specific response to the previously articulated—and at least partially justified—fierce criticism of the state-centrism, faddishness, and epiphenomenalism of regime theorization.

The development outlined earlier ought to be understood as a part of a more general IR debate, known as the Third Great Debate between positivism and postpositivism (Lapid 1989) and the gradual rise of theoretical eclecticism in IR (Lake 2013), with an emphasis on mid-level theorization. One of the effects could also be observed at the level of the label itself: "regime theory" was largely replaced by "theories of regimes" for this wave of theorization (Hasenclever, Mayer, and Rittberger 1997; Haggard and Simmons 1987). And became just "theorization of regimes" for the third wave of scholarship, as it has drawn on theoretical approaches, many of them originating from outside of IR, rather than substantive IR theories. It is here where the distinction between regime-theoretical "thinliners" and "thickliners" can be invoked (Stokke 2012, 5) with the moderation of his overly optimistic view of a "heathy conceptual and methodological debate" supposedly taking place between the two positions (2012, 5; cf. Hynek and Teti 2010). The ontological and epistemological opening for the second "wave" of regime theorization was already made by Kratochwil and Ruggie (1986, 774) who sparked off the discussion on a dialogical character of such analysis: "we proposed a more interpretive approach that would open up regime analysis to the communicative rather than merely the referential functions of norms in social interactions. . . . The ontology of regimes consists of an intersubjective basis." They also highlighted the importance of epistemic politics (1986, 775). Methodologically, Puchala and Hopkins's (1982) work on inductive analysis and qualitative research investigating participants' perceptions, understanding, and convictions paved the way for the cognitivist—and comparativist—shift (Rublee 2009).

The most systematically developed research program within this wave of scholarship has been represented by a European take on theories of regimes: the *Tübingen School* under the intellectual leadership of Volker Rittberger (Hasenclever, Mayer, and Rittberger 1997). Not only did the authors provide the IR field with a rich understanding of cognitivism and its versions but they too attempted to link it to the previous wave and, at the same time, built up a path for the third wave of regime theorization. As this chapter makes clear, this plastic and heuristically integrative approach has been of utter significance to the power analysis outlined later and used throughout the book. Specifically, the authors divided theories of regimes into three strands (power, interest, and knowledge based). Power-based theories of regimes were said to be linked to security concerns driven by international anarchy and uneven power distribution, flagging the importance of relative gains (1997, 116–25). Theoretical inspiration was taken from hegemonic stability theory, the realist theory of cooperation (defensive positionalism), and the power-based research program based on non–Prisoner's Dilemma game theory (86–135). The central variable was said to be power, with a rationalist orientation and weak understanding of institutionalism (6). Interest-based theories of regimes were depicted as dealing with issues of overcoming collective action dilemmas (33–44), featured an analysis of institutional bargaining (68–82), and studied spillovers and their conditional circumstances (for example, intra-institutional reuse of solutions due to cost efficiency, 74–76; cf. Johnson and Urpelainen 2012). Cooperation was said to be the outcome of institutional bargaining and led to agreements and commitments (Hasenclever, Mayer, and Rittberger 1997, 20, 33, 70–72). Two specific approaches to cooperation were a broadened contractualism based on game theory ("situation-structuralism," 1997, 44–59) and "problem-structuralism" oriented on issue areas/themes (59–68). Interests served as the central variable, the sense of institutionalism being stronger than with power-based theories but weaker compared to cognitivism and absolute gains dominating a behavioral component (6).

The main contribution of the Tübingen School lies in its systematic incorporation of the cognitivist approach to regime analysis, linking it to a broader theorization of IR. As has already been made clear, a distinct feature of the second wave of regime-theoretical scholarship is *cognitivism*. Unlike the other two types of theories, cognitivist theories of regimes have sociologically derived meta-theoretical orientations (albeit of different degrees), with knowledge being the central variable. They display a strong sense of institutionalism and their behavioral model is oriented at roles dynamics (Hasenclever, Mayer, and Rittberger 1997, 6). Taking cues from the Constructivist Turn in IR, itself an effect of the Third Great Debate, cognitivists study ways and mechanisms through which knowledge, that is chiefly intersubjectively held ideas and beliefs, relates to actors' identities and actions. Codified and formalized sets of ideas, that is norms, are at the forefront of research. The authors distinguish between two types of cognitivism: weak and strong (1997, 136–39). While the former attempts to make sense of the actual behavior of an actor, the latter interrogates intersubjective structures, namely the relationship between the Self and the Other (138). The weak cognitivism mirrors a more general strategy of the "thin, complementizing" Constructivism in IR that attempts to make rationalist accounts more robust by theorization of preference formation, that is, what rationalists take axiomatically for granted (154–55; cf. Klotz 1995). It is here where the link to literature on epistemic communities and the role of science in theorization of regimes exists (cf. Lidskog and Sundqvist 2002). Scientists are portrayed as powerful interlocutors and knowledge shapers (2002, 149–52). As for strong cognitivism, itself based on "thick Constructivism" (156), Giddens's (1984, cf. Wendt 1987) structurationist approach to the agency-structure debate is taken seriously and four specific cooperation areas are highlighted: the power of legitimacy studying social fabrics of international political life and its norms and rules (Giddens 1984, 169–76); the power of arguments inspired by Habermas's communicative rationality and ethics (176–85); the power of identity where the Self/Other binary is at the forefront (186–92); and the power of history, that is, dialectical perspectives on historical creations of world orders and their structural features and maintenance mechanisms (192–208).

Radical Constructivist/Poststructuralist Theorization of Regimes

This section tackles what can be termed the third wave of theorization of regimes, namely the incorporation of radical critical social and political theory to regime analysis. While the Tübingen School contained discussion of strong cognitivism and its outlined cooperation areas promised to open up new venues of research, it has stayed at the declaratory level and never produced specimens of such theorization. Ontologically and epistemologically, this wave goes *beyond* "strong cognitivism." Rather than being linked to Wendt's substantive-theoretical version of Constructivism inspired by mind-independent, scientific realist ontology, it espouses a more radical, mind-dependent (that is, antifoundationalist) ontology and anti-essentialist epistemology (Hynek and Teti 2010, 174; cf. Sismondo 1996, 6–7, 79). As a consequence, the correspondence theory of truth and the possibility of "truth discovery" as such need to be flatly rejected (Sayyid and Zac 1998, 250–51). The previous wave managed to exclude radical constructivist and poststructural scholarship from considerations: "critical" Constructivist research on regimes became limited to Kratochwil, Ruggie, Haas, and their followers. With the theorization of regimes and also more generally, this strategy produced a disciplinary effect in the form of delegitimization of "poststructural" critiques as unscientific and unfit for regime analysis. It presented the "loyal opposition" of Kratochwil and others as the (only) critical alternative, providing at best a "thick" description of norms inside regimes and their complexes, thus backing up (and cyclically relegitimizing) "thinner" versions. Rooted in the elision of ontological differences between Constructivism and Neoutilitarianism, the demarcation between "thin cognitivism" and "thick cognitivism" policed the boundary of acceptable research on regime theorization, contributing to the more general "immunization" of mainstream IR against radical-constructivist/poststructural critiques (Hynek and Teti 2010, 180–81; Keeley 1990, 83–85).

Not only have radical approaches to regime analysis been underpinned by strikingly different ontology, epistemology, and methods, but they too have drawn on markedly different intellectual inspirations. By taking cues from outside of the discipline, continental philosophy and linguistics have played an especially important role. The third wave does not begin with denotative exercises of the previous two waves; it flees them. Endless wrangles over the difference between rules and norms and their subtypes, as far as degree of specificity, deontology, links to interests, and alike, are being replaced by the arrival of connotation. Neither interested in (re)articulating regime theory nor contributing to theories of regimes, this wave embraces the process of theorization as an end goal. As Foucault maintains, the process of theorization "is always local and related to a limited field. . . . *Theory* does not express, translate, or serve to apply practice: it *is* practice" (Deleuze and Foucault 1977, 205). In the conversation between Foucault and Deleuze, theory gets a whole new meaning: rather than synbooking or totalizing phenomena, it is seen as a "box of tools" used in order to expose power where it is most unexpected. To understand theory as practice, one needs to ask: What kind of practice? As Deleuze (1987, 19) suggests, it lies "in developing a compass" and can be comprehended as "the art of conceptual and perceptual coloring" (Lorraine 2005, 207). As a result, theorization becomes conceptual practice and is linked to a mode of experimentation. Experimentation is simultaneously theoretical and practical: it takes seriously interconnection between orders of assembled conditions and the resulting tendencies, thus investigating "what it does and what is done with it" (Deleuze and Guattari 1983, 180). Experimentation is thinking anew, tackling "the new, remarkable, and interesting that replace the appearance of truth and are more demanding than it is" (Deleuze and Guattari 1994, 110). Similarly to Foucault's (1977) genealogy based on further epistemological cultivation of Nietzsche, Deleuze also pits experimentation against history. While distancing it from historiography, experimentation requires history as it represents "the set of almost negative conditions that make possible the experimentation of something that escapes history" (1977, 111).

It is only within this wave where the four "cooperation areas" flagged by the Tübingen School (that is, power of legitimacy, narrative structures, identity-related binary separations, and conditions of possibility for emergence and transformations of historical orders) are taken seriously and theorized through the means of experimentation and conceptual practice. The best examples of regime analysis where these four areas can be found properly examined are in the scholarship of Richard Price (1995, 1997) on the chemical weapons regime and Nina Tannenwald on the nuclear weapons regime (1999, 2007). Their scholarship can be understood as radical constructivist rather than poststructuralist, in spite of their meta-theoretical orientation and intellectual sources being identical (Price's genealogy) or similar (Tannenwald's social construction). As Price (1995, 88) put it, "genealogy injects a different dimension of power into the study of norms, an element that often seems neglected in the attempt to distance the role of norms and ideas from realism's focus on material power." Unlike poststructuralists, they both still subjected themselves to testing the null hypothesis (H_0), articulating their theoretical and interpretive position vis-à-vis mainstream IR and rejecting the "residual variance" of their accounts. This is despite the fact that their accounts still reflected notable differences between the two regimes, such as the loci of their origins, presence/absence of hegemony during their formation, means of their spreading, robustness, and types of stigma, to mention but a few.

Specifically, they showed how liberal and realist—but by extension also cognitivist—approaches are indeterminate, or outright mistaken, in their inability to explain the de jure existing nonuse prohibition regime related to chemical weapons and the de facto present nonuse prohibition regime related to nuclear weapons. As the authors maintained, "with its ahistorical approach, rationalist regime theory has little to say about the origins and evolution of norms and practices that cannot be conceived as simply the rational calculation of the national interest. It is precisely because the taboos embody an 'irrational' attitude towards technology" (Price and Tannenwald 1996, 124). By virtue of being interested in wider normative contexts, Price and Tannenwald successfully attempted to problematize the rationalist explanation of the existence of those regimes as well as the motivation of states for cooperative action and general observation of related norms. Their question is therefore "how certain weapons have been defined as deterrent weapons whereas other weapons have not" (1996, 115). Simultaneously, even the "thick cognitivism" as outlined by the Tübingen School (cf. "The Critics of the Critics" in Hasenclever, Mayer, and Rittberger 1997, 208–10) seems to avoid at best this type of analysis that relies on an investigation of historical contingencies probed through the means of Foucauldian genealogy. It marginalizes an analysis of moral discourses through which power hierarchies and political separations have been achieved and upheld; ideas, knowledge, and collective identities are being rejected to be more than variables.

SIGNIFICANCE OF THE THREE GENERATIONS

The utility of the consequentialist regime theory lies in highlighting structural (material) conditions and incentives for regime formation, regime evolution and maintenance, and regime compliance. With regard to regime formation, the following questions can be posed: Did the regime result from particular interests of hegemonic powers, from a different "tier" of states, or another type of actor? How precisely was the issue area specified and subsequently institutionalized? What role did "norm entrepreneurship" play in a given regime formation? Was it pursued through coercive diplomacy? What kind of reasoning drove the other states when joining the regime (following rational interest, specification of cost/benefit, coercion, bandwagoning, etc.)? As for regime evolution, one's attention is steered, inter alia, toward these questions: Did the regime evolve along the lines of great power interests, and if not, why? How has the evolutionary dynamic changed after the initial stage of formation (from power/interest driven to path-dependency or even normative persistence)? Did the regime become more coherent due to the substantial economy of transaction costs/information sharing procedures? Last but not least, questions related to compliance relate to reasons why states complied with the regime—bargaining for profit, procedural calculations, rewards, coercion, compellence, and/or normative compliance.

Were effective verification mechanisms formed within the regime, and why? What were the outcomes of noncompliant behavior and the impact on the robustness of a regime? Did the motivations among the members to comply with a given regime change over time? More recent studies drawing on this type of scholarship have further contributed by examination of interplays of international regimes (Muzaka 2011; Stokke 2003), cross-scale interactions (Young 2000), regime complexity (Gómez-Mera 2015), and ontological pluralization, especially incorporation of other types of actors (Biermann and Pattberg 2008; Arts 2000).

To make a few remarks on the utility of the cognitivist wave of regime analysis, it can be divided into three areas: actors and identities involved in regimes, regime-related processes and outcomes, and ideas through which knowledge is produced and politically used. In regard to actors and their identities, it is to study primary and secondary agents and their identities, push-pull dynamics vis-à-vis IOs and their politico-scientific justification, transnational dynamics, as well as links between ideas and national interests. Role conceptions/playing are also important objects of examination for regime analysis, not least because they render foreign policy analysis relevant by virtue of bridging domestic and international environments. With respect to processes and outcomes, focus ought to be steered toward cognitive and communicative mechanisms such as persuasion, coercion, and forms of legitimation; network analysis related to workings of epistemic communities (and other types of actors) and thematic analysis; as well as research on formation and use of narrative structures more generally. Finally, relationships between ideas and norms need to be scrutinized, their specific types (principled, causal, etc.) and codification (that is, treaty regimes, cf. Sitaraman 2009) as well as an interplay between cognitive, regulatory, and behavioral components and how those contribute to identity formation and reproduction. How do actors' identities affect their stance on norm determinacy in the formation and recreation of regimes? What is the role that ideas play in the best possible achievement of a desired social and political purpose as far as regimes are concerned? How is cognitional (and political) success influenced by a degree of intersubjectively shared knowledge?

As for the third "wave," that is, radical constructivist/poststructuralist theorization of regimes—the utility is manifold. Ontologically, it goes beyond the dichotomy, or juxtaposition, of state-centered and transnational analytical frameworks (for these, cf. Lipson 2005–2006). It is capable of examining regime complexes, understood as a plural mix comprising actors, networks, and artefacts, both material and ideational, and their coproductions and hybrids. Deleuze and Guattari's (1983, 1987) and Foucault's (1991) analyses are vital for studying assemblages and the ways in which they have been linked to state apparatuses and their rationalities, thereby creating governmentalized assemblages (Hynek 2012, 31–34; Joseph 2012; Krause 2011). This wave takes seriously ethics and

culture and examines them as socially constructed, if contingent, categories (Tannenwald 2013). Relevant scholarship recognizes the necessity of
flexible analytical toolboxes comprehending structures as contingent,
open, where seeds of resistance come from within:

> Increasing interdependence among issues and issues-areas may thus
> produce increasing strains on regimes. In such circumstances, argu-
> ments that specific regimes order the entire system become problematic
> even if some issue-areas, regimes, or instruments are more significant
> than others. Theoretical approaches that rely on a grand unifying order
> become particularly suspect. "The system" may be a fragmented, ill-
> coordinated thing; it may be broken-legged and limp along according-
> ly. (Keeley 1990, 95–96)

Importantly, such an analysis also avoids siren songs of prescription and
normativity, be they explicit or implicit (cf. Taylor 1985). Finally, collective identities are taken seriously and scrutinized: on one hand, their
conditions of emergence, on the other, their structural and productive
effects (see the next session). Last but not least, this wave attempts to
expose forms (for example, informal empires) and sources (for example,
use of knowledge) of international anarchy, hierarchy, and heterarchy
(Wendt and Friedheim 1995; Crumley 1995).

A POWER-ANALYTICAL APPROACH TO INTERNATIONAL
SECURITY REGIMES

No one would likely dispute that when it comes to the complexities of
international security regimes, robust ex post understandings, that is, the
thrust of work IR scholars do every day (except for their dealings with
piles of bureaucracy and administration), are the best way to comprehend the dynamics and cross-cutting effects (cf. Drezner 2009). Theoretical robustness often involves the necessity of combining different
metatheoretical leanings as well as the reliance on limited, contingent
generalizations of examined phenomena, that is, "small-t(heory)-claims"
(Price and Reus-Smit 1998, 275). The evolution of the IR field clearly
shows the rise of theoretical and analytical eclecticisms, what Reus-Smit
(2013, 589) has labeled "bracket metatheory thesis," thereby going beyond sweeping generalizations. However, there are still different kinds
of eclecticisms. This chapter in particular and the book in general shuns
"progressivist" theoretical eclecticism, which has usually been associated
with an examination of microfoundations and production and testing of
mid-range theories (Lake 2013; Sil and Katzenstein 2010). Despite their
cagey aversion to the discussion of metatheoretical assumptions, research
design and methods used by many of these mid-range studies have repli-
cated problems of conventional IR theorization, just one level of theoretical ambition down.

Rather than mid-range progressivism, the type of eclecticism embraced here is what Lake (2013, 574) dubs "open-ended eclecticism." Arguably, not only does such open-endedness allow for unique and specific features of various issue areas under the microscope to be considered and theorized accordingly, but it too underlines the primacy of "questions/concerns 'in the world,'" thus staying away from "pathological implications" of "current textbook configuration of multiple 'isms'" (Lake 2011; cf. Krause 2002, 252–56). While regime analysis was being formulated as a mid-range project from the beginning, it has not overcome those pathologies, as was demonstrated in the previous part of the chapter. Simultaneously, the identified three waves of regime theorization and featured assessment of their metatheoretical leanings helps to cushion what Reus-Smit (2013, 589) correctly associated with this kind of theorization, a research project not being "structured by epistemological and ontological assumptions, making it an exclusively empirical-theoretic project with distinctive ontological content."

The meta-organizing and conceptual device chosen here to order regime analysis is what we term the *power-analytical approach*. It is the means to bring the previously heeded theorizations and conceptualizations in through considerations of multiplicity of power relations. As Foucault (1980, 98) put it, power is relational rather than substantial, it is not perfectly possessed or controlled by anybody, it is not the property of anyone or anything, it passes through subjects and manifests its loci in objects, it constitutes and actuates networks and apparatuses. The position embraced here begins with an acknowledgment of multiple types of dynamic power structures becoming intertwined (with)in regimes and among them (cf. Guzzini 1993). As Allen (1998, 178) held it, "the proper alternative to power is not defeat but indifference." In particular, as the following lines show, these are political *hierarchies*, that is, formal or informal, less or more rigid tree-like structures, oriented vertically and unitarily, what Deleuze and Guattari describe as "arborescent assemblages" (1987, 5; for an alternative conception, cf. Cooley 2005). Other systems where power is located and through which it passes are *heterarchies*— what Deleuze and Guattari (1987, 7–9) would call rhizomatic assemblages: these are forming, maintaining, and reconfiguring security regimes in a flexible and horizontal fashion, fleeing attempts of being overcoded and rendered arborescent, thus allowing for reconstitution and resistance inside of formal organizations and rigid spaces (for hierarchy-heterarchy nexus, cf. Crumley 1995).

Foucault (1982, 216–22) identifies several starting questions for power analysis: "*How is power exercised? . . . By what means is it exercised? . . . What constitutes specific nature of power? . . . What happens when individuals exert (as they say) power over others? . . . How is one to analyse the power relationship?*" Essentially, the power-analytical approach deals with an analysis of "economies of power," that is, its various configurations (based on modalities of efficiency/effectiveness and informed by types of power involved, see discussion shortly). In the process of their excavation, a few guidelines (G1–5) were put forward by Foucault (1982, 223):

> G1. *The system of differentiation* that features legal conditions, traditions of status and privilege, economic disparities, transformations in production, differences in culture and language, as well as in know-how and competence; relations of power create differentiations and these are its conditions and results simultaneously. This guideline is particularly important for the analysis of productive power.
>
> G2. *The types of objectives* such as "the maintenance of privileges, the accumulation of profits, the bringing into operation of statutory authority, the exercise of a function or a trade" (1982, 223). This guideline helps to sharpen the analysis of structural power.
>
> G3. *The means of bringing power relations into being*—through coercion, military means, and discourses; also by means of economic differences, of control, by surveillance, with the help of archives, through informal rules, with/without technological means. Compulsory power lends itself to be analyzed through these means.
>
> G4. *Forms of institutionalization*—can involve traditional predispositions with customs/fashions and legal systems; expressed through (sometimes very complex and elaborate) apparatuses with their loci, regulations, hierarchies, and autonomies; also feature "the distribution of all power relations in a given social ensemble" (223). How institutional power is exercised can be found out with the deployment of this guideline.
>
> G5. *The degree of rationalization*—can be understood "in relation to the effectiveness of the instruments and the certainty of the results," contains different kinds of costs—economic, for example, putting new instruments into practice, or costs associated with reactive resistance (224). This principle ought to be heeded especially when operations of institutional and compulsory power get examined.

These questions and guidelines may serve as the springboard for the following conceptual analysis of types of power. For reasons of theoretical sophistication and comprehensiveness, this chapter draws on the conceptualization of power offered by Barnett and Duvall (2005). Their typology takes inspiration, inter alia, from Guzzini (1993), who was the first to problematize uses of power analysis inside IR and offered a conceptual remedy. Redistribution of power understood as capabilities was enriched by the introduction of structural power and its different renderings, namely indirect institutional power, nonintentional power, and impersonal power. He proposed "that any power analysis should necessarily include a pair or dyad of concepts of power, linking agent power and impersonal governance" (Guzzini 1993, 443). Barnett and Duvall (2005) opt for two organizing dyads as far as their conceptualization: first, in relation to expressions of power, one can make a difference between *interaction* and *constitution*; and second, in connection to specificity of social relations of power, *direct* and *diffused* relations can be identified (2005, 45–48). When put together, four types of power can be rendered: compulsory, institutional, structural, and productive. While utilizing Barnett and Duvall (2005), I deliberately reverse the order of types of power in the subsequent lines. Indeed, what takes theoretical and conceptual precedence in the beginning of an analysis has important consequences (cf. Reinalda and Verbeek 2004, 27–28). Due to the fact that theorization of wider normative considerations, general constitution of subjectivities, and their historical and structural conditionings are seen as especially relevant, I move from systemic to specific and from diffused to direct. This should not be read, however, as the preference for a structuralist approach to power analysis but rather a counterbalance, as far as the research strategy is concerned, to a conventional, state-centered regime analysis. The latter managed to tackle unit-level interactions between and among (important) states and IOs, that is, chiefly relying on compulsory and institutional conceptions of power.

While usually being dealt with marginally at best or completely ignored at worst, *productive power* is crucial for understanding the nature of regime dynamics and conditions, or the lack thereof. This type of power allows for the construction—or rather production (considering that their very physical makeups are at stake)—of political subjects through diffuse social relations. While productive power shares several features with other types (especially the focus on constitutive sociopolitical processes, actors' capacities, as well as their self-perception), it notably differs in relational specificity. In their analysis of power, Barnett and Duvall (2005, 55) therefore discussed a difference between structural power as structural constitution, that is, "the production and reproduction of internally related positions of super- and subordination, or domination, that actors occupy" and productive power as "the constitution of all social subjects with various social powers through systems of knowledge and discursive practices of broad and general social scope." Therefore productive power permeates systems of meaning/knowledge production and relates to general processes of signification. Following the first guideline, that is, to grasp productive power through systems of differentiation, this advancement is predicated upon the constitutive role—and materiality—of the discourse. To investigate productivity of power, its differentiating capacity needs to be revealed: "Rather than analysing power from the point of view of its internal rationality, it consists of analysing power relations through the antagonism of strategies. For example to find out what our society means by sanity, perhaps we should investigate what is happen-

		Relational Specificity	
		Diffuse	Direct
Conduit of power	Social relations of constitution	PRODUCTIVE (G1) Impersonal intersubjective power (doxa, dispositif, episteme) desiring-production	STRUCTURAL (G2) Impersonal positional power (Cultural hegemony, transnational historical bloc and its maintenance)
	Interactions of specific actors	INSTITUTIONAL (G4, G5) Indirect/unintended institutional effects; lags and feedback between power base and regime	COMPULSORY (G3, G5) Possessive (power as resources and their shifts) and relational (direct control over outcomes)

ing in the field of insanity. And what we mean by legality in the field of illegality" (Foucault 1982, 220).

With direct implications for seeing how productive power permeates, signifies, and conditions international security regimes, the constitutive role of *ethics and culture* is seen as cardinal. Produced moral and cultural discourses (Price 1995) function as legitimizing "regimes of truth," that is, "the types of discourse which it accepts and makes function as true, the mechanisms and instances which enable one to distinguish true and false statements, the means by which each is sanctioned" (Foucault 1980, 131). Thus, they play the role of "codes of intelligibility" (Weldes et al. 1999, 16), serving both as conditions of possibility and horizons of the taken for granted. It is through these that the constitutive differentiation between "the civilized" and "the uncivilized," what Price (1995, 95) called "the discipline of civilization" in relation to prohibitionary chemical weapons regime, can be enacted. Of course, those systems are ordered contingently, therefore succumbing to numerous transformations and changes in/of intensities. How can we understand possible relationships between prohibition/regulation and productive power? What are the conditions for and effects of productive power's perpetuation/neutralization in and around security regimes? For instance, nuclear weapons being portrayed as the rich man's bomb versus chemical weapons being depicted as the poor man's bomb (1995, 98) with different expectations and courses of action and involvement of three other types of power mediating and moderating operations of productive power. The history of humanitarian arms control and disarmament is full of these separations and differentiations (Cooper 2011; Hynek 2011) but also of their dialogical reversals (for example, the subversion of the dual standards through a complete subversion of what was to be an integrative category of WMDs by "poor men," cf. Price 1995, 99). Contingent yet potent symbolic and legal differentiation between small arms and light weapons, antipersonnel landmines (which used to be part of the former), and cluster bombs (which had been separate but were later narratively linked to antipersonnel landmines) can partially explain different fortunes when it comes to their respective regulations and prohibitions.

Roles of productive power in stigmatization and tabooization politics (with its principles of contingency, hierarchy/domination through civilizational discipline and resistance, cf. Price 1995, 89–93) help the analyst to expose how moral opprobrium articulated in and around security regimes is being linked to more general moral and cultural horizons. Moreover, productive power helps to constitute seemingly noble discourses (for example, many international security regimes are greased by narratives on humanitarianism), which in turn stimulate positive effects. Deleuze and Guattari (1983, 11–11) call them micropolitical "desiring production," that is, the investment of psychical energy into the production of what is taken as reality, and "social-production" articulated as the utilization of corporeal energy, that is, labor. These have been neglected though very important parts of the so-called political rationalities, or governmentalities, function as wider discourses of rules that structure sociopolitical orders and within which grid subjects are constituted (Foucault 1988, 161). What else can explain, apart from generous financing by many actors, the reasons why NGOs and civil society in general have been more and more involved in the molding of many of international security regimes, from agenda setting all the way to their verification, and why they have been increasingly using humanitarian language even in agendas such as the push for nuclear disarmament (cf. Hynek and Smetana 2016)? Positive inducement—and looping—through effects is beyond any doubt linked to "ethics creep" (Slim 2013, 3).

The next type there is is *structural power*. This type of power sheds light on the creation of actors' capacities. Such creation is based on mutual—and positionally oriented—constitution and occurs through direct interactions between/among actors. While structures constrain actors' options in terms of who they are and what they want, they are, simultaneously, the products of actors' direct relations. In the words of Barnett and Duvall (2005, 52–53), this type of power "produces the very social capacities of structural, or subject, positions in direct relation to one another, and the associated interests, that underlie and dispose action . . . A, exists only by virtue of its relation to structural position, B. The classical examples here are master-slave and capital-labor relations." Structural asymmetry indeed has consequences. That is, especially, different distribution of benefits, obligations, and self-awareness (including one's understanding concerning how much determined its fate is). The key concept for structural power is the notion of hegemony, especially in the neo-Gramscian sense. As Cox (1987, 7) maintained,

> hegemony is more than the dominance of a single world power. It means the dominance of a particular kind where the dominant state creates an order based ideologically on a broad measure of consent, functioning according to general principles that in fact ensure the continuing supremacy of the leading state or states and the leading social classes but at the same time offer some measure or prospect of satisfaction to the less powerful. In such an order, production in particular countries becomes connected through the mechanisms of the world economy and linked into world systems of production.

Lukes (1975, 24) queried hegemony hiding itself behind the veil of false conscience and thin legitimacy as follows: "is it not the supreme and most insidious exercise of power to prevent people, to whatever degree, from having grievances shaping their perceptions, cognitions, and preferences in such a way that they accept their role in the existing order of things?"

The importance for regime analysis can be understood in relation to the (re)production of power hierarchies. This is where the notion of cultural hegemony and neo-Marxist analysis in particular can help to reveal them (but also cf. Wendt and Friedheim 1995). Cultural production of actors' political identities plays an important role in this regard. When it comes to direct, functionally determined power relations and capacities, sound regime analysis inquires into the nature, extent, and direction of contestation within a given regime. Of particular importance for regime theorization is the "un-politics" of regimes, here understood as hegemonic attempts to block initiatives concerning regime proposals through exercises of structural power and reproduction of power asymmetries (Newell 2008, 2005; Crenson 1971). Strange (1994, 24–32) recognized four components of structural power relevant for theorization of regimes, namely capacity to exercise control over the sphere of security, knowledge production, finance, and material production. Explicitly from a regime-theoretical perspective, Gale (1998) analyzed meso-level structures in this light, and specifically strategies of contestation and recreation of normative structures, privileges, and compliance mechanisms by global civil society actors. To him, international regimes could be comprehended as "instances of institutionalized hegemony" (1998, 275) and with its focus on nonstate actors, and their counter-hegemonic struggles, testifies to the link between political heterarchies and structural power (cf. Paterson, Humphreys, and Pettiford 2003). What is the dominant character of such contestation, that is, does it take place among actors who subscribe to the hegemonic discourse (and can therefore be described as "technical"); among those actors and designated "free-riders," or among these and those who seek to more radically change, break, or break *out* of the regime and establish alternative associations based on existing, temporarily subjugated types of knowledge or on appropriation and subversive reinterpretation of existing norms? What are, on the other hand, ideational and material reasons for nominally politico-juridically independent actors to embrace norms and obligations associated with dominant actors of a given period (Ikenberry and Kupchan 1990; Kennedy 1988)?

Still more, there is *institutional power*. While its operations through specific interactions among actors is what it shares with the next in the line, that is, compulsory power, its relational quality is diffuse, or indirect. As Barnett and Duvall (2005, 51) maintain in this context, "the conceptual focus here is on the formal and informal institutions that mediate between A and B, as A, working through the rules and procedures that define those institutions, guides, steers, and constrains the actions (or non-actions) and conditions of existence of others." Thus, where it differs from compulsory power is particularly in the mediatory, international-institutional locus of power workings. Therefore A and B do not enter into direct interaction here as temporal, bureaucratic, and/or social distance kicks in. Indeed, temporal and bureaucratic distances require the use of historical institutionalist and rational-choice institutionalist accounts. Forms of institutionalization and degrees of rationalization, that is, Foucault's fourth and fifth guidelines, highlight the significance of institutional power and its particular workings. As Hanrieder (2015) showed, complex political, legal, and bureaucratic relations between states and IOs account for the design of IOs often being "circumscribed by path-dependent power dynamics," leading to rationally explicable inertia and preferences for certain types of policy/norm diffusion (2015, 215). Here, an analysis of institutional programs, themselves derived from wider political rationalities effectuated by productive power, should be stressed as one of their most important functions is its regulatory function: "practices of bureaucratic hierarchism and proceduralism spread from state institutions into 'non-state' realms. . . . This dispersal of the . . . regulation and government throughout society also illustrates the governmentalization of society" (Sharma and Gupta 2006, 17).

When it comes to relevance for regime analysis, operations of power such as decisional rules (either hegemonically or collectively established), formal/informal lines of responsibility and its division, configurations of linear path dependence—or on the other hand shifts through critical junctures—as well as diffused reciprocity are being investigated. With a theoretical and empirical focus on international regulatory regimes, manipulation of power configuration through collective institutional entrepreneurship becomes crucial for understanding the fashion in which institutional power operates on/through those regimes (Wijen and Ansari 2007). As the authors put it, there is an "agency-structure paradox or the ability of institutional entrepreneurs to spearhead change despite constraints. In many complex fields, however, change also needs cooperation from numerous dispersed actors. This presents the additional paradox of ensuring that these actors engage in collective action when individual interests favor lack of cooperation" (2007, 1079). How has an established regime subsequently evolved, in relation to original hegemonic interests and calculations? Also, importantly for regime analysis, it is a question of durability, intensity, and evolutionary trajectories related to the formation/application of institutional rules. As Barnett and Duvall (2005, 52) argue, while "institutions . . . are established to help actors achieve mutually acceptable, even Pareto-superior, outcomes also create 'winners' and 'losers,' to the extent that the ability to use the institution and accordingly, collective rewards—material and normative—are unevenly distributed into the future and beyond the intentions of the creators." Therefore an integral part of analyzing the institutional power is a focus on indirect (and often unintended) consequences, such as institutional effects of particular agenda-setting, facilitating/mediating conditions, forms of interdependence, as well as nesting and/or path-dependency pathologies (cf. Clegg, Courpasson, and Phillips 2006; Barnett and Finnemore 1999; Finnemore 1993). Indeed, such an analysis also needs to consider institutional mediation from the position of the subaltern, or weak actors. Sometimes, and perhaps surprisingly, it may be linked, in terms of indirect effects, to the institutional limits of hegemonic power (consider the subversive discourse of the weak states on chemical weapons enabled by the previously established Western legal and political connection between those weapons and hegemonic possession of nuclear weapons).

Finally, there is *compulsory power*. It is based on a series of unit-based interactions through which actors get into relations with each other directly. As Barnett and Duvall (2005, 48) maintain, "compulsory power exists in the direct control of one actor over the conditions of existence and/or the actions of another." It is here where Dahl's (1957, 202–3) classical definition of power, defined as the ability of A to get B to do what B otherwise would not do, applies. In this context, one can think about one's direct influence over other actors exercised through practices and discourses. Both material and ideational resources are thus being utilized and put into workings. The important feature, which goes beyond Dahl's formulation and is noted by Barnett and Duvall (2005, 50), is the possibility of compulsory power operating in an unintended fashion. It is for this reason that "compulsory power is best understood from the perspective of the recipient, not the deliverer, of the direct action" (2005, 50). Indeed, this does not square readily with existing IR scholarship which has—both generally and in regime analysis—traditionally focused on deliverers, especially the wielding of compulsory power by dominant states in the system.

When it comes to the significance of compulsory power for theorization of regimes, three points are highlighted in particular. First, great power politics and diplomacy need to be examined. Specifically to focus on how, and for what reasons, great powers form and maintain international regimes. Systemically, hegemony and its specific manifestations need to be studied. Can we identify a specific hegemon in a given regime? What has been the nature of legitimization of regime formation? How has it been accepted internationally? In terms of mechanisms of power, can we recognize coercion, peer pressure, normative compliance, bandwagoning, bribery, etc., in this context? What has been their specific configuration, both in terms of spatiality and temporality? What have been directly produced unintended consequences, especially in light of resistance and subversion from other actors and their coalitions? Second, the role of IOs needs to be studied when it comes to compulsory power and regime analysis. When it comes to this type of power operation, especially the use of their specific targeting needs to be systematized. What have been ways in which IOs have put into use their sources of authority? What kinds of authority and/or their configuration (for example, expert, moral, delegated, political/legal) have been deployed to alter the behavior of specific actors? What have been the specific mechanisms and technologies of power (for example, teaching, persuasion, and sanctions) used for this alteration? Last but not least, the compulsory power of nonstate actors needs to be scrutinized. When it comes to regime analysis, especially the role of NGOs and broader transnational advocacy networks have been well documented (Risse, Ropp, and Sikkink 2013; Arts 2000; Price 1998; Keck and Sikkink 1998; Risse 1995). What have been their sources of compulsory power (for example, moral authority, field knowledge and recognized history of practice, informal/formal standing and/or status)? What specific technologies and mechanisms of power did they utilize to alter other actors' interests and identities (for example, naming, shaming, tabooization, whistleblowing)? However, while those actors are usually perceived positively, their possible blocking and/or disruptive potential needs to be factored in too (for example, actors representing business/legal interests that clash with international prohibitive/ regulatory attempts and targeting directly other actors; actors physically fighting against such attempts and their proponents).

CONCLUSION

Theorization of regimes—and that includes international security re- gimes—is not dead, though Strange's (1982) five criticisms, or "dragons," have been swirling around theoretical grounds ever since she used them to critique what she believed were major deficiencies of the theory. Judged by the number of regime analysis publications in academic jour- nals and books, theorization of regimes has seen its peak, with more recent contributions having focused on refinements and new venues of limited ambition, such as regimes interplay, complexity, etc. Therefore theorization of regimes has had many features of an explicit, progressive scientific research program—to invoke Lakatos's (1970) understanding of scientific work—for much of its life. The move from neorealism and heg- emonic stability theory to neoliberal institutionalist regime theory, and from there to theorization of cognitivism and stronger incorporation of the role of ideas and norms, can be understood as "progressive problem shifts," both theoretically and empirically. That is, however, within an image of the IR field remaining intact when it comes to the nature of its general paradigm (Kuhn's "normal science") and "disciplinary" stan- dards. As was shown, the development in and around the field of IR experienced two trends that coincided with the existence and refinement of normal-scientific regimes theorization.

The trends—that is, the opening of disciplinary boundaries (since the Third Great Debate) and the rise of theoretical and analytical eclecti- cism—which are still visible and even stronger today, have synergistical- ly—and irreversibly—worked to change the IR landscape. For some, this has been for the better, for others, the perception has not been so positive, as the special issue of the *European Journal of International Relations* on the end of IR theory showed (Dunne, Hansen, and Wight 2013; Reus-Smit 2013; Lake 2013). Be that as it may, it could be argued that the develop- ment of a regime-theoretical research program has displayed signs of what Lakatos would have called "negative heuristics," that is, certain propositions of a research program that are nonrevisable. Here it was regime theorization based on an "ism" of one sort or another, just with a more limited range, state-centralism, and marginalization of insights from radical constructivism and poststructuralism. For these reasons, this chapter, and the entire book, embraces a cautiously open-ended, eclectic position that puts into the center the discussion conceptualization of power, its exercises, multiplicities, as well as the general outline of rele- vance for theorization of international security regimes. From the Lakatosian "hardcore" research programmatic perspective, this looks like an example of epistemological pluralism, but for reasons driven by plastic understanding of workings of those regimes vis-à-vis operations of power. This is including productive power, for many reasons the most underdeveloped one when it comes to normal science of regime theorization, and which cannot be ignored for the sake of its constitutive effects.

REFERENCES

Aceves, W. J. 1997. "Institutionalist Theory and International Legal Scholarship." *American University International Law Review* 12, no. 2: 227–66.

Adler, E., and P. Greve. 2009. "When Security Community Meets Balance of Power: Overlapping Regional Mechanisms of Security Governance." *Review of International Studies* 35, no. S1: 59–84.

Alker, H. R., and W. J. Greenberg. 1977. "On Simulating Collective Security Regime Alternatives." In *Thought and Action in Foreign Policy*, edited by G. M. Bonham and M. J. Shapiro, 263–305. Basel: Birkhäuser Verlag.

Allen, B. 1998. "Foucault and Modern Political Philosophy." In *The Later Foucault: Politics and Philosophy*, edited by J. Moss, 164–98. London: Sage Publications.

Alter, K. J., and S. Meunier. 2009. "The Politics of International Regime Complexity." *Perspectives on Politics* 7, no. 1: 13–24.

Andreatta, F., and M. Koenig-Archibugi. 2010. "Which Synthesis? Strategies of Theoretical Integration and the Neorealist-Neoliberal Debate." *International Political Science Review* 31, no. 2: 207–27.

Arts, B. 2000. "Regimes, Non-State Actors and the State System: A 'Structurational' Regime Model." *European Journal of International Relations* 6, no. 4: 513–42.

Baldwin, D. A., ed. 1993. *Neorealism and Neoliberalism: The Contemporary Debate*. New York: Columbia University Press.

Barnett, M. N., and R. Duvall. 2005. "Power in International Politics." *International Organization* 59, no. 1: 39–75.

Barnett, M. N., and M. Finnemore. 1999. "The Politics, Power and Pathologies of International Organizations." *International Organization* 53, no. 4: 699–732.

Biermann, F., and P. Pattberg. 2008. "Global Environmental Governance: Taking Stock, Moving Forward." *Annual Review of Environment and Resources* 33, no. 1: 277–94.

Breitmeier, H., O. Young, and M. Zürn. 2006. *Analyzing International Environmental Regimes: From Case Study to Database*. Cambridge, MA: MIT Press.

Bourne, M. 2007. *Arming Conflict: The Proliferation of Small Arms*. Houndmills: Palgrave Macmillan.

Clegg, S. R., D. Courpasson, and N. Phillips. 2006. *Power and Organizations*. London: Sage Publications.

Cooley, A. 2005. *Logics of Hierarchy: The Organization of Empires, States, and Military Occupations*. Ithaca, NY: Cornell University Press.

Cooper, N. 2011. "Humanitarian Arms Control and Processes of Securitization: Moving Weapons along the Security Continuum." *Contemporary Security Policy* 32, no. 1: 134–58.

Cox, R. W. 1987. *Production Power and World Order: Social Forces in the Making of History*. New York: Columbia University Press.

Crenson, M. 1971. *The Un-Politics of Air Pollution: A Study of Non-Decisionmaking in the Cities*. Baltimore, MD: Johns Hopkins University Press.

Crumley, C. L. 1995. "Heterarchy and the Analysis of Complex Societies." *Archeological Papers of the American Anthropological Association* 6, no. 1: 1–5.

Dahl, R. 1957. "The Concept of Power." *Behavioral Science* 2, no. 3: 201–15.

Deleuze, G. 1987. *Dialogues*. New York: Columbia University Press.
Deleuze, G., and M. Foucault. 1977. "Intellectuals and Power." In *Language, Counter-Memory, Practice: Selected Essays and Interviews*, edited by M. Foucault, 205–17. Ithaca, NY: Cornell University Press.
Deleuze, G., and F. Guattari. 1983. *Anti-Oedipus: Capitalism and Schizophrenia*. Minneapolis: University of Minnesota Press.
———. 1987. *A Thousand Plateaus: Capitalism and Schizophrenia*. London: Athlone.
———. 1994. *What Is Philosophy?* London: Verso.
Dimitrov, R. S., D. F. Sprinz, G. M. DiGiusto, and A. Kelle. 2007. "International Nonregimes: A Research Agenda." *International Studies Review* 9, no. 2: 230–58.
Drezner, D. W. 2009. "The Power and Peril of International Regime Complexity." *Perspectives on Politics* 7, no. 1: 65–70.
Duffield, J. S. 1994. "Explaining the Long Peace in Europe: The Contribution of Regional Security Regimes." *Review of International Studies* 20, no. 4: 369–88.
Dunne, T., L. Hansen, and C. Wight. 2013. "The End of International Relations Theory?" *European Journal of International Relations* 19, no. 3: 405–25.
Efrat, A. 2010. "Toward Internationally Regulated Goods: Controlling the Trade in Small Arms and Light Weapons." *International Organization* 64, no. 1: 97–131.
Finnemore, M. 1993. "International Organizations as Teachers of Norms: The United Nations Educational, Scientific, and Cultural Organization and Science Policy." *International Organization* 47, no. 4: 565–97.
Foucault, M. 1977. "Nietzsche, Genealogy, History." In *Language, Counter-Memory, Practice: Selected Essays and Interviews*, edited by D. F. Bouchard, 139–64. Ithaca, NY: Cornell University Press.
———. 1980. *Power/Knowledge: Selected Interviews and Other Writings 1972–1977*. Brighton: Harvester Press.
———. 1982. "The Subject and Power: Afterword." In *Michel Foucault: Beyond Structuralism and Hermeneutics*, edited by H. Dreyfus and P. Rabinow, 208–28. Brighton: Harvester Press.
———. 1988. *Technologies of the Self: A Seminar with Michel Foucault*. Amherst, MA: MIT Press.
———. 1991. "Governmentality." In *Foucault Effect: Studies in Governmentality*, edited by G. Burchell, C. Gordon, and P. Miller, 87–104. Chicago: University of Chicago Press.
Gale, F. 1998. "Cave 'Cave! Hic Dragones': A Neo-Gramscian Deconstruction and Reconstruction of International Regime Theory." *Review of International Political Economy* 5, no. 2: 252–83.
Garcia, S. 2011. *Disarmament Diplomacy and Human Security: Regimes, Norms and Moral Progress in International Relations*. London: Routledge.
Getz, K. A. 2006. "The Effectiveness of Global Prohibition Regimes: Corruption and the Antibribery Convention." *Business and Society* 45, no. 3: 254–81.
Giddens, A. 1984. *The Constitution of Society: Outline of the Theory of Structuration*. Berkeley: University of California Press.
Goldsmith, J. 2000. "Sovereignty, International Relations Theory, and International Law." *Stanford Law Review* 52, no. 4: 959–86.
Gómez-Mera, L. 2015. "Regime Complexity and Global Governance: The Case of Trafficking in Persons." *European Journal of International Relations*. Published Online (before print) September 24.
Grieco, J. 1988. "Anarchy and Limits of Cooperation: A Realist Critique of the Newest Liberal Institutionalism." *International Organization* 42, no. 3: 485–507.
Guzzini, S. 1993. "Structural Power: The Limits of Neorealist Power Analysis." *International Organization* 47, no. 3: 443–78.
Haas, E. B. 1982. "Words Can Hurt You: Or, Who Said What to Whom about Regimes." *International Organization* 36, no. 2: 207–43.
———. 1983. "Regime Decay: Conflict Management and International Organizations, 1945–1981." *International Organization* 37, no. 2: 189–256.

Haas, P. M. 1989. "Do Regimes Matter? Epistemic Communities and Mediterranean Pollution Control." *International Organization* 43, no. 3: 377–403.

———. 1992. "Introduction: Epistemic Communities and International Policy Coordination." *International Organization* 46, no. 1: 1–35.

Haggard, S., and B. A. Simmons. 1987. "Theories of International Regimes." *International Organization* 41, no. 3: 491–517.

Hanrieder, T. 2015. "The Path-Dependent Design of International Organizations: Federalism in the World Health Organization." *European Journal of International Relations* 21, no. 1: 215–39.

Hasenclever, A., P. Mayer, and V. Rittberger. 1997. *Theories of International Regimes.* Cambridge: Cambridge University Press.

Hynek, N. 2011. "Rethinking Human Security: History, Economy, Governmentality." In *Critical Perspectives on Human Security: Rethinking Emancipation and Power in International Relations*, edited by D. Chandler and N. Hynek, 157–71. London: Routledge.

———. 2012. *Human Security as Statecraft: Structural Conditions, Articulations and Unintended Consequences.* London: Routledge.

Hynek, N., and M. Smetana, eds. 2016. *Global Nuclear Disarmament: Strategic, Political, and Regional Perspectives.* London: Routledge.

Hynek, N., and A. Teti. 2010. "Saving Identity from Postmodernism? The Normalization of Constructivism in International Relations." *Contemporary Political Theory* 9, no. 2: 171–99.

Ikenberry, G. J., and C. A. Kupchan. 1990. "Socialization and Hegemonic Power." *International Organization* 44, no. 3: 283–315.

Jervis, R. 1982. "Security Regimes." *International Organization* 36, no. 2: 357–78.

Johnson, T., and J. Urpelainen. 2012. "A Strategic Theory of Regime Integration and Separation." *International Organization* 66, no. 4: 645–77.

Joseph, J. 2012. *The Social in the Global: Social Theory, Governmentality and Global Politics.* Cambridge: Cambridge University Press.

Keck, M. E., and K. Sikkink. 1998. *Activists beyond Borders: Advocacy Networks in International Politics.* Ithaca, NY: Cornell University Press.

Keeley, J. F. 1990. "Toward a Foucauldian Analysis of International Regimes." *International Organization* 44, no. 1: 83–105.

Kennedy, E. 1988. *The Rise and Fall of the Great Powers: Economic Change and Military Conflict from 1500 to 2000.* London: Fontana Press.

Keohane, R. O. 1984. *After Hegemony: Cooperation and Discord in the World Political Economy.* Princeton, NJ: Princeton University Press.

———, ed. 1986. *Neorealism and Its Critics.* New York: Columbia University Press.

———. 1989. "Neoliberal Institutionalism: A Perspective on World Politics." In *International Institutions and State Power: Essays in International Relations Theory*, edited by R. Keohane, 1–20. Boulder, CO: Westview Press.

Keohane, R. O., and L. Martin. 1995. "The Promise of Institutional Theory." *International Security* 20, no. 1: 39–51.

Keohane, R. O., and J. S. Nye. 1977. *Power and Interdependence: World Politics in Transition.* Boston: Little, Brown.

Keohane, R. O., and D. G. Victor. 2010. *The Regime Complex for Climate Change.* Discussion Paper, January. Cambridge, MA: Harvard Project on International Climate Agreements. http://belfercenter.ksg.harvard.edu/files/Keohane_Victor_Final_2.pdf.

Klotz, A. 1995. *Norms in International Relations: The Struggle against Apartheid.* Ithaca, NY: Cornell University Press.

Krasner, S. D. 1982. "Structural Causes and Regime Consequences: Regimes as Intervening Variables." *International Organization* 36, no. 2: 185–206.

———. 1999. *Sovereignty: Organized Hypocrisy.* Princeton, NJ: Princeton University Press.

———. 2003. "Harry Kreisler's Conversation with Stephen D. Krasner." *IIS: Conversations with History.* March 31. http://globetrotter.berkeley.edu/people3/Krasner/krasner-con0.html.

Kratochwil, F. 1993. "Contract and Regimes: Do Issue Specificity and Variations of Formality Matter?" In *Regime Theory and International Relations*, edited by V. Rittberger, 73–93. Oxford: Clarendon Press.

Kratochwil, F., and J. G. Ruggie. 1986. "International Organizations: A State of the Art on an Art of the State." *International Organization* 40, no. 4: 753–75.

Krause, K. 1990. "Constructing Regional Security Regimes and the Control of Arms Transfers." *International Journal* 45, no. 2: 386–423.

———. 2002. "Multilateral Diplomacy, Norm Building and UN Conferences: The Case of Small Arms and Light Weapons." *Global Governance* 8, no. 2: 247–63.

———. 2011. "Leashing the Dogs of War: Arms Control from Sovereignty to Governmentality." *Contemporary Security Policy* 32, no. 1: 20–39.

Krause, K., and A. Latham. 1998. "Constructing Non-Proliferation and Arms Control: The Norms of Western Practice." *Contemporary Security Policy* 19, no. 1: 23–54.

Lakatos, I. 1970. "Falsification and the Methodology of Scientific Research Programmes." In *Criticism and the Growth of Knowledge*, edited by I. Lakatos and A. Musgrave, 91–196. Cambridge: Cambridge University Press.

Lake, D. A. 2011. "Why 'Isms' Are Evil: Theory, Epistemology, and Academic Sects as Impediments to Understanding and Progress." *International Studies Quarterly* 55, no. 2: 465–80.

———. 2013. "Theory Is Dead, Long Live Theory: The End of the Great Debates and the Rise of Eclecticism in International Relations." *European Journal of International Relations* 19, no. 3: 567–87.

Lapid, Y. 1989. "The Third Debate: On the Prospects of International Theory in a Post-Positivist Era." *International Studies Quarterly* 33, no. 3: 235–54.

Levy, M. A., O. R. Young, and M. Zürn. 1995. "The Study of International Regimes." *European Journal of International Relations* 1, no. 3: 267–330.

Lidskog, R., and G. Sundqvist. 2002. "The Role of Science in Environmental Regimes: The Case of LRTAP." *European Journal of International Relations* 8, no. 1: 77–101.

Lipson, M. 2005–2006. "Transgovernmental Networks and Non-Proliferation: International Security and the Future of Global Governance." *International Journal* 61, no. 1: 179–98.

Lorraine, T. 2005. "Plateau." In *The Deleuze Dictionary*, edited by A. Parr, 206–7. New York: Columbia University Press.

Lukes, S. 1975. *Power: A Radical View*. Houndmills: Macmillan.

March, J. G., and J. P. Olsen. 1998. "The Institutional Dynamics of International Political Orders." *International Organization* 52, no. 4: 943–69.

Miron, J. A. 2001. "Violence, Guns, and Drugs: A Cross-Country Analysis." *The Journal of Law and Economics* 44, no. S2: 615–33.

Müller, H. 1993. "The Internationalization of Principles, Norms and Rules by Governments: The Case of Security Regimes." In *Regime Theory and International Relations*, edited by V. Rittberger, 361–90. Oxford: Clarendon Press.

———. 1995. "Regime Robustness, Regime Attractivity and Arms Control Regimes in Europe." *Cooperation and Conflict* 30, no. 3: 287–97.

Müller, H., and C. Wunderlich, eds. 2013. *Norm Dynamics in Multilateral Arms Control: Interests, Conflicts and Justice*. Athens: University of Georgia Press.

Mutimer, D. 2000. *The Weapons State: Proliferation and the Framing of Security*. Boulder, CO: Lynne Rienner Publishers.

Muzaka, V. 2011. "Linkages, Contests and Overlaps in the Global Intellectual Property Rights Regime." *European Journal of International Relations* 17, no. 4: 755–76.

Nadelmann, E. 1990. "Global Prohibition Regimes: The Evolution of Norms in International Society." *International Organization* 44, no. 4: 479–526.

Newell, P. 2005. "Race, Class and the Global Politics of Environmental Inequality." *Global Environmental Politics* 5, no. 3: 70–94.

———. 2008. "The Political Economy of Global Environmental Governance." *Review of International Studies* 34, no. 3: 507–29.

Nye, J. S. 1987. "Nuclear Learning and U.S.–Soviet Security Regimes." *International Organization* 41, no. 3: 371–402.

———. 1988. "Neorealism and Neoliberalism." *World Politics* 40, no. 2: 235–51.

Oye, K. A., ed. 1986. *Cooperation under Anarchy*. Princeton, NJ: Princeton University Press.

Paterson, M., D. Humphreys, and L. Pettiford. 2003. "Conceptualizing Global Environmental Governance: From Interstate Regimes to Counter-Hegemonic Struggles." *Global Environmental Politics* 3, no. 2: 1–10.

Peterson, M. J. 2012. "International Regimes as Concept." *E-International Relations*. Published online December 21. http://www.e-ir.info/2012/12/21/international-regimes-as-concept/.

Powell, W. W., and P. J. DiMaggio, eds. 1991. *The New Institutionalism in Organizational Analysis*. Chicago: University of Chicago Press.

Price, R. 1995. "A Genealogy of the Chemical Weapons Taboo." *International Organization* 49, no. 1: 73–103.

———. 1997. *The Chemical Weapons Taboo*. Ithaca, NY: Cornell University Press.

———. 1998. "Reversing the Gun Sights: Transnational Civil Society Targets Land Mines." *International Organization* 52, no. 3: 613–44.

Price, R., and C. Reus-Smit. 1998. "Dangerous Liaisons? Critical International Theory and Constructivism." *European Journal of International Relations* 4, no. 3: 259–94.

Price, R., and N. Tannenwald. 1996. "Norms and Deterrence: The Nuclear and Chemical Weapons Taboos." In *The Culture of National Security: Norms and Identity in World Politics*, edited by P. J. Katzenstein, 114–52. New York: Columbia University Press.

Puchala, D. J., and R. F. Hopkins. 1982. "International Regimes: Lessons from Inductive Analysis." *International Organization* 36, no. 2: 245–75.

Reinalda, B., and B. Verbeek, eds. 2004. *Decision Making within International Organizations*. London: Routledge.

Reus-Smit, C. 2013. "Beyond Metatheory?" *European Journal of International Relations* 19, no. 3: 589–608.

Risse, T., ed. 1995. *Bringing Transnational Relations Back In: Non-State Actors, Domestic Structures and International Institutions*. Cambridge: Cambridge University Press.

Risse, T., S. C. Ropp, and K. Sikkink, eds. 2013. *The Persistent Power of Human Rights: From Commitment to Compliance*. Cambridge: Cambridge University Press.

Rosenau, J. N. 1986. "Before Cooperation: Hegemons, Regimes and Habit-Driven Actors in World Politics." *International Organization* 40, no. 4: 849–94.

Rublee, M. R. 2009. *Non-Proliferation Norms: Why States Choose Nuclear Restraint*. Athens: University of Georgia Press.

Ruggie, J. G. 1975. "International Responses to Technology: Concepts and Trends." *International Organization* 29, no. 3: 557–83.

———. 1982. "International Regimes, Transactions, and Change: Embedded Liberalism in the Postwar Economic Order." *International Organization* 36, no. 2: 379–415.

———. 1983. "Continuity and Transformation in the World Polity: Toward a Neorealist Synthesis." *World Politics* 35, no. 2: 261–85.

Sayyid, B., and L. Zac. 1998. "Political Analysis in a World without Foundations." In *Research Strategies in the Social Sciences: A Guide to New Approaches*, edited by E. Scarbrough and E. Tanenbaum, 247–67. Oxford: Oxford University Press.

Sharma, A., and A. Gupta. 2006. "Introduction: Rethinking Theories of the State in an Age of Globalization." In *The Anthropology of the State: A Reader*, edited by A. Sharma and A. Gupta, 1–42. Malden, MA: Blackwell Publishing.

Sil, R., and P. J. Katzenstein. 2010. *Beyond Paradigms: Analytic Eclecticism in the Study of World Politics*. Basingstoke, UK: Palgrave Macmillan.

Sismondo, S. 1996. *Science without Myth: On Construction, Reality, and Social Knowledge*. New York: State University of New York Press.

Sitaraman, S. 2009. *State Participation in International Treaty Regimes*. Burlington, VT: Ashgate Publishing.

Slim, H. 2013. "Humanitarian Ethics and Humanitarian Effectiveness: How Are They Related?" *Presentation to OCHA Policy Seminar Series*, New York, April 17.

Smith, R. K. 1987. "Explaining the Non-Proliferation Regime: Anomalies for Contemporary International Relations Theory." *International Organization* 41, no. 2: 253–81.

Stokke, O. 1997. "Regimes as Governance Systems." In *Global Governance: Drawing Insights from the Environmental Experience*, edited by O. R. Young, 27–63. Cambridge, MA: MIT Press.

———. 2003. "Trade Measures, WTO, and Climate Compliance: The Interplay of International Regimes." *FNI Report 5/2003*. Oslo: The Fridtjof Nansen Institute, Lysaker.

———. 2012. *Disaggregating International Regimes: A New Approach to Evaluation and Comparison*. Cambridge, MA: MIT Press.

Strange, S. 1982. "Cave! Hic Dragones: A Critique of Regime Analysis." *International Organization* 36, no. 2: 479–96.

———. 1994. *States and Markets*. Second edition. London: Pinter.

Tannenwald, N. 1999. "The Nuclear Taboo: The United States and the Normative Basis of Nuclear Non-Use." *International Organization* 53, no. 3: 433–68.

———. 2007. *The Nuclear Taboo: The United States and the Non-Use of Nuclear Weapons Since 1945*. Cambridge: Cambridge University Press.

———. 2013. "Justice and Fairness in the Nuclear Non-Proliferation Regime." *Ethics and International Affairs* 27, no. 3: 299–317.

Taylor, C. 1985. "Neutrality in Political Science." In *Philosophical Papers*, 58–90. Cambridge: Cambridge University Press.

Waever, O. 1996. "The Rise and Fall of the Inter-Paradigm Debate." In *International Theory: Positivism and Beyond*, edited by S. Smith et al., 149–85. Cambridge: Cambridge University Press.

Weldes, J., M. Laffey, H. Gusterson, and R. Duvall. 1999. "Introduction: Constructing Insecurity." In *Cultures of Insecurity: States, Communities and the Production of Danger*, edited by J. Weldes, M. Laffey, H. Gusterson, and R. Duvall, 1–35. Minneapolis: University of Minnesota Press.

Wendt, A. E. 1987. "The Agent-Structure Problem in International Relations Theory." *International Organization* 41, no. 3: 335–70.

Wendt, A. E., and D. Friedheim. 1995. "Hierarchy under Anarchy: Informal Empire and the East German State." *International Organization* 49, no. 4: 689–721.

Wijen, F., and S. Ansari. 2007. "Overcoming Inaction through Collective Institutional Entrepreneurship: Insights from Regime Theory." *Organization Studies* 28, no. 7: 1079–100.

Young, O. R. 1980. "International Regimes: Problems of Concept Formation." *World Politics* 32, no. 3: 331–56.

———. 1982. "Regime Dynamics: The Rise and Fall of International Regimes." *International Organization* 36, no. 2: 277–97.

———. 1991. "Political Leadership in Regime Formation: On the Development of Institutions in International Society." *International Organization* 45, no. 3: 281–308.

———. 2000. "Institutional Interplay: The Environmental Consequences of Cross-Scale Interactions." NAS Project Working Paper. http://dlc.dlib.indiana.edu/dlc/bitstream/handle/10535/519/youngo041300.pdf?sequence=1&isAllowed=y.

TWO

The Nineteenth-Century Security Regime Complex

This chapter opens up a series of empirical case studies presented in this book by providing insight into the dynamics of humanitarian arms control and disarmament pertinent to the nineteenth century. It sets the stage for analyzing and comprehending the case studies. In particular, it is here where we will show how humanitarianism, and eventually International Humanitarian Law (IHL), gets embedded with weapons treaties within the domain of humanitarian arms control and disarmament. Three disarmament conferences, namely the 1868 St. Petersburg Conference and the 1899 and 1907 Hague Conferences, as well as a series of outcome agreements, receive detailed scrutiny. By orienting ourselves to these manifold developments, we frame our analytical focus under the rubrics of the international regime complex, that is, an essentially composite regime. The opening section details the composition of this regime and explains the notion of regime complexity. The following sections examine operations of power, which enabled the emergence of humanitarian disarmament campaigns, related politics, and the consequent establishment of the nineteenth-century security regime complex. This scrutiny begins by showing the importance of productive power in the constitution of horizons of the possible, especially through broad, ethically anchored discourses. Politico-economic interests behind these dynamics, a feature that will also resurface repeatedly in the consequent chapters, are elucidated afterward. The power analysis performed in this chapter ultimately shows how the idea and practice of humanitarian (arms control and) disarmament originated in the nineteenth century by virtue of the interplay between productive power ("biopolitics," the standard of civilization, Christian beliefs, liberal ethics, etc.), structural and compulsory power (practices of the Red Cross and pacifists versus great power wars, colonial warfare, ongoing arms races, etc.), and institutional power (open diplomacy versus closed sessions). On balance with contemporary and emerging regulatory/disarmament regimes, the herein examined case is not odd. As this book seeks to show, while the content varies, the pivotal logics outlined in this chapter endure.

EMERGENT LEGAL BASE: AT THE CROSSROADS OF HUMANITARIANISM AND DISARMAMENT

The origins of modern *disarmament* law can be traced to the St. Petersburg Declaration of 1868 as well as the 1899 and 1907 Hague Declarations and Conventions (Docherty 2010, 10). Analyzed on balance shortly, the *laws of war* and the peaceful settlement of international disputes were also among the key objectives behind the negotiation and adoption of these documents (Best 1999). The 1899 Hague Conference in particular resulted in the adoption of the Convention for the Pacific Settlement of International Disputes (I); Convention with Respect to the Laws and Customs of War on Land (II); Convention for the Adaptation to Maritime Warfare of the Principles of the Geneva Convention of 1864 (III); Declaration Concerning the Prohibition of the Discharge of Projectiles and Explosives from Balloons or by Other New Analogous Methods (IV/1); Declaration Concerning the Prohibition of the Use of Projectiles with the Sole Object to Spread Asphyxiating Poisonous Gases (IV/2); and Declaration Concerning the Prohibition of the Use of Bullets which Can Easily Expand or Change Their Form Inside the Human Body such as Bullets with a Hard Covering which Does Not Completely Cover the Core, or Containing Indentations (IV/3). The 1907 Hague Conference in turn agreed on the adoption of the Convention for the Pacific Settlement of International Disputes (I); Convention Respecting the Limitation of the Employment of Force for Recovery of Contract Debts (II, "Drago-Porter Convention"); Convention Relative to the Opening of Hostilities (III); Convention Respecting the Laws and Customs of War on Land (IV); Convention Relative to the Rights and Duties of Neutral Powers and Persons in Case of War on Land (V); Convention Relative to the Legal Position of Enemy Merchant Ships at the Start of Hostilities (VI); Convention Relative to the Conversion of Merchant Ships into War-Ships (VII); Convention Relative to the Laying of Automatic Submarine Contact Mines (VIII); Convention Concerning Bombardment by Naval Forces in Time of War (IX); Convention for the Adaptation to Maritime Warfare of the Principles of the Geneva Convention of 1906 (X); Convention Relative to Certain Restrictions with Regard to the Exercise of the Right of Capture in Naval War (XI); Convention Relative to the Establishment of an International Prize Court (XII); Convention Concerning the Rights and Duties of Neutral Powers in Naval War (XIII); and Declaration Prohibiting the Discharge of Projectiles and Explosives from Balloons (XIV) (Scott 1915, 230–32 and 236–39; Hayashi 2017, 2–3).

What is of particular importance for this study is the nexus between *humanitarian law* and disarmament law solidified through these legal measures. Also known as the "law of war" or "law of armed conflict," IHL features a "branch of international law" concerned with the conduct of hostilities and aimed to "minimize suffering and ensure that both combatants and civilians are treated humanely" (Maresca and Maslen 2000, 7). This nexus is of particular importance because the aforementioned disarmament-oriented documents indeed largely served IHL objectives (Mathur 2017, 11). In particular, the 1868 St. Petersburg Conference with its final declaration banned projectiles with a weight below 400 grams, which were either explosive or charged with fulminating or inflammable substances (Declaration of St. Petersburg 1868). Its importance lies not with the specific weapon ban but with the general principle of humanitarian law it introduced, and that is the rejection of the use of weapons "which cause additional suffering for no military gain" (O'Connell 2013, 23). IHL continued to evolve as "a collective expression of the Geneva Conventions and the Hague Laws" (Mathur 2017, 11). As also detailed earlier, the 1899 Hague Conference banned expanding ("dum-dum") bullets, asphyxiating or deleterious gases, and the launching of projectiles or explosives from balloons (Hague Declaration 1899, IV/1, 2, 3). The 1907 Hague Conference in turn reaffirmed the ban of the discharge of projectiles and explosives from balloons (Hague Declaration 1907, XIV). Importantly, the laws and customs of war were also codified in 1899 and 1907 (Hague Declaration 1899, II; Hague Declaration 1907, IV). Humanitarian concerns were also expressed through the so-called Martens Clause that was inserted into the preamble of the 1899 Hague Convention (II). It established the protection of civilians and soldiers in those cases that were not explicitly covered by the laws and customs of war on land. The key notion was "public conscience": "populations and belligerents remain under the protection and empire of the principles of international law, as they result from the usages established between civilized nations, from the laws of humanity and the requirements of the public conscience" (cited in Ticehurst 1997). Also, the 1899 Hague Convention (III) and 1907 Hague Convention (X) adapted the 1864 and 1906 Geneva Conventions respectively (Henckaerts and Doswald-Beck 2005, xxvi). These emerging intersections were crucial because the Geneva Conventions were, in contrast to the Hague Laws, still written primarily from "the perspective of the 'victims' of armed conflict" (O'Connell 2013, 22). Therefore these legal developments of the nineteenth century agreed upon at St. Petersburg (1868) and the Hague (1899 and 1907) feature *humanitarian-disarmament* endeavors.

It is important to highlight that what is scrutinized here is an international *regulatory/disarmament regime complex*, as we term it. This is because, as detailed throughout this chapter, the emergent humanitarian regime of the nineteenth century was composed of a series of agreements between various states, with multiple regulatory focuses concerning different weapons categories and aspects of war conduct. We take the general notion of "international regime complexity," characterized by "a number of elements, building blocks or agents capable of interacting with each other," as a starting point (Alter and Meunier 2009, 13–14; Drezner 2009, 65). Here we show how this phenomenon practically manifests in the domain of arms control and disarmament as well as how it may, and should, be traced to the nineteenth century. The following sections shed light on how this regime complex came into being in a certain shape, inter alia, as a complex product of new humanitarianism, (new) imperialism, and the interplay between "old" and "new" diplomacy. In particular, attention is directed to the processes leading up to and the actual conduct and the outcomes of the St. Petersburg International Military Commission (1868), the First Hague Peace Conference (1899), and the Second Hague Peace Conference (1907) (Higgins 1909/2010, 5; Crowe and Weston-Scheuber 2013, 32–33).

PRODUCTIVE POWER: THE HUMANITARIAN DISARMAMENT EPISTEME

This section will show that an increase in humanitarianism after the end of the Cold War and the role of nongovernmental organizations (NGOs) in this process cannot be considered an unprecedented phenomenon. If one speaks about new humanitarianism, then the attention needs to be directed to the nineteenth century. What both the nineteenth-century humanitarianism and the post–Cold War humanitarianism have in common is precisely their strong attachment to liberal and neoliberal political rationality of government respectively. In both these instances, humanitarian action and campaign were discursively built around the notion of a suffering individual. The legitimization of humanitarian-disarmament campaigns suggest that both actions were framed as human security issues: in the case of the nineteenth century without an accompanying political doctrine; in the case of the post–Cold War humanitarian disarmament campaigns, this was a part of an explicit human security doctrine (the freedom-from-fear doctrine). Specifically, an intimate relationship between the constitution of an active subject/citizen in the society and the emergence of the individual in need of protection as the referent point in the security discourse can be discerned (Hynek 2008). By virtue of this relationship, one can argue that the human body began to be perceived as a vulnerable organism as far as people-centered security was concerned. In other words, while anatomo-politics disciplined the individual-as-a-subject, in both body and mind, biopolitics approached it through life sciences, regulating it at the level of the population (Foucault 1978, 139–44). In line with Foucault, biopolitics can be conceived of as the point of the strategic coordination between economy, population, and government with the aim of extracting from the population what we term "bioenergy." This is to be accomplished through the use of biopower, which includes "numerous and diverse techniques for achieving the subjugation of bodies and the control of populations . . . [that is,] techniques that govern and administer . . . human life" (1978, 140 and 143). The essential characteristic of biopower is its capillarity: once it is exercised, it works through the minds of subjects with the aim of introducing certain attitudes and behavioral patterns.

New humanitarianism (and humanitarian disarmament) of the nineteenth century emerged in connection with the establishment of new types of actors: nonstate actors (Boli and Thomas 1999). Their argumentation aiming at the creation of new human security–based legal norms reveals the essence of what Foucault (1991) calls the transformation of the individual as an effective and efficient political subject. The accumulation of humanitarian knowledge about security, with a focus shifted from the national security frame to the notion of a "suffering" individual, was successfully linked on their part to "a struggle for disarmament" (Mathur 2017, 19 and 95). The International Committee of the Red Cross (ICRC) can be considered one of the most important actors for the generation of this new type of knowledge in the field of security (Finnemore 1999). The underlying "plea" of Henry Dunant, its founder, played a crucial constructive role in this regard too (Toyoda 2009, 1109). Apart from the ICRC, other important players were mainly associations and individual activists promoting humanitarianism and humanitarian disarmament from a pacifistic perspective, as well as members of the press (Hayashi 2017, 7).

To this study, the crucial issue is that of normative resonance between the humanitarianisms and the central role of nonstate actors in their articulation, the fact enabled both in the nineteenth century and after the end of the Cold War by a certain version of liberal order and states' preferred economies of power. As Foucault (1991, 26–27) notes, the liberal rationality of government does not concern purely economic matters; rather, it engulfs the entire functional mechanism of the exercise of political sovereignty. In this light, it is not surprising that the president of the First Plenary Session during the Hague Conference of 1899 mentioned the liberal purpose of maintaining harmony and reduction of horrors of war as the basic reason why diplomatic delegations gathered in the Hague. Similarly, the Dutch government, which hosted and cofinanced the conference, appeals in its conference invitation to states to do their utmost to secure peace and disarmament (Rutherford 1999, 36 and 42). As discussed in detail in the following sections, the liberal rationality of government can be discerned in the nineteenth-century campaigns concerned with humanitarian disarmament in several directions. First of all, it is visible in related knowledge production. Knowledge was generated by nonstate actors and subsequently used to target governments that were present at the conferences. Apart from that, liberal rationality was also visible through medialization of this knowledge, with the aim to pressurize the governments and to hold them accountable. More and more, governments had to pay attention to public opinion in liberalizing polities and were under pressure from nonstate opinion makers, organizations promoting humanitarian ideals and peace, associations of lawyers and teachers, and so on. Following Foucault's guideline concerning the relationship between productive power and systems of differentiation, this underlay one of the early attempts of European states to establish what Price (1995, 95) called "the discipline of civilization." Echoing the Enlightenment thinkers, this nineteenth-century "standard of civilization," having the "civilized" society of states on the one side and the "uncivilized" remainder ("barbarians") on the other (especially regarding colonies, Japan, and the Ottomans before they joined in), was based upon "the idea of European cultural and moral superiority" (Heraclides and Dialla 2015, 31–32). This "Western civilization" was, inter alia, associated with "Christian beliefs" in particular (Caron 2000, 6).

This mixture of Christian and liberal ethics, including a more general change in *typification of security* with the individual—yet mainly a soldier in the nineteenth-century campaigns—constituted a referent object (Hynek 2011, 163), facilitated the establishment of IHL and the nineteenth- and early twentieth-century practice of *humanitarian disarmament* (Caron 2000, 6; Docherty 2010, 10). Scrutinizing the Brussels Act (1890), Cooper (2018, 444) discerned an interesting link by analyzing efforts to "graft" weapons regulatory norms onto an "established and constitutive antislavery norm." This Brussels Act, an antislavery initiative including also arms restrictions, features a crucial landmark in this normative regard (Cooper 2011, 141–42). Studying humanitarian interventions of the nineteenth century, Finnemore (2003, 54) also noted that the underlying notion of "humanity" became expanded from the early efforts to abolish slavery and the slave trade. More importantly, Price (1998, 628) highlighted that efforts to delegitimize weapons tend to build upon "the grafting of moral opprobrium" from practices generally delegitimized by the laws of war or IHL. Starting with the St. Petersburg Declaration, these ethical forces of compassion would manifest in disarmament efforts as a delicate "interplay between military necessity and humanity" in the development of the international laws of war (Docherty 2010, 10; Crowe and Weston-Scheuber 2013, 31; Hayashi 2017, 1–2). However, there are more complex operations of power bringing about broader changes in ethics, its (re)constitution through contingent evolution, and interactions with other structural forces, namely conflict and economy (Barnett 2011, 22–29). Temporality of such changes needs to be linked to the longue durée (Braudel 1982, 25–35; Purdey 2010, 63–65), or long-term time spans, and a series of epochal configurations of forces, or *dispositifs*. This reveals productive forces that need to be taken into account when one subsequently tries to engage in an analysis of specific events, or eventalization (Foucault 1996, 277) and of "instant time" (Braudel 1982, 27). Barnett (2011, 29) has used three longue durée periods to analyze the evolution of humanitarianism. Indeed, a number of characteristics between nineteenth-century humanitarianism and post–Cold War humanitarianism are then different due to historical and political contingencies that have shaped the economy, security, and politics:

> There are various ways to understand how context shapes what is imaginable, desirable, possible. . . . I foreground the global environment. I observe three ages of humanitarianism, distinguished by a global context defined the relationship between the forces of destruction (violence), production (economy), and protection (compassion). For Imperial Humanitarianism it was colonialism, commerce, and civilizing missions; for Neo-Humanitarianism the Cold War and nationalism, development, and sovereignty; and for Liberal Humanitarianism the liberal peace, globalization, and human rights. (2011, 9)

The central notion for understanding such operations of power is *dispositif*, or apparatus: "the apparatus is essentially of a *strategic* nature, which means assuming that it is a matter of a certain manipulation of relations of forces, either developing them in a particular direction, blocking them, stabilizing them, utilizing them, etc. The apparatus is always inscribed in a play of power, but it is also always linked to certain coordinates of knowledge which issue from it but, to an equal degree, condition it" (Foucault 1980, 196–97). Distinguishing between a dispositif and episteme, Foucault maintained that "the *episteme* is a specifically *discursive* apparatus, whereas the apparatus in its general form is both discursive and non-discursive, its elements being much more heterogeneous" (1980, 196–97). In the following section, it will be showed how the nineteenth-century humanitarian dispositif was framed around and set up the structural edifice of modern compassion.

STRUCTURAL AND COMPULSORY POWER: CAUGHT BETWEEN STRATEGIC-MILITARY MOTIVES AND HUMANITARIANISM

This section scrutinizes deeply intertwined operations of structural and compulsory power in and around the nineteenth-century humanitarian regulatory/disarmament regime complex. Both the forces of destruction (violence) and production (economy) are taken into consideration. In particular, the following lines systematically illustrate the convergence between subject positions in direct relation to one another (structural power) and their direct control of actions and conditions of existence of one another (compulsory power) (Barnett and Duvall 2005, 48 and 52–53). Indeed, the selected case study of humanitarian arms control and disarmament features the most vivid illustration of how the workings of these two power configurations could be virtually inseparable. This is because, in the first place, the nineteenth century was the epoch of war, violence, and dominance by a few empires or great powers by military means (Taylor 1954/1971, xix; Best 1999, 619). Although no major wars occurred between 1815 and 1914, there were numerous crises involving the then great powers, including a few particularly violent conflicts such as the Crimean War or the Austro-Prussian and Franco-Prussian Wars (Kennedy 1987/1989, chap. 4; Mulligan 2006, 401 and 406). Colonialism featured a means of particular importance for projecting imperialism in the nineteenth century (Trotha 2006, 437). As a result, for instance, France controlled significant portions of Africa and Southeast Asia, while Britain had "bits and pieces, some of them enormous, everywhere" (Best 1999, 619). This process was largely about colonial warfare because it may be characterized by (bloody) campaigns of conquest by colonial states, the (violent) anticolonialism of the colonized (Trotha 2006, 438), as well as (violent) clashes between the major powers such as the English and French (Kennedy 1987/1989, chap. 5).

Apparently, the strategic environment of the nineteenth century was relatively dynamic. Although the great powers such as France, Austria, or Russia remained the same, they still had their momentous "ups-and-downs" (Taylor 1954/1971, xxiii–xxiv). Four major developments of that time aggravated the "world of struggle" and induced shifts in the balance of world forces, especially toward the late nineteenth century (Kennedy 1987/1989, chap. 5). First, the atmosphere of the century induced broad-based fears of internal revolutions. This is because the emerging "visions of peace" were also implemented during that time through nationalism and self-determination (Ishay 2004/2008, 175). Not only did there occur two inspirational revolutions at the end of the eighteenth century, namely the French and American Revolutions (Toyoda 2009, 1101–2), but ominous revolutionary sentiments would also hang over Russia, Prussia, and Austria in the nineteenth century (Taylor 1954/1971, xxxiii). Second, the prevalent international system, long dominated by five great powers—Austria, Britain, France, Prussia, and Russia (Mulligan 2006, 401)—welcomed the "newcomers." This change was associated with the rise of the United States as a world power (Caron 2000, 6–7), of imperial Germany, as well as of Japan and Italy as great powers (Kennedy 1987/1989, chap. 5). Nationalism played a crucial role for "consolidating states" such as Japan (1868–1912), declared as the Empire of Japan in 1868, Italy (1815–1870), declared as the Kingdom of Italy in 1861, and Germany, which also emerged as a unified state in 1871 (Riall 1994, 1; Ishay 2004/2008, 175–76; Mulligan 2006, 406; Dukes 2011, 31). The newly consolidated and rising powers of the United States, Germany, Italy, and Japan were driven by revisionist aspirations to expand their territories, to emulate the existing powers and challenge the established order, with the United States and Germany having particularly tangible potential to do so (Kennedy 1987/1989, chap. 5). The striking, even surprising, success of Japan in the 1904–1905 Russo-Japanese War signified Japan was also capable of mounting a major military campaign and in fact testified to its status as a great power (Keefer 2007, 39 and 54). Third, the last quarter of the nineteenth century marked the era of new imperialism in this light, renowned as the "scramble" for Africa (Kennedy 1987/1989, chap. 4; Wintle 2006, 24). Finally, the Industrial Revolution arrived to many countries at that time. This systemic transformation directly related the power of weapons to technological advancement (Caron 2000, 6–7). This led to a major change in the technology of land war and naval weaponry and gave rise to a wide-ranging arms race and competition for superiority (Best 1999, 619; Vagts 2000, 31–32). In this era of modern, industrialized warfare, the maintenance of and competition for power became, however, increasingly dependent on a tighter link between economics and strategy (Kennedy 1987/1989, chap. 5). This novel context epitomized a double-edged sword defining the (newly) disadvantaged players in the international arena. On the one hand, it entailed staggering costs and severe pressures on government budgets (Vagts 2000, 32). On the other hand there appeared a reality of military defeats determined by the failure to adapt to this military revolution of the mid-nineteenth century (Kennedy 1987/1989, chap. 4). Possibly the most vivid illustration of this newly emerging rift is Russia's eventual precipitated "military inferiority" vis-à-vis its European rivals (Hayashi 2017, 6). Not only did this arms race heavily burden the Russian economy in general terms (Vagts 2000, 33), but it entailed such costs that were painful for Russia yet not as much for its principal enemies, Germany and Austria-Hungary (Best 1999, 622). However, this technological shift served well to reestablish the still sharpest structural power imbalance, in particular the "colonial order," and the Brussels Act (1890) was in part adopted by the powers to codify this rift via restrictions on arms trade to colonies (Cooper 2011, 143).

The strategic environment of the nineteenth century thus kept states largely preoccupied with their own "security, survival, influence, and perhaps territorial expansion," as accurately summarized by Mulligan (2006, 401). The motives behind the aforesaid developments were more complex, however, if one also considers the dominant discourses detailed in the previous section. In the first place, the expansion of European influence and colonization was accompanied by what Heraclides and Dialla (2015, 31–32) called the "idea of progress, coupled with the standard of civilization" and "a presumed historical mission to civilize the rest of the world." What may testify to this is that a portion of armed interventions of the nineteenth century were "humanitarian interventions" driven by the "humanitarian concern" (2015, 101). These included the interventions in the Greek War of Independence (1821–1832), in Lebanon and Syria (1860–1861), in Bulgaria (1875–1878), in the Balkans (1875–1878), in Cuba (1895–1898), and in Armenia (1894–1917) (Finnemore 2003, 58–64; Heraclides and Dialla 2015). However, these narratives rather reflected a selective and biased "civilization-barbarian construction" (Heraclides and Dialla 2015, 226). First, it codified conquerors or rulers' "superiority" over the uncivilized (Trotha 2006, 441; Heraclides and Dialla 2015, 31). This included an assumed preeminence of "Christendom" (Ladd 1840/2007, 17). Cooper (2011, 143) also noted that restrictions imposed on arms trade to colonies through the Brussels Act (1890) were in fact driven by "imperial concern" rather than "ethical discourse." Second, this construction disregarded "acts of barbarity and inhumanity by various 'civilized' states," as Heraclides and Dialla (2015, 38) spotted. Such then featured, for instance, a military campaign with genocidal attributes in British Australia, excesses of the British, French, and Belgians in Africa, and those associated with the US policy against the indigenous peoples or Russia conquering neighboring territories in the Caucasus and Central Asia (2015, 226). In general terms, colonial states were with no doubt violent by definition (Trotha 2006, 438). Therefore altruistic aspirations were deeply intertwined with instrumental motives. The latter encompassed one's imperialist design and/or "humanitarian prestige" (Heraclides and Dialla 2015, 229). Inter alia, it included "Christian missionizing" as part of the expansion of European influence (Trotha 2006, 443). Importantly, even the notion of humanitarian intervention was biased because it particularly implied the protection of Christians against Ottoman Turks or Muslims, while simultaneously disregarding pogroms against Jews (Finnemore 2003, 58 and 65; Heraclides and Dialla 2015, 225).

Similarly mixed were the driving forces behind the codification of international law toward the late nineteenth century. This move may be associated with the increasing recognition of the inadequacy of "informal" balancing such as the Concert of Europe for the organization of European and international security (Caron 2000, 6–7). Russia was therewith particularly interested in the arms race being halted (Best 1999, 621) and potential recourse to armed hostilities being forestalled (Crowe and Weston-Scheuber 2013, 32). Having discussed it in broader terms, Croft (1996, 136) claimed that "to avoid dangerous imbalances in weapons" is in fact one of the popular motivations behind arms control–related initiatives and designs. However, it may be argued that the trauma and growing horror of war facilitated a wide-ranging resistance to armed violence and an aspiration for peace-oriented arrangements as the general spirit of that time (Caron 2000, 5–6; Forsythe 2005, 23; Frevert 2006, 429). Although state and particularly great power (imperialist) interests still dominated the scene, public opinion came to play a prominent role in this regard (Toyoda 2009, 1099). Progressively harnessing it, peace activists strove to direct attention to the cruelties of war and compel governments to undertake the course of "peace, disarmament, and international arbitration" (Vagts 2000, 32; Hucker 2015, 405). Inter alia, they particularly sought to (re)construct the nexus between the notion of civilized nations, including that of Christianity, and those of pacifism and international order (Caron 2000, 6). Among those who actively sought to influence and report on the related matters were individual peace activists, peace movements or societies, including Quakers, as well as the press (Best 1999, 620; Caron 2000, 6 and 8; Hayashi 2017, 7). The power of public opinion was growing (Hucker 2019, 6–7), particularly against the background of the democratization of politics and liberalization of the press. This wave of change in the political climate to various extents concerned the United States, France, the Netherlands, Spain, Denmark, as well as Prussia and Germany (Toyoda 2009, 1100–102). Despite the prominence of the Swiss government's support for the creation of the ICRC (2019, 1108) and the still national character of societies and associations, international peace and press congresses were emerging (Tyrrell 1978; Kubka and Nordenstreng 1986, 44–45) and the transnational civil society was on the rise (Best 1999, 620). Nonstate actors would thus shape the views of politicians, both directly and also indirectly, including through the printed media (Tuchman 1996, chap. 5). As a direct channel for the peace and disarmament agenda to the governmental level, the Inter-Parliamentary Union (IPU) reinforced the peace movement (Best 1999, 620). It apropos issued an important resolution (1904) requesting the governments to partake in the second international peace conference (1907) (Caron 2000, 18–19). A number of individuals, including some Nobel Peace laureates, embodied the principal nonstate "driving force" of the peace movement (2000, 8). Among them were Lord Salisbury, a conservative statesmen, and Norman Angell, a passionate pacifist later awarded a Nobel Peace Prize (Vagts 2000, 34). Through their intensive lobbying activities, William Evans Darby, the Secretary of the Peace Society of London, and Bertha von Suttner, cofounder of the Austrian Peace Society and a Nobel Peace Prize laureate, also contributed to the development of the peace movement (Abrams 1962; Best 1999, 624 and 629; Goldblat 2002). With their works, Clara Barton and Florence Nightingale also facilitated the peace agenda, including the aspiration to moderate armaments quantitatively and qualitatively (Vagts 2000, 32). William Ladd, the founder and first president of the American Peace Society, inter alia contributed to (re)constructing Christian beliefs of the "Christian and civilized nations" as the foundation for international order (Ladd 1840/2007, 8; Caron 2000, 6 and 10). Another crucial person for framing and politically embedding the peace movement was Ivan Bloch. He was a prominent banker from Poland, then a railway magnate (the head of a railroad) in Russia and a member of the Russian Imperial Council. Once a student of military affairs, he was also a commentator on political and economic consequences of contemporary industrial warfare (Ford 1936, 358–59; Best 1999, 622; Vagts 2000, 33; Caron 2000, 12; Hucker 2015, 407). He significantly contributed to portraying "the destructive potential of industrial warfare," including by writing articles, giving lectures, and traveling widely (Abbenhuis 2018, chap. 2). Bloch's work on "the mounting burdens of modern war on society" had crucial positive implications for the peace movement, especially that it had a strong influence on the Russian Tsar Nicholas II and even inspired his decision to convene the 1899 Hague Peace Conference (Hayashi 2017, 6). In his book *Is War Now Impossible?* Bloch (1898, IV/153–54) acknowledged that the physical qualities of Russia provide it with a unique endurance potential when it comes to warfare. However, he warned (1898, IV/162–63) that the reduction of war preparation costs possibly featured a greater necessity for Russia, in its current economic situation, than for other European states. Another important inference in this book was that both war preparations and wars were painful and burdensome to the European nations (VI/181). Importantly, among other things, Bloch (VI/177) surmised the nexus between wars and revolutionary movements. This renowned work, originally written in Russian, was translated into English, French, and German and "carried considerable weight" beyond Russia (Vagts 2000, 33).

Another renowned individual of that time was Henry Dunant, a Swiss citizen and businessman who founded the ICRC in reaction to his immediate experience of the Battle of Solferino (1859) (Toyoda 2009, 1108). Dunant wrote a book containing his memories of the battle and distributed it to important nongovernmental actors, governments and military personnel alike. In 1863, the ICRC invited governments, international lawyers, and representatives of international pacifist and peace federation movements for a conference to discuss the principles of IHL. These principles were later inserted into the Geneva Conventions (Lavoyer and Maresca 1999; Toyoda 2009, 1108–9). Also in part due to the pressure by national Red Cross movements on their governments, this initiative was met all over Europe with collective enthusiasm for humanitarianism (Toyoda 2009, 1108–9). Dunant became the first recipient of the Nobel Peace Prize (Best 1999, 624). The ICRC emerged as the key humanitarian actor first and foremost driven by its guardianship of the Geneva Laws or IHL (Forsythe 2005, 13; Mathur 2011, 182, 2017, 4 and 95). In fact, the ICRC appeared "at the intersection of IHL and disarmament" (Mathur 2017, 15). Having initiated the process that culminated with the 1864 and 1906 Geneva Conventions, it paved the way also for the 1899 (III) and 1907 (X) Hague Conventions (Henckaerts and Doswald-Beck 2005, xxvi). What is remarkable is that the First Geneva Convention (1864), with only a few minor modifications, principally derived from the draft convention produced by the ICRC (Raboud, Niederhauser, and Mohr 2018, 153). In turn, Martens (1900, 19) made clear that the following 1899 Hague Peace Conference paved the way for its formal recognition in the field of regulation/prohibition of weapons. However, the agenda of disarmament would be "a matter of secondary importance" to the ICRC (Mathur 2017, 95). This is because this actor became, in the first place, "instrumental" in institutionalizing the principles of human warfare (Price 1998, 628). This overall pattern of development gave rise to a unique authority of the ICRC. It was conferred a "legal status vis-a-vis states in international law," while particularly in the role of a "humanitarian expert" (Mathur 2011, 182, 2017, 19).

There were also involved other formally recognized actors with certain forms of authority or expertise. In light of its "moral authority," the "moral tutelage" by the Holy See was of particular importance (Eyffinger 1999, 77–88). Still more, the "humanitarian presence" of the Sovereign Military Order of Malta, also particularly driven by the "protection of the Christian Civilization," should not be overlooked. It is remarkable that the "formal recognition" of both by the players within the institutional order of diplomacy enabled them to put into use a unique combination of resources for humanitarian purposes too (Bátora and Hynek 2014, 6, 88, 91, and 112–13). Individual international lawyers and professional associations with legal expertise featured an essential cluster of the relevant epistemic community. In particular, they drove the momentum toward the creation of an international court (Best 1999, 620; Caron 2000, 10 and 14–15). Their knowledge-based expertise also broke ground for their—rather exceptional at that time—form of authority on the part of nongovernmental actors. On par with diplomats and still pivotal (governmental) military experts (Crowe and Weston-Scheuber 2013, 31), including army and navy officers, international law experts were also taken onto national delegations to the international conferences (Best 1999, 624). They would even draft some nations' conference proposals concerning the matters of international law (Caron 2000, 15).

Overall, the peace and disarmament conferences and the subsequent codification of "humanized" international law, essentially not motivated by state interests, were built largely upon nonstate activism (Caron 2000, 8; Toyoda 2009, 1101). The latter also influenced the development of the idea of humanitarian intervention in the nineteenth century and was even able to "mount considerable pressure on policy makers" (Finnemore 2003, 64–65). Various nonstate actors flocked together for these progressive causes and provided a crucial impetus for the governments "to take such issues more seriously." However, the gap between their expectations and states' willingness to meet them was barely reconcilable, especially with respect to the question of disarmament (Hucker 2019, 6–7). The still paramount exercise for states in the prevalent strategic environment was to remain balanced between the precept of human warfare and the "necessities of war" (Frevert 2006, 429). The necessity of having arms, particularly for the (great) powers, and humanitarian (disarmament) instincts thus largely played out in what Cooper (2018, 444) correctly terms "liberal militarism." As also explained earlier, it could then be argued that those emerging, "seemingly conscientious" norms of humanitarianism were "most probably deeply entangled with state interests" (Toyoda 2009, 1101). Even a humanitarian action would never be undertaken if it jeopardized other foreign policy goals or interests of an intervening state (Finnemore 2003, 65). This angle of reasoning may indeed cast a further shadow over the humanitarian logic of that time. As Eyffinger (1999, 77–88) discussed, the Holy See was "not fully inspired by altruism" in its engagement, and severe disagreements also arose among the governments, mainly between those of Italy and Russia, over its potential involvement with the Hague Conference. Even the ICRC could be considered less a result of heroic activities of its founder, Henry Dunant, and more a product of systemic needs of states to civilize aspects of industrialized warfare, including "shoring up domestic support for war as an instrument of foreign policy" (Forsythe 2005, 18–20). What also testifies to a certain strategic reasoning behind the ICRC is that its humanitarian identity was only recognized by governments on balance with state sovereignty (Mathur 2011, 181). In particular, this was epitomized by its "principle of neutrality" (Mathur 2017, 7) and lack of credible enforcement mechanisms, particularly outside of conflict and crisis zones (ICRC 2011, n.d.-a, n.d.-b). In addition, the ICRC could be seen as the guardian of the civilization-barbarian disciplinary system, a states' product. Barnett (2011, 10) has pointed to the temporally stable paradox between universal and circumstantial characteristics of humanitarian ethics. When applied to the period in question, he maintained that "because non-Christian peoples were incapable of honouring the laws of war but might be able to do so after a colonialism that produced civilization, the ICRC possessed the ethnocentric, if not outright racist, views that were endemic to the era" (2011, 13).

INSTITUTIONAL POWER: A (DUBIOUS) TRIUMPH OF HUMANITARIANISM

This section will illustrate how the dissected hierarchies and exercises of power, as well as associated interests, embedded humanitarianism as an international *regulatory/disarmament regime complex* with all the consequences and limits. Russia, driven by its "mixed" motives detailed earlier, became the principal driving force behind this process at the governmental level (Best 1999, 622). It was Russia who summoned the St. Petersburg Conference (1868) (Higgins 1909/2010, 7), called the first conference in the Hague (1899) (Vagts 2000, 33), and assumed sponsorship of the second conference in the Hague (1907) yet originally proposed by President Roosevelt (Keefer 2007, 54). Russia not only recognized its particularly strong aspiration for pursuing this path but also assumed that there was no other civilized nation that would undertake as many efforts in favor of international order and law (Martens 1900, 24–25). With the Laws of War (LoW) also on the agenda, its more ambitious proposals envisaged general disarmament and the creation of compulsory/obligatory arbitration mechanisms for the peaceful settlement of disputes (Best 1999, 621; Caron 2000, 14–16; Crowe and Weston-Scheuber 2013, 32). Referred to as the issues long bothering "the best minds of the civilized world," the proposed initiatives were also related to the notion of civilization on the part of Russia (Martens 1900, 6). Because this impetus by Russia resonated with broader-based and deeply intertwined strategic and humanitarian rationales for the codification of international (humanitarian) law, momentum was gained for the three international conferences and a series of intergovernmental agreements.

At the end of 1868, the Declaration of St. Petersburg was adopted by the commission of international military experts assembed at St. Petersburg (Crowe and Weston-Scheuber 2013, 31; O'Connell 2013, 22). It became the first formal agreement, obligatory upon the contracting and acceding parties, that restricted the use of weapons in land and maritime warfare (Higgins 1909/2010, 6–7). The First Peace Conference was convened in the Hague from May 23 to July 24, 1899, and was undertaken in three commissions, as well as a number of subcommissions and committees of examination (Scott 1920; Caron 2000, 14). Divided into as many as six commissions, numerous subcommissions, and committees of examination, the Second Peace Conference met in the Hague from June 15 to October 18, 1907 (Caron 2000, 19; Hayashi 2017, 3). These two international conferences resulted in a number of binding agreements covering certain aspects of dispute settlement and warfighting (Hayashi 2017, 1). Not only were the doors opened to "the era of arms control" (Vagts 2000, 31) but the way was also paved for the (further) development of IHL. The Declaration of St. Petersburg (1868) codified an important customary principle of armed conflicts prohibiting the infliction of unnecessary, that is, exceeding the extent necessary to achieve military objectives, suffering (Crowe and Weston-Scheuber 2013, 31; O'Connell 2013, 22). The 1899 Hague Conference also had notable positive implications for legal regulation of the means and methods of warfare. This is because its participating delegates reaffirmed the norm of (un)necessary suffering, further cultivated restrictions on specific types of weapons and military tactics, and clarified aspects related to the treatment of prisoners of war and the obligations of occupying powers (Crowe and Weston-Scheuber 2013, 32). Most of the 1907 Hague Conventions (IV, V, VI, VII, VIII, IX, XI, and XIII) were also relevant to IHL, especially in that they similarly turned into customary law (O'Connell 2013, 27). Best (1999, 625) fairly remarked that these developments "gave our century a running start" with respect to the LoW.

However, the adopted international laws still largely reflected states' (military) interests, including those related to (violent) imperialism and colonialism as well as fear of internal revolutions. First, this is because they primarily outlawed means and methods of warfare with little to no military utility (Jochnick and Normand 1994, 68). Second, they were state-centric, rather than human-centric, because they chiefly concerned interactions among sovereigns disregarding any internal matters (Hayashi 2017, 4 and 7). Third, they were yet mainly applicable to soldiers, rather than humans or individuals in a broader sense (Hynek 2011, 163). Fourth, the newly adopted international laws unevenly addressed those originally raised concerns. The principal Russian objective of disarmament remained unfulfilled (Best 1999, 625; Hayashi 2017, 2). This is because the emerging legal framework lacked any meaningful limitations on armaments or military budgets, including on acceleration with new types and calibres of rifles and naval guns (Hayashi 2017, 1–2). As Russia lost its passion about this agenda after the 1904–1905 Russo-Japanese War, ambitious disarmament aspirations had largely been curtailed even by the time of the Second Hague Peace Conference (Keefer 2007, 39 and 54; Hayashi 2017, 3). Analyzing the dynamics of nineteenth-century international law, Toyoda (2009, 1109) precisely reckoned that the governments seemed prepared to "please the public opinion" for the most part in matters with "no serious threat to national (or governmental) interests."

Apart from the LoW, relative success was also achieved with respect to the institutionalization of the peaceful settlement of international disputes (Hayashi 2017, 4). However, the newly established legal basis served as a milestone for this legacy to build upon rather than entailing any immediate breakthroughs. A particularly "tangible accomplishment" was the creation of the Permanent Court of Arbitration (1899) (Hucker 2019, 6). The "spirit" of this development also drove the establishment of the Permanent Court of International Justice, and later the International Court of Justice. Even the foundation of the International Criminal Court was also in part premised on those rules of law originated in the late nineteenth and early twentieth century (Caron 2000, 4). However, the 1899 Convention entailed mere nonobligatory measures in regard to the pacific settlement of international disputes, and this provision was not fundamentally altered in 1907 (Hayashi 2017, 6). More ambitious initiatives concerning obligatory arbitration and a permanent court faced serious impediments, mainly as a reflection of multiple intergovernmental disagreements, in both 1899 and 1907 (Caron 2000, 20–22; Hayashi 2017, 6). It is crucial to remark that the originally established Permanent Court of Arbitration was, despite the name, not permanent in essence (Caron 2000, 18). There was voiced criticism on the part of Russia regarding the failure to adopt some credible mechanisms of the peaceful settlement of disputes. Martens (1900, 23) stressed that any outcome of international arbitration, even the most unfavorable, would still be better than the huge losses that wars entailed.

Great powers were reluctant to compromise on their national interests and jeopardize their sovereignty and defense capacity in favor of more restrictive international (humanitarian) laws (Hucker 2019, 6). As the most prominent of the then emerging powers, the United States and Germany precluded much of the progress on important issues on the stage of negotiations (Caron 2000, 16; Hayashi 2017, 2). With almost all the outcome documents signed and ratified, with minor reservations, by virtually all twenty-six powers present at the 1899 Hague Conference, the United States and Great Britain stood out as being the least successful with their respective signatures and ratifications. What is notable is that this mainly concerned the bans on the launching of projectiles or explosives from balloons (Hague Declaration 1899, IV/1), asphyxiating or deleterious gases (Hague Declaration 1899, IV/2), and expanding ("dum-dum") bullets (Hague Declaration 1899, IV/3) (Scott 1915, 230–32). In contrast to relative, though still deficient, success with signatures and ratifications on the part of the other great powers, Italy defied to ratify all the key final agreements of the 1907 Hague Conference. Notably, it did not even sign the ban on the discharge of projectiles and explosives from balloons (Hague Declaration 1907, XIV) (1915, 236–39). The mentioned instances of opposition by liberal states, particularly the United States and Great Britan, may serve as an excellent illustration of Cooper's (2018, 444) notion of "liberal militarism," also referred to earlier. The cases of opposition by Italy, Germany, and the United States may in turn exemplify how revisionist ambitions on the part of the rising powers, as discussed earlier, curtailed certain regulatory efforts. In more general terms, the three conferences were conducted with a rather discriminatory modus operandi. The Conference at St. Petersburg was composed of military delegates predominantly from the major powers (Higgins 1909/2010, 7; O'Connell 2013, 22). Although states with insignicant militaries were among the twenty-six countries that convened in the Hague in 1899 (Keefer 2006, 10; Hayashi 2017, 2), all the present states "were referred to, and referred to one another, as 'powers,' Great or otherwise" (Best 1999, 619). Even more importantly, the great powers in fact did "most of the talking," besides a few important contributions by lesser powers (1999, 624). Of the world's fifty-seven sovereign states, forty-four came together for the 1907 Hague Conference, a much bigger diplomatic endeavor (Caron 2000, 19; Hucker 2019, 5). Effective deliberations were, however, hampered by "the large multilateral format" (Keefer 2007, 60–61), and "Powers" still assumed their privileged institutional standing vis-à-vis "all nations" (Caron 2000, 22). Additionally, all three conferences were put together on the basis of invitations often characterized by shadowy selection principles (Higgins 1909/2010, 56; Best 1999, 623; Caron 2000, 19; Keefer 2006, 10). The format of negotiations had implications for the purview of the outcome documents. Not only did they solely reflect the views of the participant states, mainly major powers, but they were at best open for other states to accede. For instance, while it was the case with the St. Petersburg agreement, the 1899 Hague Convention (I) was only open to signature by those powers present at that conference (Higgins 1909/2010, 6 and 56).

A crucial part of the success associated with these conferences was the immediate access to the process by nonstate actors, that is, organized public opinion. This included their presence in corridors of the buildings in which negotiations were held and the significant space they were given in the media to share their opinions and demands (Best 1999, 623; Eyffinger 1999; Caron 2000, 15). They would also run their fora in parallel with the official sessions (Hucker 2015, 412). Withal, fringe meetings were organized and peace activists also engaged in active lobbying (Best 1999, 623). Nicholas II used his diplomatic position to allow a number of such nonstate opinion makers to attend the Hague Conference of 1899 and disseminate their work (Hynek 2011, 165). Because a decision to exclude the press would not be viable at that time, especially on the part of liberalizing polities (Best 1999, 625), the conferences were also subject to considerable press coverage internationally (Hucker 2019, 17). All of this is what British historian Alfred Zimmem (cited in Caron 2000, 14) summarized under the rubrics of the so-called open diplomacy. That was the space within which diplomats, lawyers, human rights defenders, and peace activists mingled and exchanged their views. However, the public was still highly restricted in their leverage and the press was in turn well managed (Best 1999, 625). The conference delegates denied the press too much access to their deliberations, and their meetings thus were held "behind closed doors" (Hucker 2015, 412, 2019, 17) or "in closed session" (Caron 2000, 15). The conference participants principally included states' diplomats, often also army and navy officers, and sometimes international law experts (Best 1999, 624). Despite the regular coverage of the proceedings, the press also rarely accounted for more than repeating information obtained officially via communiqués or from chairmen of committees, and unofficially via Stead's Courrier de la Conference (Best 1999, 625; Hucker 2019, 17). Therefore "old" diplomacy prevailed over "new" diplomacy, despite the growing prominence of the latter (Hucker 2015, 412). Either with respect to the non–great power states or the public opinion, Best (1999, 619) was rightly referring to the nineteenth century as still "a world managed by the powerful." On balance, Cooper (2018, 444) also accurately noted that there existed certain "mechanisms of prohibition and permission" that withal ensured "arms control as governmentality."

CONCLUSION

This chapter presented a detailed scrutiny of power configurations that gave rise to humanitarian arms control and disarmament in the nineteenth century. The 1868 St. Petersburg Conference and its Declaration, as well as the 1899 and 1907 Hague Conferences and their Conventions and Declarations were under the microscope. The opening section set the stage by introducing the nature of the herein studied security regime. First, we showed how this regime embedded itself in the nexus between disarmament and humanitarianism. Next, having pointed at its constitutive constellation of states, agreements, regulatory focuses, weapons categories, and aspects of war conduct, we defined this regime under the rubrics of an international *regulatory/disarmament regime complex*.

Through the lens of productive power, it was shown how the humanitarian disarmament episteme, based upon the emergent notion of new humanitarianism, was shaped in the nineteenth century. We discussed it as a product of the rise of nonstate actors and "biopolitics," also facilitated by the liberal rationality of governments. Two major, in part contradictory, discursive frames emerged as the dominant ideational forces of that time: (1) a more general change in *typification of security*, with a focus shifted from the national security frame to the notion of a suffering individual; and (2) the civilization-barbarian construction built upon the mixture of Christian and liberal ethics associated with this shift.

After having discussed the forces of protection (compassion), we directed attention toward the configuration of dispositifs with a particular focus on the forces of production (economy) and destruction (violence). In regard to this, we chose to examine complex and deeply intertwined exercises of structural and compulsory powers jointly. This is because the dynamic strategic environment of the nineteenth century may serve as possibly the most vivid and multiplex illustration of how some actors' relative position directly translates into their control over actions and even conditions of existence of the other. In the first place, we demonstrated that it was the era of war, violence, and military power as the means to gain and maintain structural dominance, the requisite of great power status. To properly dissect the prevalent strategic environment, we considered the then emerging powers and the rise of new imperialism, the growing nationalist and revolutionary sentiments, as well as the impact of the Industrial Revolution. With the latter, it was particularly evinced how economics and strategy interacted in shaping states' structural interests. The key finding of this section was that the new humanitarian ideals were used by the great powers instrumentally. It was, on the one hand, performed to sustain the prevalent strategic modus operandi, even order for the most part, and to codify certain principles of international law, as dictated by their national interests, on the other. Such conclusions reveal how humanitarianism, humanitarian interventions, and disarmament could be compatible with imperialism, colonialism, and arms races. In that, our findings deeply converge with Cooper's (2018, 444) inferences, also related to the analysis of this age of empires. Not to belittle the growing prominence of nonstate actors, we seriously considered the democratization of politics, the liberalization of the press, the rise of the global civil society, and the creation of the ICRC. In this light, we comprehensively reviewed how various nongovernmental groups and individuals contributed to framing and embedding the humanitarian disarmament episteme in the nineteenth century.

Through the prism of institutional power, we also demonstrated how space was progressively opened for nonstate actors to access and even moderately steer the intergovernmental negotiations. In resonance with broader-based and deeply intertwined strategic and humanitarian rationales for this move in the system, humanitarianism was codified in international (humanitarian) law. However, having juxtaposed the triumph of "new" diplomacy with the still discriminatory mode of negotiations, as well as the ambitious original expectations with moderate final outcomes, we showcased how the humanitarian logic and great power politics played out on balance. Considering and systematically pointing out the special role of Russia in sponsoring the three conferences, we considered a Russian-based evaluation of various related matters throughout this study.

The scrutinized nineteenth-century discourses and practices paved the way for those of humanitarian arms control and disarmament as we know it in the post–Cold War era. In the first place, as part of these developments, the humanitarian disarmament episteme and the civilized-uncivilized system of differentiation emerged. It was also the time when the early practice of what Price (1998, 628) later termed normative or legal "grafting" and that which Krause (2011, 23) called "arms control as governmentality" were established. A part of this contribution was also setting the stage for "new" or open diplomacy and a greater involvement of nonstate actors in the mechanisms of (global) governance. Even more importantly, the nonstate activism, in particular as part of transnational civil society, proved to underlie and steer the dynamics of weapons regulation/prohibition. At the same time, it also became clear that the recognition of humanitarianism would not necessarily entail humanitarian disarmament or even at least some severe legal restrictions. In particular, the processes of that time envisaged how expectations of the nongovernmental advocacy would likely fail to fully reconcile with great power politics. The employed power-analytical approach allowed us to comprehensively engage with how this rift manifested on the levels of dominant narratives, structural hierarchies of power, and interactions both within and outside of the principal deliberation fora, as well as played out in the adopted agreements. The following chapters will show how the post–Cold War evolution of humanitarian arms control and disarmament processes represents a firm continuation of the emerging modern discourses and practices of the nineteenth century.

REFERENCES

Abbenhuis, Maartje. 2018. *The Hague Conferences and International Politics, 1898–1915*. New York: Bloomsbury.

Abrams, Irwin. 1962. "Bertha von Suttner and the Nobel Peace Prize." *Journal of Central European Affairs* 22, no. 3: 286–307.

Alter, Karen J., and Sophie Meunier. 2009. "The Politics of International Regime Complexity." *Symposium* 7, no. 1 (March): 13–24.

Barnett, Michael. 2011. *Empire of Humanity: A History of Humanitarianism*. Ithaca, NY: Cornell University Press.

Barnett, Michael, and Raymond Duvall. 2005. "Power in International Politics." *International Organization* 59, Winter: 39–75.

Bátora, Jozef, and Nik Hynek. 2014. *Fringe Players and the Diplomatic Order: The "New" Heteronomy*. London: Palgrave Macmillan.

Best, Geoffrey. 1999. "Peace Conferences and the Century of Total War: The 1899 Hague Conference and What Came After." *International Affairs* 75, no. 3: 619–34.

Bloch, Ivan. 1898. *Будущая Война в Техническом, Экономическом и Политическом Отношениях* [*The War of the Future in Its Technical, Economic and Political Relations*, abridgement: *Is War Now Impossible?*]. St. Petersburg: Printing House of I. A. Efron.

Boli, John, and George M. Thomas, eds. 1999. *Constructing World Culture: International Nongovernmental Organizations since 1875*. Palo Alto, CA: Stanford University Press.

Braudel, Fernand. 1982. *On History*. Chicago: University of Chicago Press.

Caron, David D. 2000. "War and International Adjudication: Reflections on the 1899 Peace Conference." *The American Journal of International Law* 94, no. 4 (January): 4–30.

Cooper, Neil. 2011. "Humanitarian Arms Control and Processes of Securitization: Moving Weapons along the Security Continuum." *Contemporary Security Policy* 32, no. 1: 134–58.

———. 2018. "Race, Sovereignty, and Free Trade: Arms Trade Regulation and Humanitarian Arms Control in the Age of Empire." *Journal of Global Security Studies* 3, no. 4 (October): 444–62.

Croft, Stuart. 1996. *Strategies of Arms Control: A History and Typology*. Manchester: Manchester University Press.

Crowe, Jonathan, and Kylie Weston-Scheuber. 2013. *Principles of International Humanitarian Law*. Cheltenham, UK: Edward Elgar.

Declaration of St. Petersburg. 1868. *Declaration Renouncing the Use, in Time of War, of Certain Explosive Projectiles*. 18 Martens Nouveau Recueil (ser. 1) 474, 138 Consol. T. S. 297. Adopted and entered into force December 11, 1868.

Docherty, Bonnie. 2010. "Ending Civilian Suffering: The Purpose, Provisions, and Promise of Humanitarian Disarmament Law." *Austrian Review of International and European Law* 15, no. 1: 7–44.

Drezner, Daniel W. 2009. "The Power and Peril of International Regime Complexity." *Perspectives on Politics* 7, no. 1 (March): 65–70.

Dukes, Paul. 2011. *Minutes to Midnight: History and the Anthropocene Era from 1763*. London: Anthem Press.

Eyffinger, Arthur. 1999. *The 1899 Hague Peace Conference: The Parliament of Man, the Federation of the World*. Hague: Kluwer Law International.

Finnemore, Martha. 1999. "Rules of War and Wars of Rules: The International Red Cross and the Restraint of State Violence." In *Constructing World Culture: International Nongovernmental Organizations since 1875*, edited by John Boli and George M. Thomas, 149–68. Palo Alto, CA: Stanford University Press.

———. 2003. *The Purpose of Intervention: Changing Beliefs about the Use of Force*. Ithaca, NY: Cornell University Press.

Ford, Thomas K. 1936. "The Genesis of the First Hague Peace Conference." *Political Science Quarterly* 51, no. 3 (September): 354–82.

Forsythe, David P. 2005. *The Humanitarians: The International Committee of the Red Cross*. Cambridge: Cambridge University Press.

Foucault, Michel. 1978. *The History of Sexuality, Volume I: An Introduction*. New York: Pantheon Books.

———. 1980. *Power/Knowledge: Selected Interviews and Other Writings 1972–1977*. Brighton: Harvester Press.

———. 1991. "Governmentality." In *The Foucault Effect: Studies in Governmentality*, edited by G. Burchell, C. Gordon, and P. Miller, 87–104. Hemel Hempstead: Harvester/Wheatsheaf.

———. 1996. "Impossible Prison." In *Foucault Live: Collected Interviews, 1961–1984*, edited by S. Lotringer. New York: Semiotext(e).

Frevert, Ute. 2006. "War." In *A Companion to Nineteenth-Century Europe, 1789–1914*, edited by Stefan Berger, 417–31. Oxford: Blackwell Publishing.

Goldblat, Jozef. 2002. *Arms Control: The New Guide to Negotiations and Agreements*. Thousand Oaks, CA: Sage.

Hague Declaration. 1899 (IV/1). *Declaration to Prohibit for the Term of Five Years, the Launching of Projectiles and Explosives from Balloons, and Other Methods of Similar Nature*. 26 Martens Nouveau Recueil (ser. 2) 994, 187 Consol. T. S. 456. Adopted July 19, 1899. Entered into force September 4, 1900.

———. 1899 (IV/2). *Declaration Concerning the Prohibition of the Use of Projectiles Diffusing Asphyxiating Gases*. 26 Martens Nouveau Recueil (ser. 2) 998, 187 Consol. T. S. 453. Adopted July 29, 1899. Entered into force September 4, 1900.

———. 1899 (IV/3). *Declaration Concerning the Prohibition of the Use of Expanding Bullets*. 26 Martens Nouveau Recueil (ser. 2) 1002, 187 Consol. T. S. 459. Adopted July 29, 1899. Entered into force September 4, 1900.

———. 1907 (XIV). *Declaration Prohibiting the Discharge of Projectiles and Explosives from Balloons*. 3 Martens Nouveau Recueil (ser. 3) 745, 205 Consol. T. S. 403. Adopted October 18, 1907. Entered into force November 27, 1909.

Hayashi, Nobuo. 2017. *The Role and Importance of the Hague Conferences: A Historical Perspective*. Geneva: United Nations Institute for Disarmament Research (UNIDIR), UNIDIR Resources. https://www.unidir.org/files/publications/pdfs/the-role-and-importance-of-the-hague-conferences-a-historical-perspective-en-672.pdf.

Henckaerts, Jean-Marie, and Louise Doswald-Beck. 2005. *Customary International Humanitarian Law—Volume 1: Rules*. International Committee of the Red Cross (ICRC). Cambridge: Cambridge University Press.

Heraclides, Alexis, and Ada Dialla. 2015. *Humanitarian Intervention in the Long Nineteenth Century: Setting the Precedent*. Manchester: Manchester University Press.

Higgins, Alexander Pearce. 1909/2010. *The Hague Peace Conferences: And Other International Conferences Concerning the Laws and Usages of War—Texts of Conventions with Commentaries*. New York: Cosimo Classics (Reissued 2010). First Published 1909.

Hucker, Daniel. 2015. "British Peace Activism and 'New' Diplomacy: Revisiting the 1899 Hague Peace Conference." *Diplomacy and Statecraft* 26: 405–23.

———. 2019. "Our Expectations Were Perhaps Too High: Disarmament, Citizen Activism, and the 1907 Hague Peace Conference." *Peace and Change* 44, no. 1 (January): 5–32.

Hynek, Nik. 2008. "Conditions of Emergence and Their Effects: Political Rationalities, Governmental Programs and Technologies of Power in the Landmine Case." *Journal of International Relations and Development* 11, no. 2: 93–120.

———. 2011. "Rethinking Human Security: History, Economy, Governmentality." In *Critical Perspectives on Human Security: Rethinking Emancipation and Power in International Relations*, edited by David Chandler and Nik Hynek, 157–71. New York: Routledge.

ICRC [International Committee of the Red Cross]. 2011. *Building Respect for the Law.* May 1. https://www.icrc.org/en/doc/what-we-do/building-respect-ihl/overview-building-respect-ihl.htm.

———. n.d.-a. *The ICRC's Mandate and Mission.* Accessed October 15, 2019. https://www.icrc.org/en/mandate-and-mission.

———. n.d.-b. *Treaties, States Parties and Commentaries.* Accessed October 22, 2019. https://ihl-databases.icrc.org/ihl/WebART/375-590006.

Ishay, Micheline R. 2004/2008. *The History of Human Rights: From Ancient Times to the Globalization Era.* London: University of California Press.

Jochnick, Chris, and Roger Normand. 1994. "The Legitimation of Violence: A Critical History of the Laws of War." *Harvard International Law Journal* 35, no. 1 (Winter): 49–96.

Keefer, Scott Andrew. 2006. "Building the Palace of Peace: The Hague Conference of 1899 and Arms Control in the Progressive Era." *Journal of the History of International Law* 8: 1–17.

———. 2007. "Building the Palace of Peace: The Hague Conference of 1907 and Arms Control Before the World War." *Journal of the History of International Law* 9: 35–81.

Kennedy, Paul. 1987/1989. *The Rise and Fall of the Great Powers: Economic Change and Military Conflict from 1500 to 2000.* Vintage Books Edition (eBook 1989). First Published, hardcover 1987. New York: Random House.

Krause, Keith. 2011. "Leashing the Dogs of War: Arms Control from Sovereignty to Governmentality." *Contemporary Security Policy* 32, no. 1: 20–39.

Kubka, Jiri, and Kaarle Nordenstreng. 1986. *Useful Recollections Part I: Excursion Into the History of the International Movement of Journalists.* Prague: International Organization of Journalists.

Ladd, William. 1840/2007. *An Essay on a Congress of Nations for the Adjustment of International Disputes without Resort to Arms.* Carnegie Endowment for International Peace, Division of International Law. Clark, NJ: The Lawbook Exchange (Reissued 2007). First Published 1840.

Lavoyer, J. P., and L. Maresca. 1999. "The Role of the ICRC in the Development of International Humanitarian Law." *International Negotiation* 4, no. 3: 503–27.

Maresca, Louis, and Stuart Maslen, eds. 2000. *The Banning of Anti-Personnel Landmines: The Legal Contribution of the International Committee of the Red Cross 1955–1999.* International Committee of the Red Cross (ICRC). Cambridge: Cambridge University Press.

Martens, Feodor. 1900. "Таагская Конференция Мира: Культурно-Исторический Очерк" ["Hague Peace Conference: Cultural-Historical Essay"]. In *Вестник Европы: Журнал Истории, Политики, Литературы* [*Herald of Europe: Journal of History, Politics, Literature*]. St. Petersburg, volume II (March): 5–28. https://www.prlib.ru/item/323534.

Mathur, Ritu. 2011. "Humanitarian Practices of Arms Control and Disarmament." *Contemporary Security Policy* 32, no. 1: 176–92.

———. 2017. *Red Cross Interventions in Weapons Control.* Lanham, MD: Lexington Books.

Mulligan, William. 2006. "Restrained Competition: International Relations." In *A Companion to Nineteenth-Century Europe, 1789–1914*, edited by Stefan Berger, 401–16. Oxford: Blackwell Publishing.

O'Connell, Mary Ellen. 2013. "Historical Development and Legal Basis." In *The Handbook of International Humanitarian Law*, third edition, edited by Dieter Fleck, 1–42. Oxford: Oxford University Press.

Price, Richard. 1995. "A Genealogy of the Chemical Weapons Taboo." *International Organization* 49, no. 1: 73–103.

———. 1998. "Reversing the Gun Sights: Transnational Civil Society Targets Land Mines." *International Organization* 52, no. 3 (Summer): 613–44.

Purdey, Stephen J. 2010. *Economic Growth, the Environment and International Relations: The Growth Paradigm.* London: Routledge.

Raboud, Ismael, Matthieu Niederhauser, and Charlotte Mohr. 2018. "Reflections on the Development of the Movement and International Humanitarian Law through the Lens of the ICRC Library's Heritage Collection." *International Review of the Red Cross* 100, no. 1-2-3: 143–63.

Riall, Lucy. 1994. *The Italian Risorgimento: State, Society and National Unification*. London: Routledge.

Rutherford, Ken. 1999. "The Hague and Ottawa Conventions: A Model for Future Weapons-Prohibition Regimes?" *Non-Proliferation Review* 6, no. 3: 36–50.

Scott, James Brown, ed. 1915. *The Hague Conventions and Declarations of 1899 and 1907: Accompanied by Tables of Signatures, Ratifications and Adhesions of the Various Powers, and Texts of Reservations*. Carnegie Endowment for International Peace, Division of International Law. New York: Oxford University Press. https://archive.org/details/hagueconventions00inteuoft/page/n1.

———. 1920. *The Proceedings of the Hague Peace Conferences: Translation of the Official Texts—The Conference of 1899*. Carnegie Endowment for International Peace, Division of International Law. New York: Oxford University Press. http://www.loc.gov/rr/frd/Military_Law/pdf/Hague-Peace-Conference_1899.pdf.

Taylor, A. J. P. 1954/1971. *The Struggle for Mastery in Europe 1848–1918*. Oxford: Oxford University Press. First Published 1954, paperback 1971.

Ticehurst, Rupert. 1997. "The Martens Clause and the Laws of Armed Conflict." *International Review of the Red Cross* 37, no. 317: 125–34.

Toyoda, Tetsuya. 2009. "Influence of Public Opinion on International Law in the Nineteenth Century." *Alberta Law Review* 46, no. 4: 1099–113.

Trotha, Trutz von. 2006. "Colonialism." In *A Companion to Nineteenth-Century Europe, 1789–1914*, edited by Stefan Berger, 432–48. Oxford: Blackwell Publishing.

Tuchman, Barbara W. 1996. *The Proud Tower: A Portrait of the World before the War, 1890–1914*. New York: Ballantine Books.

Tyrrell, Alexander. 1978. "Making the Millennium: The Mid-Nineteenth Century Peace Movement." *The Historical Journal* 21, no. 1 (March): 75–95.

Vagts, Detlev F. 2000. "The Hague Conventions and Arms Control." *The American Journal of International Law* 94, no. 1 (January): 31–41.

Wintle, Michael. 2006. "Visual Representations of Europe in the Nineteenth Century: The Age of Nationalism and Imperialism." In *A Companion to Nineteenth-Century Europe, 1789–1914*, edited by Stefan Berger, 11–28. Oxford: Blackwell Publishing.

THREE

From Landmines to Cluster Munitions

Resurfacing and Spillover of Transhistorical
Humanitarian Disarmament

This chapter offers a novel understanding and theorization of humanitarian disarmament regimes and their related prohibition politics. In doing so, it goes beyond the conventional regime analysis, which is seen as epistemologically restrictive, empirically too narrowly focused, and theoretically prescriptive, and norm dynamics literature perceived to be too linear and teleological in its conclusions. Instead the chapter embraces theoretical eclecticism to develop a power-analytical framework suitable for the analysis of global regulatory/prohibition regimes. It utilizes Foucault's analytics of power, Deleuze's desiring production, and Gill's transnational historical bloc and links it to Guzzini's and Barnett and Duvall's power matrix scholarship with four conceptions of power that are being put in use: productive, structural, institutional, and compulsory. Empirically, two potent humanitarian prohibition regimes that have been formed during the past twenty-five years are examined. The ban of antipersonnel landmines (APLs) in 1997 marked a significant shift in humanitarian disarmament. Consequently, a humanitarian disarmament model emerged, consisting in bypassing permanent arms control fora ("The Ottawa Process"). The ascent of the model to the arena traditionally dominated by power interests of major powers and ossified lowest common denominator consensus was confirmed in 2008 when cluster munitions (CMs) were prohibited in a very similar fashion ("The Oslo Process") after the failure of a relevant UN regulatory process to produce their prohibition and the global public and political outcry against the controversial use of CMs by the Israeli Army in its raids against the

Hezbollah. The presented chapter, however, shuns celebratory commentary on the "success" of the respective campaigns as there is abundant literature doing so. Two main contributions to the topic are the application of the power-analytical framework specifically developed to suit an analysis of formation and workings of global prohibition regimes, including heterarchy-of-power discussion of the relationship between states and nonstate actors, and the use of multitemporal perspectivism allowing the analyst to interlink humanitarian longue durée or epochal time frames marked by contingent ethical transformations in relation to other forces, instant time frame analysis, and eventalization, that is, an analysis of events. Then, instead of the usual—and flawed at best—heroic discussions of victories of global civil society, rise of moral International Relations, and supposed progressivist teleology, a more complex regime configuration with many contradictions, artefacts, and their layering inside and about those regimes looms large.

CLEARING OUT THE LEGAL UNDERBRUSH: NATURE OF THE CONVENTIONS AND REGIMES ROBUSTNESS

The 1997 Anti-Personnel Landmines Convention and the 2008 Convention on Cluster Munitions have been the two most notable modern examples of multilateral, humanitarian disarmament treaties through which entire categories of widely used conventional weapons were banned (Convention 2008; Convention 1997). Docherty (2010, 9–17) distinguished among three types of disarmament conventions: security-related conventions banning eliminating weapons of mass destruction (for example, the 1972 Biological Weapons Convention and the 1993 Chemical Weapons Convention), hybrid arms-control/disarmament conventions trying to strike a balance between security and humanitarian concerns and following principles of international humanitarian law (for example, the 1980 Convention on Certain Conventional Weapons and its protocols, see discussion shortly), and humanitarian disarmament conventions. Modern humanitarian disarmament conventions have been characterized as

> contain[ing] preventive measures, including absolute prohibitions on not only the use but also the production, transfer, and stockpiling of certain weapons, . . . [but also the] establish[ment of] remedial obligations, including to clear unexploded weapons and provide assistance to victims, that are generally stronger than the humanitarian obligations in hybrid disarmament instruments. Finally, they adopt a cooperative approach to implementation. (Docherty 2010, 16)

Thus, the APL and CM Conventions ought to be understood as comprehensive disarmament programs of action made on humanitarian grounds, creating an inextricable connection between a successfully concluded negotiations concerning global prohibition regimes and key principles of international humanitarian law (Rutherford 2011, 5; ICRC 2007), and the CM Convention also concerning international human rights law.

As for the APL prohibition regime, the legally binding APL Convention (also known as "The Ottawa Convention" or "Mine Ban Treaty") contains an absolute prohibition norm banning the use of these landmines, as well as their development, manufacturing, stockpiling, retention, and transfer. Concerning transfers, these do not involve just physical transfers but also potential transfers of title to/control over them, all of this directly or indirectly (Goldblat 2002, 237). Stockpiles need to be destroyed within four years (Article 4 exceptions are small numbers of APLs kept for training purposes) after a given state's ratifications under the Convention term, and mine-affected countries need to be free of APLs within a decade (Article 5). The Convention establishes periodical review conferences to assess the progress, as well as to share the best practices, and allows for an invitation of nonsignatory states, IOs, and/or NGOs to be invited for participation (Convention 1997). Parties to the Convention are obliged to submit annual reports on the implementation of the Convention (Article 7 of the Convention 1997) and are expected to provide assistance to mine victims and contribute to mine risk-related education (Article 6).

When it comes to the universality of the APL global prohibition regime, the Convention was signed by 123 States in Ottawa, Canada, on December 3–4, 1997. On September 18, 1998, by virtue of the fortieth ratification, the Convention came into effect and led to the launch of the de facto monitoring regime run by the International Coalition to Ban Landmines (ICBL), a transnational advocacy network and recipient of the Nobel Peace Prize (LCMM 2015). The Convention became binding international law in a significantly short time, on March 1, 1999 (ICRC 2007). The APL Convention counts among the most widely accepted multilateral treaties globally: 162 states are states parties as of 2016 (that is, over 80 percent of states), and thirty-five states find themselves outside of this global prohibition regime (ICBL n.d.-a). Among those nonsignatories, those that stood out the most are the United States, Russia, China, India, Pakistan, Israel, and Saudi Arabia. The rest are almost exclusively secondary, developing countries with a history of territorial interstate conflicts and/or foreign invasions. Importantly, the majority of states outside of the regime have tacitly observed the prohibition norm, testifying to its "universalization" and the robustness of the underpinning regime (on the US position observing the regime from the outside, cf. HRW 2014; on recent uses of APLs by Russia directly in Crimea and Eastern Ukraine and indirectly in Syria, cf. Kochin and Jenzen-Jones 2015; ICBL 2014). Overall, the APL Convention has marked great progress compared to Protocol II adopted by the Convention on Certain Conventional Weapons (CCW) in 1980, which restricted the use of APLs and similar devices but failed to induce widespread support (Mathews 2001, 994–98). Available statistics demonstrate the multifaceted success of the APL Convention, namely the sharp drop in the number of recorded cases of casualties (20,000 per year in the early 1990s versus less than 4,000 per year now), complete clearance of thirty previously APLs-riddled countries, and 50 million stockpiled APLs having been destroyed (ICBL 2016).

Yet while the APL Convention, which relied for its own success on leaving UN diplomatic channels, absolutely banned APLs, other forms of unexploded ordnance (UXO, also known as "Explosive Remnants of War," or ERW) were—both in a literal and legal sense—left out. It was for this reason that the International Committee of the Red Cross (ICRC) initiated a process through which state parties to CCW drafted and eventually signed a new Protocol (fifth to the CCW) on ERW—including cluster munitions—on November 28, 2003 (CCW Protocol 2003; ICRC n.d.-a). The UN CCW framework, which generally regulates indiscriminate weapons and/or weapons causing unnecessary suffering, has often been the target of criticism by representatives of civil society and like-minded countries. Usually perceived as a lowest common denominator mechanism producing inefficiency and yielding anything but "nonresults" (Williams 2013, 189), the CCW has managed to attract ninety-one state parties thus far, including all major powers (out of those mentioned earlier in the context of APL Convention, only Israel has not adopted it; ICRC n.d.-b). Notwithstanding its conclusion, the Protocol has suffered from being too broad and too restrictive at the same time. As for the former, unlike the previous Protocols to CCW that regulated specific categories of weapons (a weapons design approach), ERW has not been a category in its own right but a jumble of leftovers from conflicts "that applies to any explosive conventional munition that may result in ERW" (Breitegger 2012, 135). ICRC and humanitarian NGOs' efforts to draw on a Swedish proposal to ban CMs from 1974 by zooming in on CMs within the CCW framework were killed off (Maresca 2004, 819–21). With regard to the latter, governmental negotiations on what subsequently became Protocol V to CCW showed the impossibility of restructuring an effects-based understanding of ERW with its focus on *postconflict* situations (a user cleans principle) in order to embrace a wider time frame that would have included a legally binding instrument regulating the *use* of CMs *during* the conflict in addition to general parameters of international humanitarian law (Breitegger 2012, 135).

Out of the CCW negotiations on Protocol V, more progressive states and NGOs that formed the Cluster Munition Coalition (CMC) took the process (known as "The Oslo Process") outside of the UN system. While many aspects of the process itself will be analyzed later in this chapter, its result has been the legally binding Convention on Cluster Munitions (CCM) that successfully concluded the Dublin Diplomatic Conference on May 30, 2008. CMs are specified as a conventional munition that disperses or releases explosive submunition (bomblets), each having weight under twenty kilograms and containing explosives. Cluster (sub)munitions dispersing flares, smoke, and chaff as well as those designed to produce electrical or electronic effects are excluded from the ban (Article 2, Convention 2008). However, CCM did not manage to avoid the exclusion of technologically superior types of CMs as there was no consensus among like-minded states on the breadth of the future regulation (Kimball 2012). This stood out in direct contrast to the APL Convention that established the entire category-sweeping ban. Concerning APLs, two originally evasive issues got rejected: the US proposal to exclude APLs laid "near" antitank landmines from the ban, where the former were to be understood as parts of the latter due to their function rather than design; and then the distinction between the "smart" and "dumb" APLs on the basis of presence/absence of their self-destruct or self-deactivating mechanism (Rutherford 2011, 83). The final wording of the APL Convention (1997, Article 2) excluded only those equipped with an "antihandling device" and otherwise banned all the other types. The CCM, on the other hand, left the door open for future technological development of CMs as it excluded those CMs that simultaneously contained less than ten bomblets of weight greater than four kilograms, were exclusively engaging a single target object, and had electronic self-destruction and self-deactivating mechanisms (Article 2.1, Convention 2008).

As the CCM was modeled on the APL Convention, a number of features—as well as the Convention structure—have been similar. Thus, CCM proposed that state parties had to destroy all CMs within an eight-year period (with a possible four-year extension) after the Convention would have entered into force. Several provisions known from the APL Conventions were reintroduced here too: those concerning the retention of small quantities of CMs intended for training purposes and development of detection techniques (Article 3, Convention 2008); the nature and principles of clearance, destruction of CMs, and the provision of risk-reduction education (with explicit references to Mine Action Standards, cf. Article 4); victim assistance schemes (Article 5); and a particular set of transparency measures and consultations related to implementation and compliance, sharing best practices and periodic review conferences (Articles 6–12). The CCM remains the only legal instrument on CMs. Although the conclusion of the CCM did not stop the UN-based CCW process through which a possibility of specific regulation of CM was being explored and that involved major producers and users, this process failed, however, on November 25, 2011. The reason was that many of the signatories of the CCM refused a draft text with a very narrow specification of CMs proposed for regulation (Kimball 2012).

After its adoption in Dublin, Ireland, the CCM was signed on December 3–4, 2008, in Oslo, Norway, and entered into force on August 1, 2010, six months after it was ratified by thirty states. After this date, states cannot sign the CCM but need to accede to it. When it comes to attempts to make the CM prohibition regime universal, 108 states have signed the CCM at the time of writing, out of which 100 have ratified it (including half of former exporters), thereby becoming parties to the CCM (LCMM 2015, 3). After the CCM came into effect, the previously existing de facto monitoring regime run by the ICBL was extended to cover CMs, and in 2011, the ICBL and CMC merged their monitoring arms to form a single structure, the Landmine and Cluster Munition Monitor, on grounds of operational efficiencies and similar expertise required to work on APLs, CMs, and other ERW. The last available statistics show that between 2010 and 2015, twenty-seven state parties destroyed 88 percent of CMs and 90 percent of submunitions previously declared as stockpiles. Additionally, no state within the prohibition regime has used CMs and eight signatories and two nonsignatories completed clearances of contaminated areas (LCMM 2015, 1, 3).

Similarly to the APL ban, several important past users and producers have gradually come to observe the prohibition regime from the outside. Out of these, the United States has imposed an export moratorium on CMs, the position upheld on May 27, 2016, by the United States's latest refusal to transfer CMs to Saudi Arabia, which has been using them in Yemen (Hudson 2016). Additionally, the United States has been unilaterally restricting its own use of CMs on the basis of the 2008 US Department of Defense directive attempting to minimize civilian harm and maintaining that after 2018, used CMs cannot result in more than 1 percent of ERW (Kimball 2012). In February 2015, the United States reported the actual removal and destruction of half of the target specified in the directive: 500,000 tons of CMs being demilitarized by the end of 2018 (LCMM 2015, 2). Out of fifteen nonsignatory states known to be producing CMs or reserving the right to do so, only three have been known to use them: the United States, Russia, and Israel. Existing reports recorded the use of CMs in seven nonsignatory states since the CCM's entry into force (2015, 1).

PRODUCTIVE POWER: LONGUE DURÉE, HUMANITARIAN
DISPOSITIFS, AND DESIRING PRODUCTION

This section analyzes ways in which productive power has interacted with—and helped to constitute—the general structural terrain of humanitarianism within which the two examined prohibition regimes have been formed. It is maintained that this perspective has been the single biggest omission when it comes to existing analyses of APL and CM prohibition regimes and their respective theorization. Productive power is charged with impersonal, interactionist, and dispositional features and is linked to the constitution of (inter)subjectivities (Guzzini 1993, 447). It is impersonal "because the origin of the produced effect is not located at the level of actors" (1993, 461–62). Rather, it relates to "the constitution of all social subjects with various social powers through systems of knowledge and discursive practices of broad and general social scope" (Barnett and Duvall 2005, 55). Therefore productive power is instrumental in the formation and rearticulation of underlying and orderly structures, which occupy specific spaces between "unconscious" conditions of emergence and intersubjectively shared horizons of possibility (Foucault 1994, 71–76).

Indeed, if one is to study humanitarian dispositifs and their inscriptions in productive power, such an analysis needs to operate synchronically as well as diachronically, in terms of historical, albeit contingent layering of constitutive forces and their limitations. It is argued that reliance on time frames of the APL and CM campaigns respectively is insufficient as these have been, in many ways, *products* of wider forces, forming together humanitarian dispositifs. Indeed, this is not to marginalize humanitarian agency. Rather, it is to show that even individual and/or collective choices and actions are always located in wider structural contexts that serve as enablers or, conversely, limiters. Importantly, it is these contexts that have been too often ignored in existing, heroic narratives on the establishment of APL and CM prohibition regimes. These have usually been focused on advocacy campaigns and represented them as notable victories of global civil society, with the rise of moral international relations as a consequence (Garcia 2011, chap. 5; Borrie 2009; Moszynski 2008; Goose and Williams 2004; Williams 2000; Wapner 2000; Clegg 1999; Cameron, Lawson, and Tomlin 1998). Therefore one cannot agree with Wapner (2004, 252) who argued that "one could not possibly explain the Mine Ban Treaty without mentioning the activities of the non-state actors. There would be no story to tell, no process to explain." In fact, there is plenty left out for an analysis—and related theorization—of the two regimes.

The stigmatization success and prohibitionary character of the APL and CM Conventions have usually been linked by experts and campaigners to the 1972 Biological Weapons Convention and the 1993 Chemical Weapons Convention (Cluster Munition Coalition n.d.; Breitegger 2012, 11–12; Nystuen and Casey-Maslen 2010, 110; Goldblat 2002, 239). Although there have been recent attempts to "inject" theorization of regimes with a dose of humanitarianism, one of the remaining problems of such accounts is their relative ahistoricity. While Garcia (2015, 2011) examined APLs and CMs in her otherwise interesting study, she did so as a part of research focused on "*established, recent* and *developing* regimes" (Garcia 2015, 56, emphasis in original), where all of these regimes have either been established or in the making after the end of the Cold War. This stands in direct contrast with an attempt to uncover structural changes in forces of compassion upon which those regimes were being built up.

When it comes to operations of productive power related to APL/CM prohibition regimes, a humanitarian dispositif—and associated structural conditions of emergence—needs to be examined. Three general conditions are recognized in this regard: change in forces of compassion (contingent yet potent construction of ethics), shifts in typification of security, and the rise of the economic within the political. All of them are firmly linked to exercises of productive power. The structural confluence of these forces has two implications for the APL and CM regimes: despite the fact that there were attempts to tightly regulate/ban the use of those categories of weapons during the Cold War, they could only record limited success. For APLs, it was especially the ICRC's legal contribution that resulted, inter alia, in the adoption of CCW in 1980 and its Protocol II regulating the use of APLs (CCW 1980; CCW Protocol 1980; for its detailed analysis, cf. Maresca and Maslen 2009). Having identified landmines as weapons of "special concern" already in the 1950s, the ICRC became particularly active in stigmatizing them since the 1970s (Maresca and Maslen 2009, 15–16 and 20). In respect of CMs, it was Sweden-led efforts to ban "cluster warheads" in 1974 that did not make it to the CCW at all (Gillespie 2011, 67). With *sovereignty* having assumed the role of the force of *compassion* during the Cold War, it was near impossible to reverse the military utility of those weapons. A macrojuridical argument coupled with states' emphasis on APLs/CMs' key role in the geopolitical conflict and thus national security stalled any transformative efforts. On the other hand, the subsequent macroshift and replacement of sovereignty by *human rights* and *human security* in the position of the systemic ethical force after the end of the Cold War was certainly a structural enabler. What this meant for transnational political action dominated by humanitarian and human rights NGOs making their case will be further analyzed in the section on structural power.

As already pointed out in the previous chapter, it was only after a century that the Martens Clause reemerged in a weapons treaty: the preamble of the APL Convention (1997) mentioned the necessity of "stressing the role of public conscience in furthering the principles of humanity as evidenced by the call for a total ban of anti-personnel mines," and, later, the preamble of the CCM (2008) reaffirmed "the dictates of public conscience." Arguably, elements of the nineteenth-century humanitarian disarmament have resurfaced in the late twentieth-century/early twenty-first-century "new"—but not unprecedented—humanitarian disarmament. Neoliberal humanitarianism incorporated reemerging elements of the structural humanitarianism from the nineteenth century to its own dispositif. Additionally, and in accordance with Barnett's identification of forces and periodization, it managed to converge aspects of international humanitarian law with international human rights law after the end of the Cold War (on the question of their general convergence, cf. Orakhelashvili 2008; Heintze 2004). This can be seen in the CCM (but not in the

APL Convention), which for the first time invoked "human rights" in relation to the Convention on the Rights of Persons with Disabilities (Convention 2008, Preamble) and "human rights law" in relation to victim assistance (Article 5).

While the APL Convention managed to blend humanitarian provisions governed by the international humanitarian law with arms control provisions, the CCM took it even further with incorporation of human rights provisions. CCM features, as Docherty (2009, 936–37) made clear,

> the latest in a series of modern weapons treaties that date back to the 1868 St. Petersburg Declaration. . . . Early treaties strived to reduce superfluous injury to soldiers while later ones focused on minimizing the suffering of civilians. Whether safeguarding soldiers or civilians, humanitarian weapons treaties are concerned with the effects of weapons' use and the protection of individuals. . . . After the end of the Cold War, states began to negotiate weapons treaties that contained humanitarian and disarmament provisions in the same instrument. The Convention on Cluster Munitions follows the lead of the Chemical Weapons Convention and Mine Ban Treaty by combining elements of both.

Thus, the nineteenth-century transformation in typification of security, that is, the emergence of the individual as an object of security on grounds of needs (unnecessary suffering and/or weapons indiscriminacy) was extended and reinforced after the end of the Cold War by emphasis on political (human) rights of this suffering individual.

Indeed, the neo*liberal* humanitarian dispositif with its distinct governmental rationality, or what Foucault called "the art of government" (Foucault 1991, 92), produced a strong connection between the individual's position as the object of security and its subjectivity, understood through sociopolitical responsibilities. As Barnett (2011, 18) proposed, "humanitarianism is a matter of faith," the process by which liberalism cannot be seen as a mere secular ideology but, paradoxically, as the reincarnation of the sacred (Kratochwil 2013). Noble discourses—such as the one on humanitarian disarmament—stimulate positive effects. Deleuze and Guattari (1983, 10–11) call them micropolitical "desiring production," understood as the investment of mental energy into the production of what is taken as reality. They too add a component of "social production," which is directed toward utilization of corporeal energy, that is, labor. These have been neglected if very important parts of the so-called political rationalities, or governmentalities, functioning as wider discourses of rule that structure sociopolitical orders within which individual subjects are constituted (Foucault 1988, 161). Foucauldian analytics of power allow one to consider liberalism in a much broader sense, that is, as a political rationality, or governmentality, where desiring production and social production are utilized toward effective and efficient economy of power. Neoliberal governmentality thus elevates what was thought to be an economic policy, or political ideology for that sake, to the status of rationality. As Foucault himself maintains, "the art of exercising power in the form of the economy—is to have as its main objective that which we are today accustomed to call 'the economy'" (Foucault 1991, 92). The next section reflects on the emergence of an intimate relationship between emergent active subjects/citizens in the society, with their "do-gooders" desires and labor, and the rise of the individual in need of protection as the referent point. As will be shown, this has been the condition allowing for the successful exercise of structural power in APL and CM prohibition dynamics.

STRUCTURAL POWER: TRANSNATIONAL HISTORICAL BLOC AND EMANCIPATION/DOMINATION PARADOX

By virtue of structural power, actors' capacities can be exposed and theoretically reflected upon. For the purposes of the analysis concerning APL and CM prohibition politics, that is mainly the constitution of multifaceted relations between and among states and NGOs, grouped and intertwined in multiple ways. While structural power operates through impersonal, systemic, and positional constitution, direct interactions between/among actors attest to its relational specificity (Barnett and Duvall 2005, 48; Guzzini 1993, 461–62). In the words of Barnett and Duvall (2005, 52–53), structural power "produces the very social capacities of structural, or subject, positons in direct relation to one another, and the associated interests, that underlie and dispose action . . . A, exists only by virtue of its relation to structural position, B. The classical examples here are master-slave and capital-labor relations." The key concept for structural power is the notion of hegemony, especially in the neo-Gramscian sense, through which the (re)production of power structures (hierarchies and heterarchies) occur. Indeed, structural asymmetry has significant consequences. Foucault's second power-analytical guideline, which was previously tied to operations of structural power, concerns "the maintenance of privileges, the accumulation of profits, the bringing into operation of statutory authority, the exercise of a function or a trade" (Foucault 1982, 223).

In this part, I focus on the rise and transformation of the new humanitarian *transnational historical bloc* (cf. Robinson 2005; Gill 1993, 1995, 2001), or what Strange (1989) would have called "transnational empire" (and featuring states' loci of power), in the two prohibition regimes. This bloc has been composed of states (like-minded leaders and bandwagoning followers), (I)NGOs and their various umbrellas, elements of IOs, as well as epistemic communities of scientists, and the mass media, all of them in different roles and capacities (for example, NGO personnel pressurizing governments and simultaneously being incorporated into national diplomatic delegations; representatives of states sharing legal obligations yet differing vastly in their relation to humanitarian NGOs, financially as well as politically; NGOs flocking together for transnational political advocacy work yet competing for funding after the prohibitory regimes have been established). The notion of a transnational historical bloc thus needs to be linked to the discussion of heterarchies of structural power, where heterarchy gets understood

> as the relation of elements to one another when they are unranked or when they possess the potential for being ranked in a number of different ways. For example, power can be counterpoised rather than ranked. Thus, three cities might be the same size but draw their importance from different realms: one hosts a military base, one is a manufacturing center, and the third is home to a great university. Similarly, a spiritual leader might have an international reputation but be without influence in the local business community. The relative importance of these community and individual power bases changes in response to the context of the inquiry and to changing (and frequently conflicting) values that result in the continual re-ranking of priorities. (Crumley 1995, 3)

In terms of structural power reading, my approach will comprehend international regimes as "instances of institutionalized hegemony" (Gale 1998, 275), with emphasis on contestation and recreation of normative structures, privileges, and compliance mechanisms by states and NGOs within a wider structure of the transnational historical bloc.

In neo-Gramscian analysis, the transnational historical bloc has been linked to politico-economic processes dating from the 1970s onward. According to Gill (1995), the transnational historical bloc attempts to create and spread "new constitutionalism." Its three parts outlined by Gill are utilized toward better understanding of the APL/CM transnational historical bloc, and especially what Barnett (2011, 10–11) has called humanitarian paradox between emancipation and domination: disciplinary neoliberalism, panopticism oriented at surveillance, and market civilization. Gill's (1995, 2001; cf. Morton 2011) scholarship has been especially important here as he—unlike Gramsci (1971) and many of his followers (cf. Cox 1987)—allows for two moves. First, hegemony does not need to prevail for a transnational historical bloc to emerge (Gill 1993, 40, 2001). Second, operations of structural power within the bloc are not related to hegemony understood in the classical hierarchical sense but rather on what Gill (1995, 400–412) calls "politics of supremacy," that is, less apparent ways through which hegemony gets exercised over fragmented opposition. It is in relation to this novel character of the transnational historical bloc when relations between hierarchy and heterarchy ought to be invoked. When discussing heterarchies of power, Crumley (1995, 4) argued that the hierarchy-heterarchy relation admits both temporal and spatial flexibility; for example, governmental heterarchies . . . can move over time to hierarchies and vice versa . . . without invoking the rhetoric of collapse. Hierarchical relationships among elements at one spatial scale or in one dimension (members of the same club) may be hierarchical at another (the privilege of seniority in decision making). Heterarchy is both a structure and a condition.

What follows is a sketch of the rise, translocation, and multiple transformations of the transnational historical bloc through which the two prohibition regimes were being established and maintained. While its domestic structural origins had nothing to do with international development or international humanitarian action, it was subsequently stretched to include the realm of APLs and then extended further still to incorporate CMs. Reading the dynamics through operations of structural power allows one to study processes through which actors' social capacities, their mutual relations, and related objectives got constituted. Specifically, we will discuss several phases of the evolution of the transnational historical bloc: domestic structural transformations on the nonprofit and voluntary sector (NVS) in the 1970s in relation to the crisis of welfare liberalism in countries such as Canada, which will be discussed here as the leading country in the APLs ban; the 1990s incorporation of humanitarianism to the country's foreign and security policy profile that structurally allowed for subsequent articulation of APLs ban position by a group of norm entrepreneurs from the government and NGO sector; heterarchic mix of successful transnational and international political advocacy to ban APLs; depoliticization of the transnational historical bloc by the insertion of neoliberal discipline to administer the APL prohibition regime; and the bloc's extension to the realm of CMs, its repoliticization leading to a successful conclusion of the ban (by different advanced liberal countries); and the eventual depoliticization by linking the issue to APLs at the level of merger of the two transnational networks, the ICBL and CMC. This dynamic clearly shows the presence of all three components of the "new constitutionalism" identified by Gill (1995, 2001).

The benefits of this perspective over existing skewed/heroic narratives are manifold and the most important can be summarized as follow: revealing forces constituting the humanitarian paradox between emancipation and domination as embodied into the new constitutionalism; refusal of teleology that unproblematically interlinked moral progress with the two prohibition regimes; rejection of a reified, normatively laden and ontologically problematic conception of the so-called global civil society (operations of structural power actually show the importance of domestic politico-economic dynamics [Canada] and its subsequent transnationalization); and the firm critique of both the zero-sum game metaphor on which the relationship between states and nonstate actors was wrongly predicated (that is, states seen to be "losing power" as the power of the "transnational world" rises and related bifurcation of the "two worlds"; for specimens cf. Nash 2012; Matthew and Rutherford 2003, 40–52; Warkentin and Mingst 2000, 246) and reversal of push-pull dynamics, that is, to show that without state-initiated transformations and funding, there would be no humanitarian disarmament action of this nature, proportion, and "success."

The constitution of "effective and efficient" economy of power between the government and NGOs, through which structural positions for a transnational historical block were being gradually set up, happened in many liberal countries, such as Canada, the United States, the United Kingdom, Norway, and the Netherlands (Putnam 1996; Gidron, Kramer, and Salamon 1992; Flora 1986). Against the backdrop of the worn-out Keynesian welfare-liberalism model, the 1970s were especially important for this rise of disciplinary neoliberalism (cf. Gill 1995; Dean 1999). The notion of the state as a universal caretaker of the population and its needs was increasingly under fire. As Scott puts it, "it was a short step from governments reinventing themselves to demand that nonprofit and voluntary organizations should likewise reinvent themselves" (Scott 2003, 46). In Canada, the governmental efforts to reframe the role of the nonprofit and voluntary sector (NVS) and the government's reliance on it in a number of social areas were noted in the exponential growth of funding for the NVS (Gidron, Kramer, and Salamon 1992). This development coincided with procedural and substantive changes in Canada's Foreign and Security Policy and was closely linked to the return of the Liberal Party of Canada to government in 1993. One of the effects of this was the governmental pressure on the Peace Movement to professionalize. One of the outcomes was the emergence of NGOs connected to—and financially dependent upon—formal channels. As the then PM Jean Chrétien made clear, "NGOs are often very good at what they do—often better than governments—whether it is delivering aid or assistance, or saving endangered species and habitats, or working to promote a greater public awareness of international issues. . . . No one government can do it all" (Chrétien 1995). A crucial part linked to the opening of the security discourse on substantive change was acknowledged in the expressed need to have "a broader definition of national and international security" (Liberal Party of Canada 1993, 105–6), which was subsequently embodied into the governmental doctrine of human security (DFAIT 1995).

The Canadian government had already started to fund awareness-raising activities concerning APLs in 1989, that is, three years before the ICBL was founded. The Mines Action Canada, a Canadian umbrella for NGOs active in the domain of APLs and the key participant in ICBL, started to hold regular discussion with the Non-Proliferation, Arms Control, and Disarmament Division of the Department of External Relation and International Trade after the Liberals were back in power. The outcome was an announcement of Canada's export moratorium in November 1995. Common knowledge, constructed mainly by the then director of ICBL Jody Williams, suggests that ICBL persuaded pro-ban states at the UN conference on Certain Conventional Weapons, where the issue of APLs was originally negotiated, to leave the UN for an alternative process. As a Department internal memo from March 1996 (DFAIT 1996) shows, however, the Canadian government had already anticipated that the UN CCW Review Conference would remain deadlocked and made preparations for this development. The memo contained the seeds of what later became known as the Ottawa Process, which will be analyzed in the next section on operations of institutional and compulsory power.

What ensued after the successful establishment of the APL prohibition regime in 1998 was a major transformation of the transnational historical bloc in which the Canadian government, along with the Mines Action Canada/ICBL, played the key role. Indeed, this transformation could be read as the emancipation of NVS. The government managed to release and harness a significant volume of societal energy and desire to make a difference on the backbone of the global prohibition regime. To make this happen, the governmental funding of APL-related activities became massive: more than $170 million between 1998 and 2008. However, the domination side of humanitarianism demonstrates how structural power used by the state can entangle nonstate actors into a neoliberal disciplinary regime and subjugate them by giving them "responsibilities." Subjects/NGOs have been constituted within this newly constructed "reality" as effective and efficient calculating machines. One of the consequences of the advanced liberal funding regime—with activities measured strictly in terms of "risk" and "benefit" and the balance between the two—is depoliticization of the relationship. As Gill (1995) argued, the introduction of "new constitutionalism" brings regulation, discipline, and surveillance to an entirely new level. A shift in heterarchy of power could be observed: from the technology of citizenship/involvement (1993–1997) with a prevailing horizontal accountability to the top-down operations of power in the new constitutionalism with vertical accountabilities in which the main aim was to ensure an equal opportunity for NGOs to compete for contracts (Yeatman 1998). The APLs-related transnational historical bloc thus emerged through the full integration of security and economic poles. This bloc can be understood as a result of juridical government and the art of neoliberal economics together targeting international humanitarian NGOs. Put differently, the social body of the bloc was inscribed in structural power relations as a reality of transactions between governments and those NGOs.

One of the key events testing the resilience of the APL transnational historical bloc came after the ascent of Harper's Conservatives into power in Canada in 2006 where they remained without an interruption until the end of 2015. In the words of Dan Livermore, previously Canada's special ambassador on APL action, Canada "has dropped the ball and walked away, leaving the job unfinished" (cited in Westhead 2012). The loss of the previously biggest donor allowed for further transformation of the heterarchies of power within the bloc. The Canadian collective stake in ICBL significantly dwindled (Mines Action Canada 2015) as Canada, previously the political leader and biggest financial contributor to the issue, drastically reduced funding after 2008 (Westhead 2012; Canadian Landmine Foundation n.d.). However, while there was slight global decline in APL-related funding after 2012, the transnational historical bloc experienced growing diversification in sources of funding coming from countries such as Norway, Australia, and Switzerland, as well as UNICEF (ICBL n.d.-b). This has indeed helped to grease the bloc's transnational operations also at the level of funding, not just service delivery. Additionally, this played beyond any doubts a role in an increasing political interest in and advocacy for prohibition of CMs. While still referring to APLs, Livermore also noted that "maybe others like Australia will pick up the slack for us, maybe they won't" (cited in Westhead 2012). And this is what like-minded countries did: rather than just contributing to the transnational APL "social body" of the historical bloc, they extended it to cover CMs.

From the perspective of structural power, the production of CMs issue recorded ontological differences compared to the previous structural constitution of APLs. The transnational historical bloc with its multiple power heterarchies had already existed. At the level of norms dynamics, Price (1998, 627) referred to the importance of "grafting" through which moral opprobrium from other delegitimized norms or practices get manipulatively translocated to newer/other issues. Unlike Finnemore and Sikkink (1998, 908) who linked "norm adjacency" firmly to activism of NGOs and this stage of norm dynamics theoretically to the social movement literature, Price (1998, 617) allowed for states, besides "Socratic civil society," to structure actions in a decisive way. The process of legal grafting was facilitated by the fact that many CMs' dud bomblets posed a similar set of dangers as APLs once on the ground (Raccuia 2011, 474). Unlike self-excluded Canada, many of the actors involved in CMs took part in an earlier construction of the transnational historical bloc (Corsi 2009, 304). Not only did this happen in CMs dynamics but it could also be observed in a near-parallel campaign that resulted in the adoption of the international human rights Convention on the Rights of Persons with Disabilities (Convention 2007). The Convention on the Rights of Persons with Disabilities took the previously existing structural relationship between APL users and victims of their actions and linked it to the terrain of human rights principles, namely the rights and dignity of the people with disabilities. One of the connectors at the level of agency was Kenneth Rutherford, who cofounded the Landmine Survivors Network in 1995, was part of the Nobel Prize–winning ICBL umbrella, and significantly contributed to both the drafting of the UN Convention on the

Rights of Persons with Disabilities and the CM Convention. Rutherford's position as a connector serves as a reminder that agency matters in operations of structural power as related practices feed back and shape the overall structural setup. Then it is not surprising that the CM Convention makes explicit references to the former Convention, thereby creating a hybrid category of victims (previously defined solely on grounds of international humanitarian law) as fully enjoying their equal human rights.

The category of CMs—including its very extraction from a broader bundle of ERW—could have therefore relied on the existing hegemonic structure for its humanitarian manipulation, that is, what Gill called the "politics of supremacy." This structure of the transnational historical bloc had been successfully used by a group of like-minded states and the CMC—with greatly important provision of expert knowledge, legal arguments, and diplomatic facilitation by the ICRC—against opponents and counted the model of action and the existence of precedent—successfully operating APL prohibition regime—as its key features (Breitegger 2012, 135, see the next section for details). The power of events and necessity to study "instant time" came to the fore with two features that coincided to coconstitute the structure for extension of the transnational historical bloc into the realm of CMs and kickstart what became the beginning of the Oslo Process leading up to the complete ban of CMs. This was completely superfluous (ab)use of CMs by the Israeli Army against Hezbollah during their war in Lebanon in 2006, with more than 4 million CMs dropped on Lebanese soil, the thrust of it within the last seventy-two hours before the ceasefire was to take place. This served as a catalytic event to restructure the debate on humanitarian harm versus military utility of CMs (Docherty 2007; HRW 2008). Adding to this was the stalemate on CMs within the CCW framework. The CM campaign shows that the transnational historical bloc became increasingly internationalized not only at the level of funding but also when it came to political advocacy: diplomatic practices of states were much more prominent in the beginning of the process. No single country played the dominant role and it was the matter of these two synergic events within the APL-set disarmament terrain to achieve the desirable change on CMs.

Hinting at possibilities to witness flexible reordering of heterarchies of power at different scales and contexts (Crumley 1995), the transnational historical bloc has been able to accommodate varying—and at times conflicting—operations of structural power. On the one hand, it established the "new constitutionalism" with general features of disciplinary liberalism, surveillance, and depoliticization as far as the APL global prohibition regime was concerned. On the other, the CM pro-ban campaign demonstrated that a short but potent repoliticization of disarmament humanitarianism was possible within this structure, and even involving the same people. In turn, this seeming contradiction temporarily juxtaposing the technology of citizenship with technology of new contractualism, both intertwined in a transgovernmentally stretched hybrid network, helps to comprehend the swift proceeding toward the ban *once* the group of like-minded states decided to step outside of the CCW process with the issue, joining their forces with the CMC and ICRC.

Finally, the emancipation/domination paradox in the two regimes is visible in the direction of Foucault's (1982, 223) accompanying guideline, that is, in an attempt to ascertain how asymmetries in privileges and profits are being maintained. The structural power linked to the functioning of the transnational historical bloc has seen military utility of those weapons dwindle. Many states—and that has included the past first-tier producers of CMs—had already rearticulated their economic interests. The paradox can be seen in the effect of such change, namely in maintenance—if not even reinforcement—of economic asymmetries between the "West" and the "Rest." This division never ceased to exist within the transnational historical bloc (cf. Grayson 2010; Beier 2003). They had learned that restructured military utility could have been in fact used to retain this asymmetry by a shift from weapons production to their destruction both at home and in conflict zones. Part of this has been enabled by technological superiority as automatization of ERW removal and automated mapping techniques became financially lucrative areas of activity via organizations such as the United Kingdom's MAG and Aardvark or the Swedish Dynasafe. Practices such as the provision of mine risk education (MRE) and the removal and destruction of APLs and CMs have experienced isomorphic pressure with a simple message: fully professionalize. Consultancy companies such as PriceWaterHouseCooper started to provide professional advice (Mansfield 2005, 236). Militaries around the world rediscovered themselves and found their new role both in demining and MRE (Wheatley 2005; Mansfield 2003). The trendy development has been their full integration (Barlevi 2003). And Western doors operated in collusion with international NGOs and profit-making companies involved in the removal of ERW (McGrath 2000). Laurie Boulden's (1998) early account (she served on a UNDP-sponsored panel to assess related assistance programs) gives a realistic picture of the atmosphere of mutual distrust between Western donors, companies, and NGOs on the one hand and local governments and citizens on the other, as well as of the degree of bureaucratic depoliticization of demining favoring interests of the more powerful. The neoliberal funding regime and market civilization have heavily favored Western nonstate actors, nonprofit and for profit, formally on technical grounds of being able to meet fiduciary and nonfiduciary risk criteria, reporting standards, etc. One such example has been the embracement of the Result Based Management promoted by the Canadian government and spread through OECD around the world (cf. Lavergne 2002; on its adoption among NGOs such as CARE International, cf. Paterson 2005). The domination-of-demining/ MRE mindset was further reinforced by systematic targeting of financial institutions (investment banks, sovereign wealth funds, and insurance companies in particular) investing in APLs producers (now de facto non-existent) and especially CMs producers (Breitegger 2012, 203–4). This has been linked by the CMC to Article 1 of the CM Convention on prohibition of assistance to production of CMs (IKV Pax Christi 2014).

INSTITUTIONAL/COMPULSORY POWER NEXUS: CAUGHT BETWEEN THE POWER BASE AND REGIME

The following lines analyze operations of institutional and compulsory power and their complex workings in and around the two prohibition regimes. A common feature for these two types of power lies in their operation through interactions of specific actors; where they differ is relational specificity, which is diffuse for institutional power and direct for the compulsory kind (Barnett and Duvall 2005, 48). As Barnett and Duvall (2005, 51, emphasis added) explained in relation to institutional power, "the conceptual focus here is on the *formal* and *informal* institutions that *mediate* between A and B, as A, working through the rules and procedures that define those institutions, guides, steers, and constraints the actions (or non-actions) and conditions of existence of others." Thus, where it differs from compulsory power, which is said to exist "in the direct control of one actor over the conditions of existence and/or the actions of another" (2005, 48), is particularly in the mediatory, international-institutional locus of power workings. The analysis of their joint exercises is seen as a particularly suitable strategy for the analysis of the two prohibition regimes as even their creation was deeply immersed in workings of informal institutions: the Ottawa and Oslo Processes (see discussion shortly). Then Foucault's power-analytical guidelines (1982) can further link the two. That is through focus on forms and degrees of rationalization (G5), understood both as "putting new instruments into practice" and "costs associated with reactive resistance" (1982, 224), as well as a set of complex interactions between "forms of institutionalization" (G4) with their expressions "through (sometimes very complex and elaborate) apparatuses with their loci, regulations, hierarchies, and autonomies" and "the means of bringing power relations into being" (G3) through "coercion, military means, and discourses; also by means of economic differences, of control, by surveillance" (223).

The perspective of institutional/compulsory power nexus accounts for the thrust of regime analysis scholarship (especially its first and second generation) and focuses on ways of gaining individual and collective control over outcomes, utilization of power as resources, as well as on links between indirect/unintended institutional effects and original reasons for regime creation, or lags and feedback between power base and regime (Guzzini 1993, 451; Krasner 1982, 499). As Krasner (1982, 499) maintained, "regimes may assume a life of their own, a life independent of the basic causal factors that led to their creation in the first place," thereby creating lags between reasons for their creations, autonomous regime change, and deeper, collective transformation of perceptions and interests of those inside. Additionally, after a time lag, one can consider feedback regimes can provide independently of its original power base(s) to a wider—normative and material—structure of the system. As Guzzini (1993, 451) argued, "changes of regimes alter the context in such a way as to render particular resources more important for power capability than others. The approach thereby recovers part of what one could call the historically contingent character of power resources." Power then displays both relational and possessive characteristics:

> Relational power behavior refers to efforts to maximize values within a given set of institutional structures; meta-power behavior refers to efforts to change the institutions themselves. Relational power refers to the ability to change outcomes or affect the behavior of others within a given regime. Meta-power refers to the ability to change the rules of the game. Outcomes can be changed both by altering the resources available to individual actors and by changing the regimes that condition action. (Krasner 1985, 14)

The distinction made by Krasner and discussed by Guzzini between relational power and metapower is utilized here to focus on two distinct phases and workings of institutional/compulsory power complex: regime formation, that is, dynamics preceding the two bans and leading to the formalization of prohibition regimes; and autonomous workings of the two prohibition regimes, once they were established, both inside (Krasner's relational power) and toward nonsignatories (Krasner's metapower). The reason why broader categories of institutional power and compulsory power, though they have been distinguished between conceptually, are studied in forms of joint complexes is given by empirical dynamics, namely that the two prohibition regimes examined here—unlike economic regimes against which background the regime theorization was being formed—never experienced hegemons in the conventional sense. As Barnett and Duvall (2005, 67) argued, "we reject a gladiatorial competition between these conceptions; after all, they capture the different ways in which social relations shape and limit actors' ability to determine their fates."

This is also the reason why it seems to be particularly suitable to accent the role of institutional power, as even the phases leading to their establishment (Ottawa/Oslo Processes) were marked by "collective institutional entrepreneurship" of wider coalitions led by like-minded countries. Put differently, rather than the conventional regime theorization, which focuses on how hegemons project their interests to the nature of regimes they initiate and help to create, the dynamic here was the opposite, beginning with a structural reversal of hegemonic preferences (great power interests to lock negotiations in the CCW format due to its procedural and path-dependent characteristics and its subsequent failure to ban APLs and CMs as some secondary states and TANs—that is, distinct norm entrepreneurs—aimed for) and continuing with exercising of power outside of the UN system (Ottawa/Oslo Processes for APLs and CMs respectively), which simultaneously contained characteristics of institutional power and compulsory power. When it comes to institutional power inscribed in the two regimes and ways in which compulsory power has been linked to it, two examples for workings inside the regimes will be shown: victim assistance and user state responsibility. As for the utilization of institutional/compulsory power complex against nonsignatories, two issues will highlight their operations: an unprecedented legal obligation of the signatories to promote the acceptance of the norm (CCM) and what we term the creation of the field of visibility bringing together uses of regulatory apparatuses, informal heterarchies of power, surveillance, and coercion.

The exercise of institutional/compulsory power complex in the APL case saw the assumption of Canadian leadership when the government, after consultations with MAC/ICBL, suggested to a group of like-minded countries to leave the UN CCW process in order to continue diplomatic discussions of the absolute ban (DFAIT 1996). Human Rights Watch and the Pax Cristi Netherlands assisted with selection of the countries invited for the first meeting in Vienna, producing the list of twenty "good" countries to be invited for separate discussion (Short 1999, 482). This was preceded by Pope John Paul II's use of his moral authority in the call for a "definite end to the production and use" of APLs and incessant support of the action by the ICRC, a sui generis actor, which in addition to its legal expertise and diplomatic standing allowing for effective facilitation launched an international media campaign in favor of the ban (ICBL n.d.-c, 5). In regard to its legal expertise, it is crucial to remark that this long concerns the convergence of international humanitarian law and international human rights law, discussed throughout this chapter (Fortin 2012). The second meeting took place in Geneva and saw notable help and involvement of the Quakers and David Attwood in particular, which also reinforced the line to the UNIDIR. The initial core group of countries involved, apart from Canada as the patron, consisted of Austria, Belgium, Germany, Ireland, Mexico, Norway, Philippines, South Africa, and Switzerland (Short 1997). Additionally, New Zealand (after Belgium set the trend in 1995) renounced the use of APLs and committed to a complete ban in the months before the 1996 Ottawa meeting, which was attended by seventy-five states (ICBL n.d.-c, 5–6). The Canadian government decided to give ICBL its own seat, and some MAC personnel were included in the government delegation. As Short (1999, 484) put it, "the ICBL remained highly centralized in its dealing with the Canadian government. In that sense the ICBL did not function entirely as a coalition of 1,000 organizations but rather as a single, homogenous bargaining voice with a unitary position." Jody Williams's repeated verbal attacks on delegates with observer status (undecided states) that were intended to coerce those states into the acceptance of the norm were in fact a clever strategy of the Canadian government to "put its message across without dirtying one's hands," as one DFAIT official put it (cited in Hynek 2008, 104). Also, they remind us about multifaceted heterarchies of institutional and compulsory power.

There were two outcomes of the Ottawa meeting, the diplomatic-structural backbone of the Ottawa Process. First, the Canadian government and the ICBL drafted the Chairman's Agenda for Action, which was simply imposed on, rather than negotiated with, other participants who subsequently embraced it. Second, the then Canadian Minister of Foreign Affairs and International Trade Lloyd Axworthy held a speech in which he pledged all participants to come to Ottawa in a year's time to sign a convention that would completely ban APLs. While Sommaruga, the director of the ICRC at that time, and Williams of ICBL delivered their prearranged speeches of support (Tomlin 1998, 20), many like-minded states were taken by surprise. Axworthy's speech started the so-called Ottawa Process (financed by Canada, approximately CDN $2 million; cf. Hynek 2008, 104) that consisted of a set of meetings sponsored by self-selected, like-minded states and that featured NGOs subsumed under ICBL.

Axworthy's pledge was embraced in the subsequent meeting in Brussels, Belgium, by 110 governments (out of 153 attending). It too pressurized the great powers outside of the process to take a stand. Russia and Singapore announced export moratoria on APLs (Wurst 1997). Thus, in a hint of reactive resistance and an attempt to remain relevant, then US President Clinton announced that his country would pursue a ban on APL transfers through the CCW format (ICBL n.d.-c, 7). Subsequently, under huge media pressure and in another ostensible attempt to gain relevance and possibly redirect/subvert the dynamics of the Ottawa Process, the United States presented an amendment to the final draft of the Convention in Oslo, Norway, in which it tried to water down the absolute nature of the ban (exceptions for US APLs laid along the border between the Koreas, nonapplicability of the ban for "times of war," and exclusion of the "smart mines" with self-deactivating or self-destructive mechanisms from the scope of the Convention; cf. Wurst 1997). It failed among the placards and stickers "No Exceptions." Also, collective and individual exercises of coercive power stemming from more general operations of institutional power in the Ottawa Process were visible when several crucial participants (Great Britain, France, and Japan) were vacillating in light of the US "amendments" and their own military concerns and tried to utilize various legal tricks such as various attempts to reclassify certain types of APLs or insert the adjective "primarily" designed in APLs' definition into the Convention draft. To no avail: the process resulted in the Ottawa Conference in December 1997 where the Ottawa Convention was signed by 122 governments.

The Ottawa Process model was also used in the dynamics leading to the eventual ban of CMs. It too contained key features of what became known as the institutional model of humanitarian disarmament, or what some commentators called "new multilateralism" (Mutimer 2012, 373; Faulkner 2007, 44; Sigal 2006, 231): a single-issue, ad hoc, self-selecting (that is, excluding the main players in CCW, mostly the United States, Russia, China, India, Pakistan, and Israel) coalition of the willing composed of like-minded states led by a patron (typically a middle power), NGOs organized under an umbrella of a centrally run transnational advocacy network, the ICRC, elements of IOs, and the mass media favoring the case. The model featured geographically spread series of conferences with host governments and a certain degree of functional division of labor. Out of the 2006 Third Review CCW Conference that failed to single out CMs as a category and proceed toward their ban, thirty like-minded states decided to step outside of the UN system. The Israeli (ab)use of CMs played a catalytic role for NGOs, which had previously formed the Cluster Munition Coalition (CMC) in the Hague, the Netherlands, in 2003. In the fall of 2006, like-minded states, the CMC, the ICRC, and the UN Secretary General made an early collective call for a mandate to further discuss CMs (Docherty 2010, 940). Although falling short of support for a complete ban, the role of UN SG Kofi Annan was particularly noteworthy as his stance represented a powerful challenge to the key CCW players (UN Statement 2006).

Norway took the lead among like-minded states (the core group comprised Austria, Ireland, Peru, Mexico, New Zealand, and Sweden as well as the Holy See) and pledged its utmost to initiate a treaty process outside of the UN to ban all CMs with unacceptable humanitarian consequences (Docherty 2010, 940). This was more than the CMC considered (Breitegger 2012, 136), although the role of "humanitarian disarmers" during the Oslo Process proved crucial (Borrie 2014, 2009). It should be pointed out that Norway had played—apart from Canada—the key role in the successful adoption of the Ottawa Treaty. This synergy had originally been extended and resulted in the establishment of the bilateral Lysoen Declaration, which was subsequently multilateralized in the form of the Human Security Network with notable ambitions. However, this platform became completely unusable for the launch of CM ban efforts (or any other humanitarian issue) due to Canada's Conservative government doing its utmost to (literally) kill human security (Davis 2009) and gradually became a talking shop. The fifteen-month diplomatic process was therefore launched by an ad hoc coalition of forty-six states in Oslo adopting the Oslo Declaration. In the Declaration, the states pledged to

conclude by 2008 a legally binding international instrument that will:
(i) prohibit the use, production, transfer and stockpiling of cluster munitions that cause unacceptable harm to civilians, and (ii) establish a
framework for cooperation and assistance that ensures adequate provision of care and rehabilitation to survivors and their communities,
clearance of contaminated areas, risk education and destruction of
stockpiles of prohibited cluster munitions. (Oslo Declaration 2007)

The most vocal opponent of the Declaration was the United States (Breitegger 2012, 138). The Declaration's inspiration by the legal wording of
the APL Convention was more than obvious, although it legally extended
several principles. The Declaration contained a road map with planned
meetings in Lima, Vienna, Wellington, and Dublin. Operations of institu-
tional/compulsory power could be observed from tensions among attending states to the Oslo Conference. The United States kept emphasizing the ongoing military utility of CMs and the importance of the CCW
framework; Germany, an eventual signatory of the Declaration and major
producer, proposed a plan for the upcoming CCW, attempting to steer
parts of the discussion back to the UN CCW. This would have further
supported the idea of two parallel processes, that is, something that the
like-minded countries attempted to completely avoid and made this clear
to Germany and others; crucially, two other key states and CMs producers—France and Great Britain—backed the Declaration (Breitegger 2012,
141). The role of the CMC was to stress humanitarian concerns and be
involved in the dialogue with diplomats to the greatest possible degree.
As Docherty (2009, 941) noted, the CMC was "directly involved in the
deliberations, sending hundreds of campaigners to meetings and participating actively in the negotiating room." The institutional pressure by the
like-minded countries was further reinforced by the ICRC, which kept
pushing major producers and users within the CCW in October 2007 and
after one presentation of evidence that CMs still had military utility and
that technological fixes were enough to address humanitarian concerns.
It concluded that no such evidence was presented, thus effectively disso-
ciating the two processes. As a result, another important diplomatic actor, the European Union, began to play the key role with its establishment of a Group of Governmental Experts, seeking the ban (Breitegger
2012, 151). One of the mechanisms through which institutional/compul-
sory power mix got exercised by the core group over other signatories
concerned several disputed technical issues where consensus was either
fragile or nonexistent (for details of these conflicts over definition and
interoperability, cf. Wisotzki 2013, 99–101). As Breitegger (2012, 165) explained, there were tactically produced several textual proposals: the official Wellington discussion text used as the "basic text" for the forthcoming negotiations in Dublin, and the Compendium of "other proposals"
with a function to increase legitimacy of the process and exercise collective institutional power over undecided states more efficiently. The wa-

vering signatories eventually overcame differences, although they expressed disappointment with the lack of transparency and democracy in ignorance of their respective proposals (2012, 165). They flocked to the official text, however, and the main reason was the definite failure of the concurrent CCW format to progress with the issue. The CCM could therefore be adopted in Dublin, Ireland, and signed on December 3–4, 2008, in Oslo, Norway.

The following lines reflect on operations of institutional/compulsory power complex once the two prohibition regimes have been established. Exercises of this power inside the regime and outside of it versus nonsignatories will be highlighted in turn. The first potent examples of the exercise inside the regimes have been remedial provisions on *victim assistance*. In its preamble, the APL Convention sets the tone by noting that "States Parties [are d]etermined to *put an end* to the suffering and casualties caused by anti-personnel mines, that kill or maim hundreds of people every week, mostly *innocent and defenceless civilians*" (Convention 1997, Preamble). The 2004 Nairobi Action Plan and 2014 Maputo Action Plan subsequently broadened the interpretation of "victim" also to those suffering *indirectly*, thereby reinforcing previously made legal obligations for state parties and showing visible lags and feedback between regime and power base, and especially autonomous and unanticipated institutional power exercised by the regime. Still in the preamble, the signatories pledge "to do their utmost in providing assistance for the *care and rehabilitation*, including the social and economic reintegration of mine victims." This, however, gets moderated in Article 6 of the APL Convention, which stipulates that "[e]ach State Party in *a position to do so* shall provide assistance for the care and rehabilitation, and social and economic reintegration, of mine   victims and for mine awareness programs" (Convention 1997, emphases added). Thus, the victim assistance measures chiefly depend on relative capacities and infrastructure of states, especially of those mine-affected ones, and can be read as an attempt to increase—both collectively and individually—pressure on richer states within the regime, especially considering that Article 6 in its entirety deals with issues of international cooperation and assistance and explicitly allows for mine-affected states to "request assistance to mine victims" (Convention 1997, Article 6). While challenges to collective responsibility have existed, such as evasion or negligence of the obligation, there have been formal and informal supervisory mechanisms through which the Landmine and Cluster Munition Monitor was able to selectively exert coercive power over those states, at least by naming and shaming their stance (Hayashi 2012).

The CCM (Convention 2007, emphases added) takes this further still (the word "victim" is mentioned eighteen times versus the APL Convention where it gets referred to three times) when it links the issue of CM victims to their human rights already (first ever weapons treaty to do so) in the preamble ("full realisation of the *rights* of all cluster munition victims and recognising their *inherent dignity*"). Still in the preamble, it furthers the determination to cover "the special needs of vulnerable groups" and links this to the Convention on the Rights of Persons with Disabilities. In Article 2, it provides a *very broad* definition of "victims" as "all persons who have been killed or suffered physical or *psychological* injury, *economic loss, social marginalisation* or substantial *impairment of the realisation of their rights* . . . as well as their affected *families and communities*" (Convention 2007, emphases added). It contains a dedicated Article 5 solely on "victim assistance," which operationalizes in a detailed way what state parties need to do. Much greater pressure is exerted on mine-affected countries themselves, which is in line with the general tradition of international human rights law (a de facto subsidiarity principle), especially when it comes to their obligations to "collect data on victims," the "development of national plans and budgets," incorporation of (Western neoliberal) "guidelines and good practices," and embracement of "International Mine Action Standards" and "transparency measures" (Convention 2007, Articles 4, 5, and 7). The analogue to Article 6 of the APL Convention remains, however (Convention 2007, Article 6).

The second issue where complex intraregime workings of institutional/compulsory power can be observed is the issue of *user state responsibility*. This unprecedented and legally binding principle appears only in the CCM. The reason is that unlike APLs that function as designed in post-conflict environments, the presence of CMs on the ground is due to their *failure* to explode (Docherty 2009, 953). Thus, the CCM stipulates that a state party that abandoned CMs within the territory of another signatory *"prior to entry into force* of this Convention for that State Party" is "strongly encouraged . . . to facilitate the marking, clearance and destruction of such cluster munition remnants," including the provision of "information on types and quantities of the cluster munitions used, precise locations of cluster munition strikes and areas in which cluster munition remnants are known to be located" (Convention 2007, Article 4.4., emphasis added). Essentially, this principle creates *retroactive* user state responsibility and gives hope to many CMs-affected countries and, at the same time, increases legal institutional pressure on those responsible. As Corsi (2009, 308) held in this regard, "linking past use and present danger to contemporary user state obligations, this provision also strengthens the concept that states must consider the foreseeable and long-term effects of a weapon when evaluating its legality under IHL." Indeed, the CMC has been the key actor to exert selectively operating coercive power on such responsible actors, drawing on collectively operating institutional power that has targeted all "responsible" state parties in a diffuse way.

The complex exercises of institutional/coercive power can also be extracted from the ways in which the regimes worked against nonsignatories. In respect of the CCM, it contains another precedent-setting, legal obligation that consists of the duty of state parties to promote the acceptance of the ban among nonsignatories and gives them a legal duty to discourage those nonparties from the use of CMs:

> *Each* State Party *shall encourage* States not party to this Convention to *ratify, accept, approve or accede to this Convention,* with the goal of attracting the adherence of all States to this Convention. . . . Each State Party *shall notify* the governments of all States not party to this Convention . . . of its obligations under this Convention, *shall promote the norms* it establishes and *shall make its best efforts to discourage* States not party to this Convention *from using cluster munitions.* (Convention 2007, Article 21, emphases added)

The APL Convention does not have this provision and limits itself to a declaratory emphasis on "the desirability of attracting the adherence of all States to this Convention" in its preamble (Convention 1997, Preamble).

Finally, both prohibition regimes contain what we term the *field of visibility,* which mixes exercises of institutional power of these established regimes linked to compliance and verification, with coercive power related to launches of supervisory mechanisms operated by nonstate actors and funded by states. The field of visibility works both inside (insistence on upholding the states parties' legal obligations) and outside (public naming and shaming) of these regimes simultaneously. In both the post-1997 APL prohibition regime and the post-2007 CM prohibition regime, advanced liberal government and, more specifically, the technology of new contractualism have been expressed through the establishment of the field of visibility, which can simultaneously be conceived of as a technique of *performance* because all actors use it to report on their activities. According to Dean (1999, 30), visibility is a necessary condition for the operation of a particular technology as it renders possible the exchange of knowledge and experience through the use of tables, graphs, and statistics. What needs to be added is its disciplinary character, working toward certain ends. This role has been served in the APL regime by the ICBL's Landmine Monitor, an internet-based clearinghouse run by ICBL. The Landmine Monitor was founded in 1998 and features a global reporting network and database. After the CCM came into effect, the monitor was extended to cover CMs, and in 2011, the ICBL and CMC merged their monitoring arms to form a single structure, the Landmine and Cluster Munition Monitor, on grounds of *operational efficiencies* and *similar expertise.* As the merged body explains, "the Monitor is not a technical verification system or a formal inspection regime. It is an attempt by civil society to *hold governments accountable* for the legal obligations they have accepted with respect to antipersonnel mines and cluster munitions. This is done through extensive collection and analysis of publicly available information, including via field missions in some instances" (LCMM 2015).

CONCLUSION

The presented chapter sought to analyze complex workings of power in and about APL and CM global prohibition regimes. The chapter opened with a legally oriented analysis charting evolution from what could be considered a relationship between general regulatory qualities of international humanitarian law and lex specialis regulating "special aspects" of this general corpus, namely the areas of APLs and CMs (in CCW Protocol V as a part of ERW) toward more robust prohibition regimes established through the APL and CM Conventions. They may be regarded as laying down the general law of these categories. This could also be seen in an unprecedented interconnection, in a weapons treaty, between the international humanitarian law and international human rights law as in the CM Convention. Subsequently, the universality and robustness of those regimes was put under the microscope, including norm observance by those outside of the regimes.

What followed was the utilization of the power-analytical framework through which four conceptions of power were being put into use in respect of the two regimes. An argument in favor of a reversal in which these types of power had previously been discussed was made and the analysis thus started with the examination of productive power, continued with revealing operations of structural power, only to complete the discussion with an outline of complex, and interrelated, workings of institutional and compulsory power. The part on productive power took a long view, in which longue durée epochal reconfigurations were studied in relation to transformations of ethics and humanitarian dispositifs. This allowed for establishment of the temporal and legal connection between humanitarian disarmament of the nineteenth century and its post–Cold War echoes. A set of similarities such as in typifications of security and legal reasoning was displayed. Conversely, differences got identified too, especially the emergence of human rights as an ethical force and different economies of power being used to govern the relationship between states and nonstate actors. Here, the ascent of neoliberal disciplinary governmentality bringing along depoliticization and specific desiring production were highlighted.

Next, the attention was directed toward structural power. This part relied on the notion of the transnational historical bloc to explain the rise of the role of the nonprofit sector in state-sponsored political activism and service delivery; charted its emergence and embeddedness in domestic politico-economic transformations through which many Western countries—including Canada in its position of the eventual patron state in the APLs ban—left welfare liberalism behind; and became advanced liberal states with distinct neoliberal governmentality fixated on efficiency and effectiveness. Also, in order to account for multiple reconfigurations of geometries of power inside this bloc, the notion of heterarchy was introduced. Then it was possible to explain contradictory, and sometimes even concurrent, operations of structural power in relation to NGOs working first on APLs and then on CMs, next to APLs. The heterarchy of power governing transnational and international political advocacy to ban APLs was highlighted, along with its subsequent depoliticization in administration of aspects of the APL prohibition regime. Subsequently, the bloc's extension to the realm of CMs got outlined, and its brief yet potent repoliticization leading to the successful conclusion of the ban was analyzed. The eventual depoliticization linking the issue of CMs to APLs at the level of merger of the two transnational networks, the ICBL and CMC, was shown. Gill's depiction of new constitutionalism underpinning the transnational historical bloc was confirmed in relation to the two bans.

Finally, the nexus of institutional and compulsory power operating both within the two regimes and about them was up under the microscope. Indeed, while all types of power can be said to work together, synergistically reinforcing each other, the degree of complex interlocking of institutional and compulsory power was the reason why they were heuristically studied together. Their complex operations were oriented at both the regime's formation, that is, the dynamics preceding the two bans and leading to the formalization of prohibition regimes, and their autonomous workings once they were established, both inside toward the state parties and about the regimes, that is, toward nonsignatories. As the examples provided to demonstrate the distinct dynamics showed, compulsory power was often used by nonstate actors targeting both state parties and nonsignatories on the basis of obligations/norms inscribed in workings of institutional power of the two respective regimes.

REFERENCES

Barlevi, H. 2003. "The Mine Action/Mine Risk Education Integrated Approach." *Journal of Mine Action* 7, no 1: article 38. http://www.jmu.edu/cisr/journal/7.1/notes/barlevi/barlevi.htm.

Barnett, M. 2011. *Empire of Humanity: A History of Humanitarianism.* Ithaca, NY: Cornell University Press.

Barnett, M., and B. Duvall. 2005. "Power in International Politics." *International Organization* 59, no. 1: 39–75.

Bátora, J., and N. Hynek. 2014. *Fringe Players and the Diplomatic Order: The "New" Heteronomy.* London: Palgrave Macmillan.

Beier, J. M. 2003. "'Emailed Applications Are Preferred': Ethical Practices in Mine Action and the Idea of Global Civil Society." *Third World Quarterly* 24, no. 5: 795–808.

Borrie, J. 2009. *Unacceptable Harm: A History of How the Treaty to Ban Cluster Munitions Was Won*. New York: United Nations Publications.

———. 2014. "Humanitarian Reframing of Nuclear Weapons and the Logic of Ban." *International Affairs* 90, no. 3: 625–46.

Boulden, L. H. 1998. "De-Politicizing Demining." *Bulletin of the Atomic Scientists* 54, no. 4: 17–19.

Braudel, F. 1982. *On History*. Chicago: University of Chicago Press.

Breitegger, A. 2012. *Cluster Munitions and International Law: Disarmament with a Human Face?* New York: Routledge.

Cameron, M. A., R. J. Lawson, and B. W. Tomlin, eds. 1998. *To Walk without Fear: The Global Movement to Ban Landmines*. Oxford: Oxford University Press.

Canadian Landmine Foundation. n.d. *The Canadian Landmine Foundation: A History*. Accessed June 13, 2016. http://canadianlandmine.org/the-foundation/history.

CCW (Convention on Certain Conventional Weapons). 1980. *Convention on Prohibitions or Restrictions on the Use of Certain Conventional Weapons which May Be Deemed to Be Excessively Injurious or to Have Indiscriminate Effects*, adopted 10 October 1980, 1342 UNTS 137, entered into force 2 December 1983.

CCW Protocol. 1980. *Protocol on Prohibitions or Restrictions on the Use of Mines, Booby-Traps and Other Devices (Protocol II)*. 1342 UNTS 168. Adopted October 10, 1980. Entered into force December 2, 1983.

———. 2003. *Protocol on Explosive Remnants of War (Protocol V)*. UN Doc. CCW/MSP/2003/2. Adopted November 28, 2003. Entered into force November 12, 2006.

Chrétien, J. 1995. *Speech by Prime Minister Jean Chrétien to the National Forum on Canada's International Relations*. Toronto, September 11.

Clegg, L. 1999. "NGOs Take Aim." *The Bulletin of the Atomic Scientists* 55, no. 1: 49–51.

Cluster Munition Coalition. n.d. *Global Ban*. Accessed June 13, 2016. http://www.stopclustermunitions.org/en-gb/the-treaty/global-ban.aspx#.

Convention. 1972. *Convention on the Prohibition of the Development, Production and Stockpiling of Bacteriological (Biological) and Toxin Weapons and on Their Destruction (Biological Weapons Convention)*. 1015 UNTS 163. Opened for signature April 10, 1972. Entered into force March 26, 1975.

———. 1993. *Convention on the Prohibition of the Development, Production, Stockpiling and Use of Chemical Weapons and on Their Destruction (Chemical Weapons Convention)*. 1974 UNTS 45. Adopted January 13, 1993. Entered into force April 29, 1997.

———. 1997. *Convention on the Prohibition of the Use, Stockpiling, Production and Transfer of Anti-Personnel Mines and on Their Destruction (APL Convention)*. 2056 UNTS 211. Adopted September 18, 1997. Entered into force March 1, 1999.

———. 2007. *Convention on the Rights of Persons with Disabilities*. UN Doc. A/RES/61/106. Adopted December 13, 2006. Entered into force May 3, 2008.

———. 2008. *Convention on Cluster Munitions*. CCM/77. Adopted May 30, 2008 at the Diplomatic Conference for the Adoption of a Convention on Cluster Munitions. Entered into force August 1, 2010.

Corsi, J. 2009. "Towards Peace through Legal Innovation: The Process and Promise of the 2008 Convention on Cluster Munitions." *Harvard Human Rights Journal* 22, no. 1: 145–57.

Cox, R. W. 1987. *Production Power and World Order: Social Forces in the Making of History*. New York: Columbia University Press.

Crumley, C. L. 1995. "Heterarchy and the Analysis of Complex Societies." *Archeological Papers of the American Anthropological Association* 6, no. 1: 1–5.

Davis, J. 2009. "Liberal-Era Diplomatic Language Killed Off." *Canadiun*, July 1. http://canadiuns.blogspot.cz/2009/08/canadas-foreign-policy-train-wreck.html.

Dean, M. 1999. *Governmentality: Power and Rule in Modern Society*. London: Sage.

Declaration of St. Petersburg. 1868. *Declaration Renouncing the Use, in Time of War, of Certain Explosive Projectiles*. 18 Martens Nouveau Recueil (ser. 1) 474, 138 Consol. T. S. 297. Adopted and entered into force December 11, 1868.

Deleuze, G., and F. Guattari. 1983. *Anti-Oedipus: Capitalism and Schizophrenia.* Minneapolis: University of Minnesota Press.

DFAIT [Department of Foreign Affairs and International Trade]. 1995. *Canada in the World.* Ottawa: Government of Canada. http://dfait-aeci.canadiana.ca/view/ooe. b2644952E/1?r=0&s=1.

———. 1996. *Canadian Action Plan to Reduce the Global Use of Land Mines.* Internal Memo, Ottawa: DFAIT, IDA Division.

Docherty, B. 2007. "The Time Is Now: A Historical Argument for a Cluster Munitions Convention." *Harvard Human Rights Journal* 20: 53–87.

———. 2009. "Breaking New Ground: The Convention on Cluster Munitions and the Evolution of International Humanitarian Law." *Human Rights Quarterly* 31, no. 4: 943–63.

———. 2010. "Ending Civilian Suffering: The Purpose, Provisions, and Promise of Humanitarian Disarmament Law." *Austrian Review of International and European Law* 15: 7–44.

Faulkner, F. 2007. *Moral Entrepreneurs and the Campaign to Ban Landmines.* Amsterdam: Rodopi.

Finnemore, M., and K. Sikkink. 1998. "International Norm Dynamics and Political Change." *International Organization* 52, no. 4: 887–917.

Flora, P., ed. 1986. *Growth to Limits: The Western European Welfare States since World War II. Vol. 1: Sweden, Norway, Finland, Denmark.* Berlin: Walter de Gruyter and Co.

Forsythe, D. 2005. *The Humanitarians: The International Committee of the Red Cross.* Cambridge: Cambridge University Press.

Fortin, Katharine. 2012. "Complementarity between the ICRC and the United Nations and International Humanitarian Law and International Human Rights Law, 1948–1968." *International Review of the Red Cross* 94, no. 888 (Winter): 1433–54.

Foucault, M. 1980. *Power/Knowledge: Selected Interviews and Other Writings 1972–1977.* Brighton: Harvester Press.

———. 1982. "The Subject and Power: Afterword." In *Michel Foucault: Beyond Structuralism and Hermeneutics,* edited by H. Dreyfus and P. Rabinow, 208–28. Brighton: The Harvester Press.

———. 1988. *Technologies of the Self: A Seminar with Michel Foucault.* Amherst, MA: MIT Press.

———. 1991. "Governmentality." In *The Foucault Effect: Studies in Governmentality,* edited by G. Burchell, C. Gordon, and P. Miller, 87–104. Hemel Hempstead: Harvester/Wheatsheaf.

———. 1994. *The Order of the Things: An Archaeology of the Human Sciences.* New York: Vintage Books.

———. 1996. "Impossible Prison." In *Foucault Live: Collected Interviews, 1961–1984,* edited by S. Lotringer. New York: Semiotext(e).

Gale, F. 1998. "Cave 'Cave! Hic Dragones': A Neo-Gramscian Deconstruction and Reconstruction of International Regime Theory." *Review of International Political Economy* 5, no. 2: 252–83.

Garcia, D. 2011. *Disarmament Diplomacy and Human Security: Regimes, Norms and Moral Progress in International Relation.* London: Routledge.

———. 2015. "Humanitarian Security Regimes." *International Affairs* 91, no. 1: 55–75.

Gidron, B., R. M. Kramer, and L. M. Salamon. 1992. "Government and the Third Sector in Comparative Perspective: Allies or Adversaries?" In *Government and the Third Sector: Emerging Relationship in Welfare States,* edited by B. Gidron, R. M. Kramer, and L. M. Salamon, 1–30. San Francisco: Jossey-Bass Publishers.

Gill, S. 1993. "Epistemology, Ontology and the 'Italian School.'" In *Gramsci, Historical Materialism and International Relations,* edited by S. Gill, 21–48. Cambridge: Cambridge University Press.

———. 1995. "Globalisation, Market Civilisation and Disciplinary Neoliberalism." *Millennium: Journal of International Studies* 24, no. 3: 399–423.

————. 2001. "Constitutionalising Capital: EMU and Disciplinary Neo-Liberalism." In *Social Forces in the Making of New Europe: The Restructuring of European Social Relations in the Global Political Economy*, edited by A. Bieler and A. D. Morton, 47–69. Basingstoke, UK: Palgrave Macmillan.

Gillespie, A. 2011. *A History of the Laws of War: Volume 2: The Customs and Laws of War with Regards to Civilians in Times of Conflict*. Oxford: Hart Publishing Ltd.

Goldblat, J. 2002. *Arms Control: The New Guide to Negotiations and Agreements*. London: SAGE Publications Ltd.

Goose, S., and J. Williams. 2004. "The Campaign to Ban Antipersonnel Landmines: Potential Lessons." In *Landmines and Human Security: International Politics and War's Hidden Legacy*, edited by R. A. Matthew, B. McDonald, and K. Rutherford, 239–50. New York: State University of New York Press.

Gramsci, A. 1971. *Selections from the Prison Notebooks*, edited and translated by Q. Hoare and G. Nowell-Smith. London: Lawrence and Wishart.

Grayson, K. 2010. "Human Security, Neoliberalism and Corporate Social Responsibility." *International Politics* 47, no. 5: 497–522.

Guzzini, S. 1993. "Structural Power: The Limits of Neorealist Power Analysis." *International Organization* 47, no. 3: 443–78.

Hague Declaration. 1899, IV, 1. *Declaration to Prohibit for the Term of Five Years, the Launching of Projectiles and Explosives from Balloons, and Other Methods of Similar Nature*. 26 Martens Nouveau Recueil (ser. 2) 994, 187 Consol. T. S. 456. Adopted July 19, 1899. Entered into force September 4, 1900.

————. 1899, IV, 2. *Declaration Concerning the Prohibition of the Use of Projectiles Diffusing Asphyxiating Gases*. 26 Martens Nouveau Recueil (ser. 2) 998, 187 Consol. T. S. 453. Adopted July 29, 1899. Entered into force September 4, 1900.

————. 1899, IV, 3. *Declaration Concerning the Prohibition of the Use of Expanding Bullets*. 26 Martens Nouveau Recueil (ser. 2) 1002, 187 Consol. T. S. 459. Adopted July 29, 1899. Entered into force September 4, 1900.

————. 1907, XIV. *Declaration Prohibiting the Discharge of Projectiles and Explosives from Balloons*. 3 Martens Nouveau Recueil (ser. 3) 745, 205 Consol. T. S. 403. Adopted October 18, 1907. Entered into force November 27, 1909.

Hayashi, M. 2012. "The Convention on Cluster Munitions and the Clearance of Cluster Munition Remnants: Whose Responsibility and How to Ensure Effective Implementation." *Journal of International Humanitarian Legal Studies* 3, no. 2: 322–43.

Heintze, H. J. 2004. "On the Relationship between Human Rights Law Protection and International Humanitarian Law." *International Review of the Red Cross* 86, no. 856: 789–814.

Hudson, J. 2016. "Exclusive: White House Blocks Transfer of Cluster Bombs to Saudi Arabia." *Foreign Policy*, May 27. http://foreignpolicy.com/2016/05/27/exclusive-white-house-blocks-transfer-of-cluster-bombs-to-saudi-arabia/.

HRW [Human Rights Watch]. 2008. *Flooding South Lebanon: Israel's Use of Cluster Munitions in Lebanon in July and August 2006*. February 16. https://www.hrw.org/report/2008/02/16/flooding-south-lebanon/israels-use-cluster-munitions-lebanon-july-and-august-2006.

————. 2014. *United States Landmine Policy: Questions and Answers*. October 3. https://www.hrw.org/news/2014/10/03/united-states-landmine-policy-questions-and-answers.

Hynek, N. 2008. "Conditions of Emergence and Their (Bio)Political Effects: Political Rationalities, Governmental Programmes and Technologies of Power in the Landmine Case." *Journal of International Relations and Development* 11, no. 2: 93–120.

ICBL [International Campaign to Ban Landmines]. n.d.-a. *Treaty Status*. Accessed June 13, 2016. http://www.icbl.org/en-gb/the-treaty/treaty-status.aspx.

————. n.d.-b. *Who We Are*. Accessed June 13, 2016. http://www.icbl.org/en-gb/about-us/who-we-are/donors.aspx.

————. n.d.-c. *Timeline of the International Campaign to Ban Landmines*. Accessed June 13, 2016. http://www.icbl.org/media/342067/icb009_chronology_a5_v4-pages.pdf.

———. 2014. *Allegation of Russian Use of Landmines in Ukraine*. April 8. http://www.icbl.
    org/en-gb/news-and-events/news/2014/reports-of-russian-landmine-use-in-crimea-
    requires.aspx.

———. 2016. *The Mine Ban Treaty Turns 17*. March 1. http://www.icbl.org/en-gb/news-
    and-events/news/2016/the-mine-ban-treaty-turns-17.aspx.

ICRC [International Committee of the Red Cross]. 2007. *Overview of the Convention on
    the Prohibition of Anti-Personnel Mines*. August 15. https://www.icrc.org/eng/
    resources/documents/legal-fact-sheet/landmines-factsheet-150807.htm.

———. n.d.-a. *Protocol on Explosive Remnants of War (Protocol V to the 1980 CCW Con-
    vention)*. Accessed June 13, 2016. https://www.icrc.org/applic/ihl/ihl.nsf/Treaty.xsp?
    documentId=22EFA0C23F4AAC69C1256E280052A81F&action=openDocument.

———. n.d.-b. *Protocol on Explosive Remnants of War (Protocol V to the 1980 CCW Con-
    vention)*. Accessed June 13, 2016. https://www.icrc.org/applic/ihl/ihl.nsf/States.xsp?
    xp_viewStates=XPages_NORMStatesParties&xp_treatySelected=610.

IKV Pax Christi. 2014. *Worldwide Investments in Cluster Munitions a Shared Responsibil-
    ity*. Report no. 5. Utrecht, NL: PAX.

Kimball, D. 2012. "Cluster Munitions at a Glance." *Arms Control Association*, November
    4. https://www.armscontrol.org/factsheets/clusterataglance.

Kochin, I., and N. R. Jenzen-Jones. 2015. "Russian PMN-4 Anti-Personnel Landmines
    in Syria." *Armament Research Services*, October 1. http://armamentresearch.com/
    russian-pmn-4-anti-personnel-landmines-in-syria/#.

Krasner, S. D. 1982. "Regimes and the Limits of Realism: Regimes as Autonomous
    Variables." *International Organization* 36, no. 2: 497–510.

———. 1985. *Structural Conflict: The Third World against Global Liberalism*. Berkeley:
    University of California Press.

Kratochwil, F. 2013. "Politics, Law, and the Sacred: A Conceptual Analysis." *Journal of
    International Relations and Development* 16, no. 1: 1–24.

LCMM [Landmine and Cluster Munition Monitor]. 2015. *De Facto Monitoring Regime of
    the Mine Ban Treaty and Convention on Cluster Munitions*. Accessed June 13, 2016.
    http://www.the-monitor.org/en-gb/home.aspx.

Lavergne, R. 2002. *Results-Based Management and Accountability for Enhanced Aid Effec-
    tiveness*. CIDA Policy Branch, July 30.

Liberal Party of Canada. 1993. *Creating Opportunity: The Liberal Plan for Canada*. Otta-
    wa: Liberal Party of Canada.

Mansfield, I. 2003. "The Role of the Military in Mine Action." *UNIDIR Disarmament
    Forum*, no. 3.

———. 2005. "The Coordination and Management of Mine Action Programmes." In
    Mine Action: Lessons and Challenges, 209–22. Geneva: Geneva International Centre
    for Humanitarian Demining.

Maputo Action Plan. 2014. Adopted June 27, 2014. http://www.
    maputoreviewconference.org/fileadmin/APMBC-RC3/3RC-Maputo-action-plan-
    adopted-27Jun2014.pdf.

Maresca, L. 2004. "A New Protocol on Explosive Remnants of War: The History and
    Negotiation of Protocol V to the 1980 Convention on Certain Conventional Weap-
    ons." *International Review of the Red Cross* 86, no. 856: 815–35.

Maresca, L., and S. Maslen, eds. 2009. *The Banning of Anti-Personnel Landmines: The
    Legal Contribution of the International Committee of the Red Cross, 1955–1999*. Cam-
    bridge: Cambridge University Press.

Mathews, R. J. 2001. "The 1980 Convention on Certain Conventional Weapons: A
    Useful Framework Despite Earlier Disappointments." *International Review of the Red
    Cross* 83, no. 844: 991–1012.

Matthew, R. A., and K. R. Rutherford. 2003. "The Evolutionary Dynamics of the Move-
    ment to Ban Landmines." *Alternatives: Global, Local, Political* 28, no. 1: 29–56.

McGrath, R. 2000. *Landmines and Unexploded Ordnance: A Resource Book*. London: Pluto
    Press.

Mines Action Canada. 2015. *Breaking News and Press Releases*. November 26. http://www.minesactioncanada.org/media-centre, 13 June 2016.

Morton, A. D. 2011. "Social Forces in the Struggle over Hegemony: Neo-Gramscian Perspectives in International Political Economy." In *Rethinking Gramsci*, edited by M. E. Green, 147–66. London: Routledge.

Moszynski, P. 2008. "Ban on Cluster Bombs a 'Victory for Humanity,' Say Campaigners." *British Medical Journal* 336, no. 7656: 1268–69.

Mutimer, D. 2012. "International Arms Control." In *Routledge Handbook of Diplomacy and Statecraft*, edited by B. J. C. McKercher, 365–75. London: Routledge.

Nairobi Action Plan. 2004. *The Final Report of the First Review Conference of the States Parties to the Convention on the Prohibition of the Use, Stockpiling, Production and Transfer of Anti-Personnel Mines and on Their Destruction*. APLC/CONF/2004/5. February 9. http://www.nairobisummit.org/fileadmin/APMBC-RC1/documents/final_report/RC_Final_Report_en.pdf.

Nash, T. 2012. "Civil Society and Cluster Munitions: Building Blocks of a Global Campaign." In *Global Civil Society 2012: Ten Years of Critical Reflection*, edited by M. Kaldor, H. L. Moore, and S. Selchow, 124–41. Basingstoke, UK: Palgrave Macmillan.

Nystuen, G., and S. Casey-Maslen, eds. 2010. *The Convention on Cluster Munitions: A Commentary*. Oxford: Oxford University Press.

Orakhelashvili, A. 2008. "The Interaction between Human Rights and Humanitarian Law: Fragmentation, Conflict, Parallelism, or Convergence?" *European Journal of International Law* 19, no. 1: 161–82.

Oslo Declaration. 2007. *Final Declaration, Oslo Conference on Cluster Munitions*. Oslo: Norwegian Government, February 23. https://www.regjeringen.no/globalassets/upload/ud/vedlegg/oslo-declaration-final-23-february-2007.pdf.

Paterson, T. 2005. "Capacity Development in Mine Action. In: Geneva International Centre for Humanitarian Demining." In *Mine Action: Lessons and Challenges*, 305–38. Geneva: Geneva International Centre for Humanitarian Demining.

Price, R. 1995. "A Genealogy of the Chemical Weapons Taboo." *International Organization* 49, no. 1: 73–103.

———. 1998. "Reversing the Gun Sights: Transnational Civil Society Targets Land Mines." *International Organization* 52, no. 3: 613–44.

Protocol. 1925. *Protocol for the Prohibition of the Use in War of Asphyxiating, Poisonous or Other Gases, and of Bacteriological Methods of Warfare (Geneva Protocol)*. 94 LNTS 65. Adopted June 17, 1925. Entered into force February 8, 1928.

Purdey, S. J. 2010. *Economic Growth, the Environment and International Relations: The Growth Paradigm*. London: Routledge.

Putnam, R. D. 1996. *The Decline of Civil Society: How Come? So What?* The J. L. Manion Lecture. Ottawa: Canadian Centre for Management Development. February 22, 1–28.

Raccuia, D. J. 2011. "The Convention on Cluster Munitions: An Incomplete Solution to the Cluster Munition Problem." *Vanderbilt Journal of Transnational Law* 44, no. 2: 465–97.

Robinson, W. I. 2005. "Gramsci and Globalisation: From Nation-State Transnational Hegemony." *Critical Review of International Social and Political Philosophy* 8, no. 4: 559–74.

Rutherford, K. R. 1999. "The Hague and Ottawa Conventions: A Model for Future Weapons Ban Regimes?" *Non-Proliferation Review* 6, no. 3: 36–50.

———. 2011. *Disarming States: The International Movement to Ban Landmines*. Santa Barbara, CA: Praeger.

Scott, K. 2003. *Funding Matters: The Impact of Canada's New Funding Regime on Non-profit and Voluntary Organizations*. Ottawa: Canadian Council on Social Development.

Short, N. 1997. "International Efforts to Ban Landmines: The Vienna Conference." *CESD Briefing Notes*, March 5.

———. 1999. "The Role of NGOs in the Ottawa Process to Ban Landmines." *International Negotiations* 4, no. 3: 481–500.

Sigal, L. V. 2006. *Negotiating Minefields: The Landmines Ban in American Politics*. New York: Routledge.

Strange, S. 1989. "Towards a Theory of Transnational Empire." In *Global Changes and Theoretical Challenges: Approaches to World Politics for the 1990s*, edited by E. O. Czempiel and J. N. Rosenau, 161–76. Lexington, MA: Lexington Books.

Ticehurst, R. 1997. "The Martens Clause and the Laws of Armed Conflict." *International Review of the Red Cross* 37, no. 317: 125–34.

Tomlin, B. W. 1998. "On a Fast-Track to a Ban: The Canadian Policy Process." *Canadian Foreign Policy* 5, no. 3: 3–24.

Tuchman, B. W. 1996. *The Proud Tower: A Portrait of the World before the War, 1890–1914*. New York: Ballantine Books.

UN Statement. 2006. *Secretary-General's Message to the Third Review Conference of the Convention on Certain Conventional Weapons*. Delivered by Sergei Ordzhonikidze, Director-General, UN Office at Geneva, November 7. http://www.un.org/sg/statements/?nid=2289.

Wapner, P. 2000. "The Resurgence and Metamorphosis of Normative International Relations: Principled Commitment and Scholarship in a New Millennium." In *Principled World Politics: The Challenge of Normative International Relations*, edited by P. Wapner and L. E. J. Ruiz, 1–22. Lanham, MD: Rowman & Littlefield.

———. 2004. "The Campaign to Ban Antipersonnel Landmines: Potential Lessons." In *Landmines and Human Security: International Politics and War's Hidden Legacy*, edited by R. A. Matthew, B. McDonald, and K. Rutherford, 251–68. New York: State University of New York Press.

Warkentin, C., and K. Mingst. 2000. "International Institutions, the State, and Global Civil Society in the Age of the World Wide Web." *Global Governance* 6, no. 2: 237–56.

Westhead, R. 2012. "Bosnia and Herzegovina: Why Has Canada 'Dropped the Ball' on Landmine Removal Effort?" *The Star*, December 26. https://www.thestar.com/news/world/2012/09/22/bosnia_and_herzegovina_why_has_canada_dropped_the_ball_on_landmine_removal_effort.html.

Wheatley, A. 2005. "Mine Risk Education. In: Geneva International Centre for Humanitarian Demining." In *Mine Action: Lessons and Challenges*, 133–68. Geneva: Geneva International Centre for Humanitarian Demining.

Williams, J. 2000. "David with Goliath: International Cooperation and the Campaign to Ban Landmines." *Harvard International Review* 22, no. 3: 87–88.

———. 2013. *My Name Is Jody Williams: A Vermont Girl's Winding Path to the Nobel Peace Prize*. Berkeley: University of California Press.

Wisotzki, S. 2013. "Humanitarian Arms Control: The Anti-Personnel Mine Ban Treaty, the Programme of Action on Small Arms and Light Weapons, and the Convention on Cluster Munitions." In *Norm Dynamics in Multilateral Arms Control: Interests, Conflicts, and Justice*, edited by H. Müller and C. Wunderlich, 82–108. Athens: University of Georgia Press.

Wurst, J. 1997. "Closing in on a Landmine Ban: The Ottawa Process and U.S. Interests." *Arms Control Association*, June 1. https://www.armscontrol.org/act/1997_06-07/wurst.

Yeatman, A. 1998. "Interpreting Contemporary Contractualism." In *Governing Australia: Studies in Contemporary Rationalities of Government*, edited by M. Dean and B. Hindess, 227–41. Melbourne: Cambridge University Press.

FOUR

Small Arms and Light Weapons

From Humanitarian Disarmament to Arms Trade Treaty

The focus of this chapter falls to small arms and light weapons (SALW). Through the prism of the power-analytical approach, it dissects the dynamics and conditions having determined the contours of their security regulation. While there lacks a universally accepted definition of SALW, the most widely accepted detailization of their composition comes from the 1997 report of a UN Panel of Governmental Experts on Small Arms and the 2005 International Tracing Instrument (ITI). The report has associated *small arms* with firearms designed for personal use and carried by one person, while *light weapons* are larger weapons used by several persons or a crew and transportable by two or more people, a pack animal, or a light vehicle. The former therein include revolvers and self-loading pistols, rifles and carbines, assault rifles, submachine guns, and light machine guns. The latter in turn encompasses heavy machine guns, hand-held underbarrel and mounted grenade launchers, portable antitank and anti-aircraft guns, recoilless rifles, portable launchers of antitank missile and rocket systems and anti-aircraft missile systems, and mortars of less than 100-millimeter caliber. The ITI has integrated the cluster of SALW under a joint umbrella definition of any man-portable lethal weapons that expel or launch, are designed to expel or launch, or may be readily converted to expel or launch a shot, bullet, or projectile by the action of an explosive (SAS 2016, 14; IANSA 2017, 6). A renowned and broadly referred to group of SALW is firearms. They are defined by the UN Firearms Protocol, the principal related international document, as any portable barreled weapons that expel, are designed to expel, or may be readily converted to expel a shot, bullet, or projectile by the action of an explosive (Firearms Protocol 2001). However, this definition virtually covers all small arms (SAS 2016, 15), implying that these two terms usually have "the same meaning" (IANSA 2017, 6). In this chapter, small arms and firearms are thus used interchangeably, unless explicitly indicated otherwise.

Against the background of a wide-scale campaign advocating for a global regulatory regime on SALW, there has indeed emerged a framework of the sort by virtue of both international and regional endeavors. However, the uniqueness of this case is manifold, and this inquiry aims to dissect and interpret the related nuances. First, the case of SALW embodies a model of how stigmatization has evolved with no stigma ultimately imposed upon the deviant weapons category. Second, a part of the explanation for this setup lies with strong (nongovernmental) gun lobby advocacy, which is rather unconventional in the area of humanitarian arms control and disarmament. Third, besides being variously inclined, all states share powerful incentives in preserving the disputed weapons category and its flows. Finally, while occasionally echoing the pattern of humanitarian disarmament and deeply convergent with its underlying norms, the case of SALW has not followed this scenario. The power-analytical approach is considered as a particularly suitable intellectual framework for this complex and multifaceted analysis. Inter alia, it allows us to show how the dominant discourse has taken shape within its (un)favorable conditions of emergence. It also helps to discover how efforts to confine SALW and the existing resistance to such have corresponded to categorically identical actors as well as to examine their related motivations and sources of authority. Withal, it enables effective study of how the prevalent structural and institutional circumstances have embedded the discourse as a particular regulatory regime with certain powers and limitations. In doing so, we also systematically illustrate another offbeat feature of the SALW case, which is critical convergence between the involved actors' standing and leverage. Considering antipersonnel landmines (APLs) as an ad hoc legally proscribed (Hynek 2018b) category of SALW (Renner 1997, 9; Laurance 1999, 5), signs of interrelatedness in the matter of APLs and SALW security regulation are noted throughout this study. As the recent culmination of regulatory politics in the domain of SALW and conventional weapons more generally, the Arms Trade Treaty (ATT) is scrutinized, with implications of this study for understanding its future prospects flagged.

REGULATION OF TRANSFERS: FROM CONVENTIONAL WEAPONS TO SALW

The existing international legal framework regulating SALW derives from a long journey of various efforts aimed at regulating conventional weapons more generally. The international humanitarian law (IHL) and the international human rights law (IHRL), in particular including the UN Charter, the Universal Declaration of Human Rights, and the Geneva Conventions, form the very foundation of legal control of weapons-related practices (Peters n.d.). Their provisions, though, had largely remained marginalized until the end of the Cold War because piecemeal regulatory efforts had afore primarily reflected states' or rather major powers' security interests. For example, a "hegemonic imposition" was enacted through the Brussels Act (1890), the only prevalent and broadly ratified international treaty concerning certain aspects of conventional weapons (Bromley, Cooper, and Holtom 2012, 1031–34). Further restraints on conventional arms trade, though never enured because of major powers' divergent security priorities, came along with the Convention of the Trade in Arms and Ammunition or St. Germain Convention (1919) and the Geneva Traffic Convention (1925). Proposed by the United States at the League of Nations Disarmament Conference, another draft convention aimed at governing manufacture and trade in conventional arms also did not culminate in an international agreement. The Cold War gave rise to full-fledged export control regimes, namely the Coordinating Committee for Multilateral Export Controls (COCOM) on the part of the United States and similar restrictions by the Soviet Union. Such efforts, however, similarly reflected the then prevailing bipolar hostility and hegemonic order (Bromley, Cooper, and Holtom 2012, 1031–35; Hunter 2013, 229–30). Regardless of the overwhelming number of deaths caused by SALW, they had principally remained "off the arms control agenda" until the 1990s (Krause 2001, 8). Though aimed to succeed COCOM (Whang 2015, 120) while also bridging "the East-West divide" (Bromley, Cooper, and Holtom 2012, 1035), the Wassenaar Arrangement on Export Controls for Conventional Arms and Dual-Use Goods and Technologies (1995) included a reference to the notion of SALW (SAS 2016, 84). The 1991 United Nations (UN) Register of Conventional Arms, originally adopted to increase transparency in international arms transfers, was expanded in 2003 in part to consider the devastating effect of SALW. But a truly remarkable achievement in the issue area was the 2001 UN Programme of Action to Prevent, Combat, and Eradicate the Illicit Trade in Small Arms and Light Weapons in All Its Aspects (UN PoA) that drew together SALW and human(itarian) concerns (Bromley, Cooper, and Holtom 2012, 1037; Hunter 2013, 230–33). Its ambition was complemented by the 2005 International Instrument to Enable States to Identify and Trace, in a Timely and Reliable Manner, Illicit Small Arms and Light Weapons, known as the ITI and aimed to advance international marking, record-keeping, and tracing measures. Known as the UN Firearms Protocol, the 2001 UN Protocol against the Illicit Manufacturing of and Trafficking in Firearms, Their Parts and Components and Ammunition criminalized the link between (illicit manufacturing and trafficking of) "firearms" in particular and crime for the sake of public health and safety (SAS 2016, 27 and 52). The crowning achievement has to date been the 2013 ATT putting together the seven categories of conventional weapons from the UN Register and SALW as an officially distinct cluster under the "7+1 formula" (Bromley, Cooper, and Holtom 2012, 1043–44). It has thus concerned battle tanks, armored combat vehicles, large-caliber artillery systems, combat aircraft, attack helicopters, warships, missiles, and missile launchers, as well as small arms and light weapons (SAS 2016, 68). In particular, the treaty has formalized and curbed the nexus between illicit or unregulated trade in all of these and negative consequences on human beings. As the first legally binding international treaty concerning a broad spectrum of conventional arms, particularly including SALW, it has filled a critical "regulatory gap" (Balga 2016, 584–85 and 589–90).

This global-level process has been greatly reinforced by over sixty regional and subregional agreements and initiatives framing SALW around the world, mostly in the Americas, Europe, and Africa (Bourne 2019, 144). Though not all of them, many have entailed legally binding commitments (SAS 2016, 85–89). The UN PoA has explicitly encouraged and highlighted the significance of such regional efforts (Hunter 2013, 233). Of particular importance in setting the stage for "firearms" in particular was the Inter-American Convention Against the Illicit Manufacture of and Trafficking in Firearms, Ammunition, Explosives, and Other Related Materials adopted by the Organization of American States (OAS) in 1997 (Krause 2001, 29–30). The EU and its member-states have in turn "gone the furthest in integrating human security principles" with the EU Code of Conduct of Arms Exports (1998) later succeeded by the legally binding EU Common Position (2008) (Bromley, Cooper, and Holtom 2012, 1036).

Apparently, the case of SALW echoes the nineteenth-century humanitarian arms control and disarmament regime in that it also features an international *regime complex*. This is because it may similarly be characterized by "a number of elements, building blocks or agents capable of interacting with each other" (Alter and Meunier 2009, 13–14; Drezner 2009, 65). The overall pathway to this emerging global security regime in the realm of SALW may be characterized by the three intertwined trends: an evolving regulation of conventional weapons chiefly from the angle of arms transfers, a delimitation of SALW as a separately standing category, and a shifting focus from traditional security considerations toward public and human(itarian) security concerns. In the following sections there is a deep inquiry into the underlying and inner dynamics of the case, with the discerned trends systematically addressed and interpreted. While the contribution of the aforementioned precedents is also considered, the key post–Cold War (global and regional) agreements in the matter of SALW are at the core of this analysis. To the extent necessary for comprehending the nature of the regime they constitute, light is shed on their origins, character, promises and key limitations. There is also a consistent reflection on how and why this piecemeal regime for SALW has built upon and around the issue of arms transfers rather than the agenda of humanitarian disarmament. Both practical and discursive drivers and constraints in this regard are extensively discussed. Inter alia, the link between the IHL/IHRL and the emerging regulatory framework is analytically dissected.

PRODUCTIVE POWER: DISARMAMENT VERSUS ARMS (FLOWS) CONTROL

While dissecting how and why SALW have become subject to stigmatization but never been stigmatized, this section seeks to clear out the ideational underbrush of the emerging SALW-oriented global regime. In the first place, stigmatization of SALW has built upon a diligent delineation of their *profile* in relation to the otherwise broad cluster of conventional weapons. A benchmark was provided by the Conventional Forces in Europe Treaty (1980) and its five categories of Major Conventional Arms, later expanded into seven by the UN Register of Conventional Arms (1998). A critical role in elucidating the configuration of SALW was then played by the groups of experts preparing for the 2001 UN Conference. They defined SALW as a "residual category" that was ultimately incorporated as a further, separate class of conventional weapons to the UN register reporting in 2003. Solidifying the trend, the ATT incorporated all of the hitherto recognized eight categories. Case study research and reports concerning the prevalent conflicts in Afghanistan, Colombia, Pakistan, Somalia, Mali, and the wider Sahara-Sahel, as well as Boutros Boutros-Ghali's call for "microdisarmament" have assisted in framing the group of SALW (Bourne 2019, 151). This group has ultimately embodied an assembly of weapons traditionally, in fact for centuries, produced and traded on legal terms (Krause 2002, 249). It is essentially a sophisticated value-laden boundary between the legal and the *illegal* that underlies the stigmatization of SALW:

> Retiring or demobilizing soldiers frequently keep the guns they previously used for work, a custom which is legal in some countries. However, an ex-soldier, unable to find another job, sometimes uses the gun to rob a store (illegal); or sells it to a friend (illegal). In a non-conflict country like the USA, a private citizen with no criminal record might buy a gun from the ex-soldier (legal) or a gunshop (legal), and later sell it at a garage sale to a stranger (legal or illegal, depending on local state or city law). The stranger may transfer it to a criminal gang (illegal); or he may simply keep the gun at home (possibly legal), from where it may be stolen by a burglar (illegal), or taken to school by his adolescent son to impress his friends (illegal). (Peters n.d.)

What is noteworthy is that the thrust of condemnation has in this light fallen to both the unauthorized or unlawful *use and users* of SALW (Whang 2015, 134). Stigmatization of these deviant values has proceeded through "the attribution of a wide range of possible negative consequences" to the proliferation, accumulation, availability, and (mis)use of SALW (Laurance 1999, 5; Krause 2002, 251). All of this has been associated with the outbreak, escalation or intensification, prolongation, and resurgence of conflicts, insecurity of vulnerable groups (women, children, refugees, and minorities), genocide, crimes against humanity and war crimes, colossal (civilian) deaths, severe injuries and public health burdens, poverty and large-scale criminal activity, socioeconomic devastation, and the erosion of development prospects and gains. What has always formed the core of this composite discourse, as reaffirmed by the ATT, are humanitarian or IHL and human rights (HR) or IHRL concerns (Laurance 1999, 5 and 7; Krause 2001, 26, 2002, 250–51, 257, and 260, 2007, 2; Whang 2015, 114; Lustgarten 2015, 571–72 and 594; Balga 2016, 589–90; UNODC 2016, 6; IANSA 2017, 8–13; Amnesty International 2019; Peters n.d.). This exemplifies how the new (SALW-oriented) norms originate through legal "grafting," that is, in resonance with the already established norms, the ones also erstwhile critical for the ban on APL and the similar framing of weapons of mass destruction (Price 1998, 628–30). Both normative and causal claims have constituted the body of knowledge related to SALW (Laurance 1999, 5; Krause 2002, 260). Its ultimate product has manifested as an image of SALW as "the primary instruments of contemporary armed violence" (Krause 2010, 28), "the real weapons of mass destruction" (Krause 2007, 1; Lustgarten 2015, 571; Balga 2016, 597), and "an epidemic" (Peters n.d.). Their "indiscriminate" character has also been underscored (Krause 2001, 24). What is worth illuminating is that both "war deaths" and "peacetime deaths" have been considered (IANSA 2017, 7). Given the overwhelming civilian possession of SALW for sports, hunting, and in the household as well as overlaps in their peaceful and violent applications, stigmatization of SALW has not neglected the *civil-military nexus* (Amnesty International and IANSA 2012, 25; SAS 2016, 14; IANSA 2017, 10; Peters n.d.). Solicitude for the recurrence of suicides, accidental deaths, and injuries associated with civilian arms has contoured the narrative (Krause 2007, 1, 2010, 31). Even concerns about unauthorized recourses to lethal force in policing have been voiced (IANSA 2017, 6).

However, the agenda underlying these traits of stigmatization has been "relatively broad and open-ended." Unlike clear-cut prohibition campaigns such as the one to ban antipersonnal landmines (APLs), the SALW-oriented endeavor has projected a broad range of policy suggestions (Krause 2001, 18 and 25–26). Among them have been postconflict weapons collection and destruction, adjustments to national gun control legislation, and supplier states' export legislation, transparency in transfers, weapons marking and tracing, cross-border customs and police controls, identification and destruction of surplus stocks, and deceleration of the stream of new weapons (Krause 2001, 18 and 25, 2002, 257; Peters n.d.). Even the aspiration for (conventional) (micro)disarmament of both governments and civilian populations, particularly in the context of prevalent conflicts, has occasionally been articulated (BICC 1996, 5; Lustgarten 2015, 571; UNODA 2018, part III; Peters n.d.). The dominant narrative, though, has settled upon a subtle distinction between legal and illicit *flows* evaluated through a broader perspective of the weapons lifecycle from production and possession to trade and circulation (Firearms Protocol 2001; IANSA 2017, 14–15). Importantly, the deviant category itself has often been disaggregated for this purpose to encompass not only weapons as such but also their *parts or components* as well as *(am)munitions* (Firearms Protocol 2001; SAS 2016, 68–69). Because legal transfers have often underlied violations of human rights and humanitarian law (Krause 2001, 25), the key stipulated criteria for distinguishing an illicit flow has become the *potential* for SALW to be subsequently used in their violation (Lustgarten 2015, 594). From a more general perspective, the notion of illicit arms trade has been associated with any related trade practices that are "in conflict with national law, treaty law, or customary international law" (Whang 2015, 133). The thrust of criticism has thus concentrated on the *illicit, unregulated, and irresponsible flows* of SALW generating unauthorized end-users (abusers) and unauthorized end-use (misuse), especially in unstable and volatile regions (Whang 2015, 133; Balga 2016, 589–90; Peters n.d.). Also speculatively referred to as "the terror trade," these are such transfers, implying a certain practice in the realm of SALW, that have ultimately become stigmatized (Amnesty International 1999, 2002, 2003).

A combination of favorable structural conditions, often pointed to while propelling the aforesaid discourse, have allowed for this campaign to gain a strong foothold. Numerous wars with devastating humanitarian, economic, and social consequences in the Global South have gained momentum after the end of the Cold War (Lustgarten 2015, 571). Progressively covering Cambodia, El Salvador, Somalia, Rwanda, Angola, Mozambique, and other conflict-ridden areas, they have reflected a sharply increased profile of internal or communal conflicts vis-à-vis more traditional interstate conflicts (BICC 1996, 5; Krause 2001, 10). The problematic of transnational crime and that of failed states (Bourne 2019, 145 and 151), as well as the resurgence of (transnational and local) terrorism in a fourth (religious) wave (Rapoport 2004, 63), have all complemented the realities of instability and insecurity. All of this may generally be considered as the context of "high insecurity" (Greene and Marsh 2012, 2). By virtue of their low cost, easy transportation, or portability and easy application with minimum training and concealability, SALW (including APLs) have become weapons of choice for government armies as well as guerrilla groups, paramilitaries, rebel forces, insurgents, criminal bands, separatist groups, and terrorists (BICC 1996, 10; Renner 1997, 10–12; Laurance 1999, 5–6; Klare 1999/2018; Krause 2007, 1; Lustgarten 2015, 571; Balga 2016, 597; IANSA 2017, 6). The situation has been aggravated by the post–Cold War worldwide dispersion of surplus stocks as well as the expansion of an illicit faction and generally engrained lack of transparency in SALW trade (Klare 1999/2018; IPB n.d.; Peters n.d.). Illicit, in particular "craft," production of SALW has withal settled down in many parts of the globe (Hall 2014, 52). On top of this, comprehensive international standards for marking as well as registers for tracing SALW have also been lacking (Berkol 2002, 17). The economics of SALW production and trade has consistently stimulated a generally broad availability and distribution of SALW (Krause 2007, 2). What has been particularly important for framing the discourse is the fact that it is "the legal market" rather than "an illicit market" that has underlay the flow of SALW to conflicts (Bourne 2012, 30). The growing lethality of SALW, on top of what has already been brought to the fore, also must be mentioned (Klare 1999/2018). All these factors largely account for the principal focus of the campaign falling to SALW flows through the prism of a wider examination of their manufacture, stockpiling, and transfers (Krause 2001, 18, 2002, 249; Lustgarten 2015, 571–72; IANSA 2017, 14). The realization that the legal character of a gun is ambiguous, because it depends on the circumstances rather than its inherent characteristics, has given rise to a complementary objective of tracking the "journey" or provenance of SALW (Peters n.d.).

Another pivotal condition of possibility has been the concurrent emergence of a "normative space" for advancing the aforesaid discourse in the 1990s (Krause 2001, 11). The shifting balance between interstate and intrastate conflicts has engendered the reorientation from traditional security concerns of states and regimes to societal or human security concerns of communities and individuals (Krause 2001, 12–13, 2002, 259–60; Bromley, Cooper, and Holtom 2012, 1036). A notable facet of this transformation is the altered perception of sovereignty, with the human dimension of security pulled out from "the sovereign purview of states" for the sake of international oversight, transparency, and accountability (Krause 2002, 259–60). Finally, a nonlinear series of agenda-setting precedents have also stimulated the SALW-oriented campaign. The deep-rooted path has been paved by such fractionary milestones as the 1890 Brussels Act (1890), the Convention of the Trade in Arms and Ammunition or the St. Germain Convention (1919), the Geneva Traffic Convention (1925), and the Coordinating Committee for Multilateral Export Control established by the United States during the Cold War (Bromley, Cooper, and Holtom 2012, 1031–33; Hunter 2013, 229). Also falling to the category of agenda-setting developments are (unsuccessful) attempts by Amnesty International and the Stockholm International Peace Research Institute to challenge SALW during the Cold War (Krause 2001, 11). A decisive impetus for the SALW-oriented agenda has still been provided by the Nobel Peace Laureates' International Code of Conduct on Arms Transfers (1997) (Bromley, Cooper, and Holtom 2012, 1038; Hunter 2013, 234) and particularly the successful campaign to stigmatize and ban APLs (Krause 2002, 256), an "important category" of SALW (Renner 1997, 10).

However, a number of serious hurdles have not only blocked a prohibition campaign in the first place but also impeded the pervasive embeddedness of the aforesaid discourse. From a strategic-military perspective, some "traditional understanding of armed violence" has become firmly entrenched (Bourne 2019, 152). It has generated and embedded a complex layered structure of SALW spread (the global, regional, and conflict-complex levels) (Bourne 2007) "dominated by the legal (authorised) trade" (2019, 55). Unlike chemical, biological, or atomic weapons, these are particularly conventional weapons and even more so SALW that have been the most common means of violence, as also a reflection of the truly globalized market (Krause 2007, 2, 2010, 29; Lustgarten 2015, 570; Peters n.d.). This is where sovereignty understood as sovereign decision making, noninterference, and the UN Charter's right to self-defense contradicts a human-oriented reading of sovereignty. An essential facet of this overall tension between the understandings of sovereignty is also that between IHL and the existing arms export deals and defense cooperation frameworks (Bourne 2019, 152). Such considerations have legitimized most types of conventional weapons and prevented their alike stigmatization in parallel with the weapons of mass destruction (Krause 2001, 9; Lustgarten 2015, 570). Given the same concerns, the stigmatization and legal prohibition of APLs and cluster munitions may in turn be well explained by their declining role in the new (Western) way of warfare and defense strategies (Bromley, Cooper, and Holtom 2012, 1037).

There have also been substantial legal and cultural barriers to SALW stigmatization from a civilian perspective. This cluster of conventional weapons has entailed a deep-seated tradition of legitimate civilian uses. Their legally permitted applications have encompassed those related to sports, hunting, leisure, and collection as well as other traditional and nonthreatening uses (Krause 2001, 9, 2010, 29–30; Cukier and Sidel 2006, 113). An unconventional case for the weapons-oriented campaign is that the overwhelming majority of weapons under consideration have in fact rested in private hands (SAS 2011, 1). Civilian ownership of SALW has often been coupled, particularly by the United States, with individual rights (Krause 2010, 30; Whang 2015, 115; Bourne 2019, 155). An essential layer of this habitude has been the "gun culture" reified by Hollywood action films, media, and television more generally and simulated war games such as paintball as well as video games. Firearms and gun possession have ultimately grown into a representation of masculinity in many cultures (Cukier and Sidel 2006, 109 and 128–29; Stroud 2012, 216 and 218). The observability of guns and the normalization of their "symbolic significance," at the very least on the part of police officers, security guards, or soldiers, have also coconstituted the positive imaginary of SALW (Cukier and Sidel 2006, 125). To sum up, a rather extensive availability of SALW in military and civilian markets shows how the framing of such weapons by the campaign has also been informed by reconciling their "commercial image" with emerging narratives (Mutimer 2000, 52).

STRUCTURAL AND COMPULSORY POWER: AT THE CROSSROADS OF STANDING AND LEVERAGE

This section examines operations of structural and compulsory power in and around the emerging SALW regulatory regime. In particular, structural power hierarchies and associated interests that define the key stakeholders and their standing as well as their related leverage grips are studied. These power configurations are studied jointly because the listed aspects have often been deeply intertwined in the case of SALW, often to an extent of being virtually inseparable. The following lines comprehensively discuss the workings of these power displays, while systematically illustrating the convergence between subject positions in direct relation to one another (structural power) and their direct control of actions and even conditions of existence of one another (compulsory power) (Barnett and Duvall 2005, 48 and 52–53).

In part inspired by the campaign to ban APL, a group of Washington- and London-based nongovernmental agencies also took an interest in the problematic of SALW in the 1990s (Krause 2002, 256). The campaign launched through an international arms trade agreement by Nobel Peace Prize laureates in 1995 provided a critical momentum for this agenda to flourish (Hunter 2013, 234). In October 1998, its culmination came with the formation of the International Action Network on Small Arms (IANSA), a coherent campaign increasingly uniting hundreds of organizations and individuals from many countries (Krause 2001, 18–19, 2002, 256). To further reinforce efforts on the part of the IANSA grassroots network, the Control Arms Coalition was launched in 2003 (Macdonald and Pytlak 2015, 199). The key (international) nongovernmental organizations (I)NGOs involved have included Saferworld, the British-American Security Information Council (BASIC), International Alert, Federation of American Scientists, Amnesty International, and Human Rights Watch. With humanitarian and human rights (I)NGOs at the core of this campaign, other organizations oriented at the issues of conflict and disarmament, development and refugees, as well as gun control, have also become actively engaged. It is worth accentuating that development and faith groups such as Oxfam, CARE, the World Council of Churches, Pax Christi, and the Quakers have formed a crucial facet of this movement. Normative and diplomatic facilitation by the International Committee of the Red Cross (ICRC), possessing a distinct authority in the realm of humanitarian and human rights law, as extensively discussed in the previous chapters, has also been of particular importance (Krause 2001, 18–19, 23–24, and 26). Harnessing their "normative authority," such groups have repeatedly resorted to various discursive and practical strategies for steering ambitions of decision makers in the desired direction (Bourne 2019, 153). The tabooization of SALW has been performed by the means of telling the stories of gun violence survivors (IANSA 2017, 12), lobbying governments, and organizing campaign actions (Macdonald and Pytlak 2015, 199; IANSA n.d.), as well as naming and shaming via the Biting the Bullet project or IANSA "Red Book" reports (IANSA 2005; Bourne 2019, 161). All of this has been carried out in order to mobilize public support, broaden the stakeholder base, and push governments to develop certain policies (Krause 2002, 258; Macdonald and Pytlak 2015, 199). Such initiatives have been greatly favored by the concurrent "development of an 'expert' consensus that a problem exists" (Krause 2001, 14–15). It is remarkable that the nexus between "epistemic communities" and advocacy groups has been extraordinarily strong, with most of the inclined (I)NGOs individually and collectively concerned with active research and reporting (Krause 2002, 259; Macdonald and Pytlak 2015, 199). Since the early 1990s, numerous studies have been sponsored by major national and international NGOs such as the American Academy of Arts and Sciences, BASIC, Human Rights Watch, Pugwash, and the UN Institute for Disarmament Research (UNIDIR) (Krause 2001, 14–15). The "central authority of research expertise" though has rested particularly with the Small Arms Survey (SAS) (Bourne 2019, 153). Case studies of particular zones of conflict written by regional specialists have been particularly relevant for shaping the agenda (BICC 1996, 9; Krause 2001, 14–15). Ultimately, policy research interactions at the crossroads of the research, advocacy, and decision-making communities have become embedded within and across global, regional, and national levels (Batchelor and Kenkel 2014, 3–4). All of this has been critical for framing the problem and informing the related policy making (Krause 2002, 258–59).

Seriously challenging the notion of the *humanitarian transnational historical bloc* introduced in the previous chapter, (nongovernmental) gun lobby advocacy has consistently countervailed the humanitarian agenda in the case of SALW. Under the leadership of the US National Rifle Association (NRA), the World Forum on the Future of Sport Shooting Activities (WFSA) has grown into a global coalition of organizations lobbying for the preservation of civilian gun ownership rights (Rogers 2009, 184). The role played by the United States has been paramount because it is a longstanding leader in civilian gun ownership rates (SAS 2011, 2). Numerous other North and South American as well as European, Australian, and South African gun lobby organizations have supported the endeavor and contributed to the normalization of civilian firearm ownership around the world (Cukier and Sidel 2006, 116–21). The principal concern has been the potential for the same arguments warning against SALW more generally to be directly applicable to the domain of civilian gun ownership (NRA-ILA 2012). Invoking the principles of individual rights and personal safety, the cultural tradition of hunting and sport shooting and the general notion of masculinity (Cukier and Sidel 2006, 114–15; Krause 2010, 30; Whang 2015, 115; Bourne 2019, 155), they have engaged in what may accurately be termed the "counter-stigmatization" (Sauer and Reveraert 2018, 11–12) of SALW.

Both coalitions of nongovernmental actors have operated in a strong "nexus" with like-minded governments (Krause 2001, 26–27). Mutual reinforcement activities, often via direct engagements with each other's mandates or joint efforts, have ultimately boosted "the leverage of both" sides (Krause 2002, 259). States such as Belgium, Canada, Denmark, the Netherlands, Norway, Sweden, Switzerland, and the United Kingdom have, for instance, extensively sponsored such projects as Biting the Bullet, IANSA, the Norwegian Initiative on Small Arms Transfers, the Small Arms Survey, Saferworld, and the Institute for Strategic Studies. State sponsorship, including that of related meetings, consultations, seminars, and workshops, has been critical for the development of such nongovernmental activism and mobilization, and even for the emergence of certain initiatives altogether (Krause 2001, 30, 2002, 258). Nongovernmental agencies have in turn considerably influenced domestic policy formulation, as exemplified by the Institute for Security Studies in South Africa, Viva Rio in Brazil, or the NRA in the United States (Krause 2002, 257–58). This synergism has gotten as far as for even NGO representatives and researchers to be incorporated into national delegations (Krause 2002, 256; Bourne 2019, 158–59). To illustrate, NRA representatives complemented the US delegation at the 2001 conference (Bourne 2019, 154).

Nongovernmental advocacy groups have also acquired recognition and endorsement at the UN level. Publications by the SAS have been among the key sources cited in various issue-oriented resolutions and documents produced by the UN (Bourne 2019, 153). The NRA has inter alia enjoyed a consultative status at the UN Economic and Social Council (ECOSOC). The incorporation of its views into the text of the UN PoA has signaled that its agenda-setting impact eventually stretches beyond, though by the means of, the US foreign policy making (Rogers 2009, 183–84). Upon the adoption of the ATT, UN Secretary-General Ban Ki-moon explicitly recognized a synergy between governments, nongovernmental actors, and the UN with regard to the SALW process (Bourne 2019, 154). However, as already exemplified, the influence of nongovernmental actors on the international level foremost derives from their authority on the national level (Krause 2002, 257). Their involvement has also not been absolute and unconditional because a number of key intergovernmental agreements such as the UN Firearms Protocol and the 1997

OAS Convention have evolved with relatively little input from them (Bourne 2019, 150).

States and (elements of) some international organizations (IOs) have still been the key actors with legal "authority" to speak and decide, often enacted through exercising compulsory power (Bourne 2019, 153 and 159). A group of like-minded states, including the United Kingdom, France, Germany, Finland, Japan, Australia, Argentina, Costa Rica, Cambodia, Mozambique, South Africa, Mali, and Kenya, have adhered to the humanitarian agenda. In its favor, they have acted individually or under the umbrella of the Human Security Network (HSN) and collectively sponsored the UN process on the matter (Krause 2007, 11–12; Woolcott 2014; Macdonald and Pytlak 2015, 199 and 201). Favoring the case, the UN General Assembly (UNGA) has served as a forum for the formal expression of the general opinion and will of UN member-states (SAS 2016, 76–77). Various related resolutions adopted by the UNGA have been momentous for incrementally advancing the SALW process and framing the emerging international regime (Cîrlig 2015, 16–17). Political facilitation has also been provided by the UN Secretary-General (UNSG). The principal means have included SALW-oriented reports regularly submitted to the UNGA or the UNSC and the compilation of the UN member-states' and regional organizations' views for further deliberations (Krause 2007, 11; Cîrlig 2015, 16–17; Balga 2016, 586). A benchmark of such engagement by the UNSG was Boutros Boutros-Ghali's *Supplement to an Agenda for Peace* (1995), that is, a call for "microdisarmament" in the context of prevalent conflicts (BICC 1996, 5; Krause 2001, 16; Lustgarten 2015, 671). A clear indication of support on the part of the UN High Representative for Disarmament Affairs has been evidenced, for example, by Angela Kane expressing her highest endorsement for the ATT (Kane 2013) or Izumi Nakamitsu stoutly advocating for better small arms control (Nakamitsu 2019). What has additionally contributed to building up the case is a strong practical engagement with the agenda by the UN, including field missions in places such as Mali and Albania (Krause 2007, 11). Regional multilateral processes in the European Union (EU), the Organization of African Unity (OAU), the Organization for Security and Cooperation in Europe (OSCE), or the Organization of American States (OAS) have also favorably steered positions and commitments of many member-states, while also exerting peer pressure beyond (Krause 2002, 256). A complementary channel for the humanitarian agenda to squarely penetrate (further) governments has been the Parliamentary Forum on Small Arms and Light Weapons. The latter has brought together parliamentarians from around the world for the good of reducing and preventing SALW-related violence (PF-SALW n.d.). However, a number of states have in turn constantly resisted severe restrictions on SALW, often including even the underlying humanitarian bit. These have most notably included China, Russia, and the United States as well as some nations from the Arab League and the Association of Southeast Asian Nations such as Egypt, Iran, Pakistan, and India (Krause 2007, 11; Whang 2015, 132). Such an intergovernmental rift has reflected a subtle balance between humanitarian interests, combined with certain regulatory tradeoffs and national interests such as foreign policy, national security, and commercial interests (Hunter 2013, 236; Whang 2015, 117–18).

The possession of SALW has traditionally been considered indispensible to the (potential) fruition of a state's inherent legal right of self-defense and territorial integrity (Hunter 2013, 237; Lustgarten 2015, 570). From a general weapons-oriented perspective, this is a vivid illustration of how compulsory power (potentially) is effected "through relations of raw coercive force and violence" (Barnett and Duvall 2005, 61). Perceived as compulsory prudence in this regard, various sized stockpiles of SALW have been maintained, often via purchases, by all states. With only half of the world's countries actually producing them though (Peters n.d.), SALW have been distributed through bare commercial deals (SAS 2018b), strategic arms export deals, and defense cooperation agreements (Bourne 2019, 152), as well as licences and production rights (Hall 2014, 51). This rigid structural distribution mechanism thus portrays possibly the most extreme version of compulsory power, that is, the "direct control" exercised by arms providers over mere recipients' "conditions of existence" (Barnett and Duvall 2005, 48). However, given the plethora of available sources, patron-client dependences with respect to SALW have been rather diffuse (BICC 1996, 10). In turn driven by the pursuit of power (and by implication wealth) in the prevailing environment (Krause 1992, 98), "first-tier" manufacturing countries have largely corresponded to the top global providers of SALW (Hall 2014, 46). The giant exporters have long been the United States, Russia, China, France, Italy, and Germany (Hall 2014, 45–46; Whang 2015, 137; SAS 2018b; Amnesty International 2019). Among the considerable importers have been India, concurrently a noteworthy exporter, as well as the United Arab Emirates (UAE) and Saudi Arabia (Whang 2015, 137; SAS 2018b). Thinking of compulsory power also as the ability of A to get B to do what B otherwise would not do (Dahl 1957, 202–3), it is likewise possible to observe a reversed leverage. In particular, this is demand for certain weapons that has regularly leaned on the respective producers to manufacture and export them in a "demand-pull and supply-push" manner (Krause 1992, 27).

Despite the deep convergence of interests, a particular facet of this mutual relationship between providers and recipients has defined the split. It concerns a tension between transparency and opacity and a wider tension between the legal principles of territorial integrity and self-determination (Bourne 2019, 152). Both largely reflect the contentious issue of "putting human security into prohibitions and criteria for arms transfers" (Bromley, Cooper, and Holtom 2012, 1042). Interstate and intrastate conflicts with often involved nonstate actors (NSA) have generated a high demand for (il)licit arms transfers and practically extensive flows of SALW to and within the Middle East and North Africa (Whang 2015, 115; SIPRI 2018, 5–6; Amnesty International 2019). In turn motivated by profit, diplomatic goals, or the projection of power, major arms-dealing countries, including Northern democracies, have repeatedly provided weapons to countries with internal conflicts, domestic oppressions, and HR abuses (Whang 2015, 134; Lustgarten 2015, 572; Amnesty International 2019; UNODC 2019, 9). In particular, "the 'major producer' states" have often been "the major culprits in the arming of autocratic governments and brutal rebel movements" (Bourne 2012, 30). However, France, Germany, Italy, and the United States as "humanitarian interest supporters" among the others have responsibly demonstrated an increasing transparency in their arms transfers (SAS 2010, 32–33; SAS 2018a, 8–9). Such increases in transparency might be considered a relative departure from "sovereign arms control practices" toward "arms control as governmentality" (Krause 2011, 23). China and Russia have in turn stayed on a lesser transparency record implying a greater degree of flexibility (SAS 2010, 39–40; SAS 2018a, 8–9). Chinese and Russian opposition to arms embargoes on Sudan, Burma (Myanmar), Zimbabwe, and Syria has, for example, been indicative of their relative reluctance to incorporate human

security concerns with decision making in the matter of arms export (Bromley, Cooper, and Holtom 2012, 1038). India has also remained on a comparatively modest transparency record with its arms exports (SAS 2018a, 8–9). Subject to the UN arms embargoes and aspiring to secure their residual arms flows, Iran and Syria have been inimical to these blockades being reinforced with any further international mechanisms (MacFarquhar 2013). Iran, the UAE, and North Korea, the latter withal under the UN arms embargo, have inter alia long been among the exporters with "zero" level of transparency (SAS 2010, 39–40; Charbonneau 2013; SAS 2018a, 8–9). In assurance of its ability to import weapons, Egypt has also objected to ambitious transparency standards on the grounds of national sovereignty (Krause 2002, 253). The rift has further been contoured by the controversy regarding arms transfers to NSA. Regardless of a failure to properly define (un)authorized NSA for the cause, several states such as Russia, India, and Syria have endorsed a prohibition on such transfers and criticized the lack of this clause in the ATT (Holtom 2012; Mehta 2013; BBC 2013; MacFarquhar 2013; SIPRI 2018, 6). Conversely, the United States has opposed any coverage of transfers to NSA as part of the SALW process likely "to retain the option of supplying arms to allied rebel forces" (SIPRI 2018, 6). In addition, Iran has also been accused of supplying arms to Hezbollah and Houthi forces in Yemen; Saudi Arabia and the UAE have also been denounced as arms suppliers to antigovernment forces in Syria. Arms exports to Saudi Arabia and the UAE, mainly from the United States and Europe, have similarly been condemned on the assumption of their involvement in the Yemeni war (SIPRI 2018, 5 and 7). It is important to remark at this point, though to be addressed further in the following chapters, that Russia, the United States, China, India, and Pakistan as producers and users of such weapons have also been at the core of opposition to outlawing APL and cluster munitions (Bromley, Cooper, and Holtom 2012, 1038).

At the very least, the "structural power of sovereignty" has still favored opposition to severely restrictive arms trade provisions (Bourne 2019, 159). A deeper inquiry even reveals their structural dominance in the realm of SALW and related decision making. Ultimately caught on the same side as detailed in the previous paragraph, the United States, Russia, and China account for over 60 percent of global SALW flows. Such a distribution of power makes their sentiments toward the emerging international standards critical to their actual implementation and enforcement (Whang 2015, 132; Balga 2016, 648). These three giants have opposed strong regulatory measures, also in part by virtue of their leadership in current new weapons production (Krause 2007, 2). Acceleration on this front opens further space for them to reestablish their privileged position in the stratified but dynamic global arms transfer and production system. This is because the first-tier states are traditionally defined by "the locus of technological innovation" (Krause 1992, 208). What has structurally reinforced their nearly unparallelled dominance in the domain of SALW is their veto power in the UNSC (Olvera 2014, 243). It is a crucial facet of their global authority because this body is the most structurally favored one in the UN system of governance and decision making with respect to international peace and security (Ruhlman 2015, 37–38). Although the UNSC has issued the renowned 2013 and 2015 resolutions to strengthen the global response to SALW-related threats (Cîrlig 2015, 16), their language has not entailed binding legal obligations (UNSC 2013, 2015; Breakey 2014, 53). On the contrary, the UNSC has repeatedly restated the key UN Charter principles such as the rights of individual and collective self-defense and of each state to import, produce, and retain SALW for self-defense and security needs (Amnesty International and IANSA 2012, 8). Veto power was also invoked over 260 times between 1946 and 2008 to block arms embargoes, the only universal and legally binding instrument concerning illicit transfers to NSA (Olvera 2014, 243 and 248). This all, however, is not to belittle the still strong link between the UN SALW process and related signs of a "broader responsibility of states." The latter encompass UN arms embargoes, as well as programs of Disarmament, Demobilization, and Reintegration (DDR) and Security Sector Reform (SSR), sponsored by the United States among others (Krause 2007, 8–9; SAS 2016, 76). As "efforts at humanitarian disarmament," DDR and SSR initiatives may particularly be considered another manifestation of "arms control as governmentality" on balance with assertions of sovereignty (Krause 2011, 29–30).

The arms industry features the next key cluster of stakeholders in the realm of SALW. Arms manufacturers and traders have been critical in fueling the widespread availability of SALW. This is because they are driven by powerful corporate incentives, possess the necessary technical expertise, and often have greater operational flexibility than governments (Rogers 2009, 201; Hall 2014, 48–50). Importantly, arms brokers, transporters, and financiers have often been implicated in supplying SALW to the conflict and HR crisis zones, including those under UN embargoes (Macdonald and Pytlak 2015, 195–96). With regard to the challenge of unauthorized activities or the "black market" (Rogers 2009, 201), implicit authorization for such flows has in part derived from the inadequacy of national-level regulation of international arms brokering, transporting, and financing (Macdonald and Pytlak 2015, 195–96). The Control Arms Coalition has not neglected such stakeholders, and some arms manufacturers and financial investors have ultimately supported the campaign. Also in pursuit of their own "ethical" image, several groups from the defense sector in Europe have, for example, endorsed the ATT. Apart from emerging ties between the nongovernmental sector and the arms industry, certain governments such as the United Kingdom, Sweden, and Australia have in turn taken industry representatives onto their national delegations (Macdonald and Pytlak 2015, 194 and 201). There have also occurred even more complex interactions among NGOs, governments, and the arms industry. For example, by virtue of the influx of funds from the domestic arms industry, the NRA has sponsored certain politicians to ensure "the ongoing defence of gun-users' rights and the advancement of certain corporate interests" at the political level (Rogers 2009, 183).

To summarize, the campaign promoting the humanitarian approach to SALW has been diverse in membership, enabling it "to advocate with credibility across many sectors" (Macdonald and Pytlak 2015, 201). However, the rift dividing preferences on the matter has concerned virtually all the principal clusters of stakeholders: states and IOs, the arms industry, and even, rather unconventionally, nongovernmental advocacy groups. The campaign has thus never ruled the sphere of security, despite resistance within the UNSC, the domain of knowledge, given gun advocates a strong legal and cultural foothold, as well as the realm of finance and material production, especially considering the unparalleled global dominance of the reluctant United States, Russia, and China (Strange 1994, 24–32; Hynek 2018a).

INSTITUTIONAL POWER: TRADEOFFS BETWEEN
CONSENSUS AND MAJORITY

The institutional framework directly related to framing the issue of SALW embodies a miscellaneous structure of conference loci. Inter alia, pivotal venues have included the UN Conference on the Illicit Trade in Small Arms and Light Weapons in All Its Aspects (2001) as well as subsequent regular Biennial Meetings of States and Review Conferences, a series of UN Conferences on the ATT and the successive Conference of States Parties to the ATT (SAS 2016, 36, 42, 50, 66–67, and 71). The fundamental principle of decision making in the UN SALW process, and simultaneously a serious challenge, has been the consensus rule (Bourne 2019, 155). Hindering progress on important issues, several countries such as the United States, Russia, China, India, Saudi Arabia, the United Arab Emirates, Iran, Pakistan, Syria, Egypt, and North Korea have repeatedly blocked consensus by voting against more ambitious regulatory initiatives or abstaining (UNGA 2006; Krause 2007, 11; Parker 2007, 28–29; Whang 2015, 115, 132, and 137; Macdonald and Pytlak 2015, 199–200; SAS 2016, 65; SIPRI 2018, 9; Bourne 2019, 155–58). This opposition had repeatedly threatened to debar the adoption of the ATT notwithstanding a long series of deliberations over the treaty draft provisions and a number of compromises made on the criteria and scope (Bromley, Cooper, and Holtom 2012, 1038–47; Hunter 2013, 248–52; Lustgarten 2015, 583–86 and 598–99; Balga 2016, 584–89; SAS 2016, 66). Headway in the matter of SALW has often been made through compromising consensus as a preferred algorithm of decision making in favor of voting rules (Bourne 2019, 157). By virtue of its more balanced character in this regard, the UNGA has become a principal venue for building up an international SALW regime, including by the means of the UN Firearms Protocol, the UN PoA, the ITT, and eventually even the ATT (Hunter 2013, 254; Olvera 2014, 235; SAS 2016, 27, 53, and 65). Its First Committee is notably the forum where a number of such landmark developments have been reinstated, athwart consensus failures, by virtue of a bloc of like-minded countries using their quantitative leverage (Bourne 2019, 157). Although, remarkably, the UN PoA and the ITT are the products of consensus agreement, both cases illustrate how unanimity has not allowed for more than a mere politically binding form (SAS 2016, 39, 42, and 53–54).

Given this, a confined character of most of the core outcome documents should not be disregarded. To begin with a watershed event of the 1990s, the Wassenaar Arrangement features an informal agreement bearing no binding political obligations and holding no power of enforcing its standards upon the participating states (Whang 2015, 127). As accurately remarked by Hunter (2013, 238), this arrangement "provides a model for arms regulation that adheres to a state sovereignty interest framework." The UN PoA and the ITT, though applicable to all states, in turn embody politically binding instruments that do not entail any legally binding commitments (Olvera 2014, 234–35; Cîrlig 2015, 10; SAS 2016, 39, and 52). Similarly, the UN Register has been repeatedly criticized for its lack of mechanisms for review and enforcement, and thus lack of participation and effectiveness (Bromley, Cooper, and Holtom 2012, 1035; Hunter 2013, 232). Though legally binding, the UN Firearms Protocol and the ATT are both foremost subject to national implementation by state parties and lack institutional powers or external enforcement entities to duly oversee the compliance (Whang 2015, 136; Balga 2016, 584–85; SAS 2016, 64; UNODC 2016, 10–11 and 13). The utmost mechanism of control in the global SALW regime is still the collection and processing of reports submitted by states in the matter of domestic implementation of their UN PoA, ITT, and ATT commitments (SAS 2016, 50, 56, and 71; UNODC 2016, 14). Although the UN Register has also allowed states to submit reports on SALW transfers for the sake of transparency and confidence building, few states have de facto consistently reported (Hunter 2013, 231–32). Another constraining factor is that only states that have ratified or formally expressed their consent are bound by the legal provisions stipulated in the UN Firearms Protocol and the ATT (Olvera 2014, 225; SAS 2016, 27 and 64). A number of the key states, in particular including the United States, Russia, and China, have either abstained from signing or have put off ratifying these accords. These instances of self-exclusion are critical because reluctance by the three export giants to abide by the emerging international standards heralds the inadequacy of their actual implementation and enforcement (Cîrlig 2015, 15; Whang 2015, 115, 132, and 137; Balga 2016, 648).

On balance, such an international piecemeal and bounded regime regulating SALW has been greatly reinforced by multiple regional agreements and instruments, in particular those legally binding such as the OAS Convention or CIFTA (1997), the MERCOSUR Memorandum of Understanding (2004), the ECOWAS Convention (2006), the Central African Convention (2010), or the EU Common Positions (2003, 2008) (Cîrlig 2015, 18–20; SAS 2016, 85–89). However, the main drawback on the part of such regional endeavors is that they have merely put together like-minded states, with countries opposing formidable restrictions on SALW largely left out. A notable omission of the OAS Convention in this regard is the United States, with its reluctance to ratify the agreement despite being among the first countries to sign it (Krause 2002, 256; Schroeder 2004, 31–36; OAS n.d.). More generally, the development of legal commitments on the regional level has substantially bypassed Asia and the Middle East, as well as the primary issue-oriented OSCE documents are nonbinding in legal terms (SAS 2016, 85–89). All of this points at the paucity and fragility of institutional limits on the exercise of sovereign will with respect to SALW.

CONCLUSION

The presented chapter examined and disaggregated power configurations with respect to security regulation of SALW. It opened with a legal introduction to the emerging *regime complex*. This section traced how SALW have been incrementally distinguished as a separate cluster of conventional weapons for related regulatory efforts on the global and regional levels. Though the general principles of international humanitarian and HR law have always implicitly underlied SALW-related practices, it is a broader (re)orientation upon them in the 1990s that has been critical for the SALW process. This pattern was introduced in the opening section but elucidated more extensively in the following one. Here, through the lenses of productive power, we demonstrated how the humanitarian disarmament agenda has eventually been suppressed by the humanitarian arms control agenda. It was also explained how and why the latter has focused in particular around the concern of illegal, unregulated, and irresponsible flows of SALW, with a certain practice rather than a weapon itself ultimately stigmatized. In doing so, the character of the deviant category was dissected. It was found not only to feature the gradually recognized and formalized weapons category of SALW but also to specifically regard their illicit use and users, to encompass also their parts and components as well as (am)munitions, and to reflect the underlying civil-military nexus. Then we extensively discussed enabling and constraining conditions of emergence for this particular discourse to shape up in order to interpret its contours. The key findings spelled out how the disarmament agenda has never been sustainable in the issue area of SALW. It is for the reasons of the deep-rooted traditional way of warfare, the legal principles of self-defense and territorial integrity, the engrained civilian gun culture, and the truly universal distribution of SALW in the related globalized market.

Next, attention was directed toward complex and deeply intertwined exercises of structural and compulsory powers. Their joint scrutiny was chosen as a particularly suitable strategy because the case of SALW is a great exemplar of how one actor's relative position directly translates into control over actions and even conditions of existence of another (the other). In particular, three traits were discerned in this regard. First, the very character of conventional weapons presupposes their political usability, thereof manipulated with utmost credibility or utilized for steering opponents' ambitions. Second, the prevailing stratified global arms transfer and production system generates robust mutual patron-client dependences in working, albeit rather diffuse. Finally, different clusters of the involved actors have often been tightly intertwined in their operation or even essentially overlapping in their makeup. More generally, this whole analysis proceeded on the basis of consistent juxtaposition of efforts to regulate SALW and the projected resistance. In doing so, the (variously inclined) key stakeholders and their structural standing and associated interests were put under the microscope. The principal finding was that the two sides have largely mirrored each other in terms of the involved categories of actors with various sources of authority. Both the opposition to SALW and the opposition to their robust regulation were exhaustively broken down into states, (elements of) IOs, the arms industry, and non-governmental advocacy groups. Offbeat in the area of humanitarian arms control and disarmament, discord on the part of the latter challenges the notion of the *humanitarian transnational historical bloc* but does not discard it altogether. A deeper inquiry into the distribution of benefits, responsibilities, and objectives, especially that of states and (elements of) IOs, allowed us to show how the opposition to severe restraints on SALW has in fact been structurally favored. The principal identified anchor to further progress on SALW regulation has featured the convergence of the United States, Russia, and China's veto power in the UNSC, as well as their nearly unparalleled dominance and resistance to rigid regulatory measures in the domain of (new) SALW.

Finally, the workings of institutional power were scrutinized. This analysis was oriented at the core decision-making fora and principles shaping the UN SALW process as well as the character and cardinal limitations of the outcome documents. As therein shown, the existing international framework regulating SALW has evolved by virtue of regular tradeoffs between consensus and majority. Rare instances of intergovernmental consensus, having still pushed for certain key developments such as the UN PoA and the ITT, have only concerned limited restrictions and, rather more general, nonbinding provisions. Repeated failures to generate consensus over more assertive agendas have driven like-minded governments to adopt the hitherto pivotal international agreements on the basis of majority voting. However, this mechanism has in turn implied serious compromises on effectiveness of the emerging international standards. The principal discovery was that, though firmly settled on the global level and reinforced by multiple regional initiatives, the current regime regulating SALW has not traveled far enough. The discerned resistant governments responsible for a greater portion of global SALW flows have largely remained outside the evolving institutional frames, thus unbound by the related provisions. Because the ATT has not become an exception but rather consolidated the trend, the prospects of achieving an effective international control over SALW (flows) currently remain blurred.

REFERENCES

Alter, Karen J., and Sophie Meunier. 2009. "The Politics of International Regime Complexity." *Symposium* 7, no. 1 (March): 13–24.

Amnesty International. 1999. *The Terror Trade Times: Focus on Africa*. October. https://www.amnesty.org/download/Documents/140000/act310021999en.pdf.

———. 2002. *G8: Failing to Stop the Terror Trade*. Press Release, June 24. https://www.amnesty.org/download/Documents/120000/ior300032002en.pdf.

———. 2003. *The Terror Trade Times*, no. 4 (June). https://www.amnesty.org/download/Documents/100000/act310022003en.pdf.

———. 2019. *Killer Facts 2019: The Scale of the Global Arms Trade*. August 23. https://www.amnesty.org/en/latest/news/2019/08/killer-facts-2019-the-scale-of-the-global-arms-trade/.

Amnesty International and IANSA [International Action Network on Small Arms]. 2012. *Key Elements of the Arms Trade Treaty: An Annotated Guide*. London, July. https://www.amnesty.ca/sites/amnesty/files/act300682012en.pdf.

Balga, Jamil. 2016. "The New International Law of Arms Trade: A Critical Analysis of the Arms Trade Treaty from the Human Rights Perspective." *The Indonesian Journal of International and Comparative Law* 3, no. 4 (October): 583–649.

Barnett, Michael, and Raymond Duvall. 2005. "Power in International Politics." *International Organization* 59 (Winter): 39–75.

Batchelor, Peter, and Kai Michael Kenkel. 2014. "Introduction: The Past, Present and Future of the Small Arms Policy-Research Nexus." In *Controlling Small Arms: Consolidation, Innovation and Relevance in Research and Policy*, edited by Peter Batchelor and Kai Michael Kenkel, 1–12. Small Arms Survey. New York: Routledge.

BBC. 2013. *UN Passes Historic Arms Trade Treaty by Huge Majority*. April 2. https://www.bbc.com/news/world-us-canada-21998394.

Berkol, Ilhan. 2002. *Small Arms and Light Weapons: Improving Transparency and Control*. Bruxelles: GRIP. http://archive.grip.org/en/siteweb/images/RAPPORTS/2002/2002-hs1.pdf.

BICC [Bonn International Center for Conversion]. 1996. *The New Field of Micro-Disarmament: Addressing the Proliferation and Buildup of Small Arms and Light Weapons*. Brief 7, authored by Edward J. Laurance and Sarah Meek. September. https://www.bicc.de/uploads/tx_bicctools/brief7.pdf.

Bourne, Mike. 2007. *Arming Conflict: The Proliferation of Small Arms*. New York: Palgrave Macmillan.

———. 2012. "Small Arms and Light Weapons Spread and Conflict." In *Small Arms, Crime and Conflict: Global Governance and the Spread of Armed Violence*, edited by Owen Greene and Nicholas Marsh, 29–42. New York: Routledge.

———. 2019. "Powers of the Gun: Process and Possibility in Global Small Arms Control." In *Regulating Global Security: Insights from Conventional and Unconventional Regimes*, edited by Nik Hynek, Ondrej Ditrych, and Vit Stritecky, 143–68. Cham: Palgrave Macmillan.

Breakey, Hugh. 2014. "Parsing Security Council Resolutions: A Five-Dimensional Taxonomy of Normative Properties." In *The Security Council as Global Legislator*, edited by Vesselin Popovski and Trudy Fraser, 51–70. New York: Routledge.

Bromley, Mark, Neil Cooper, and Paul Holtom. 2012. "The UN Arms Trade Treaty: Arms Export Controls, the Human Security Agenda and the Lessons of History." *International Affairs* 88, no. 5: 1029–48.

Charbonneau, Louis. 2013. "Iran, North Korea, Syria Block U.N. Arms Trade Treaty." *Thomson Reuters*, March 29. https://www.reuters.com/article/us-arms-treaty-un/iran-north-korea-syria-block-u-n-arms-trade-treaty-idUSBRE92R10E20130329.

Cîrlig, Carmen-Cristina. 2015. *Illicit Small Arms and Light Weapons: International and EU Action*. European Parliament: European Parliamentary Research Service, July. https://www.europarl.europa.eu/RegData/etudes/IDAN/2015/565869/EPRS_IDA(2015)565869_EN.pdf.

Cukier, Wendy, and Victor W. Sidel. 2006. *The Global Gun Epidemic: From Saturday Night Specials to AK-47s*. Westport, CT: Praeger Security International.

Dahl, R. 1957. "The Concept of Power." *Behavioral Science* 2, no. 3: 201–15.

Drezner, Daniel W. 2009. "The Power and Peril of International Regime Complexity." *Perspectives on Politics* 7, no. 1 (March): 65–70.

Firearms Protocol. 2001. *Protocol against the Illicit Manufacturing of and Trafficking in Firearms, Their Parts and Components and Ammunition, Supplementing the United Nations Convention against Transnational Organized Crime.* New York: United Nations, June 8. https://treaties.un.org/doc/source/RecentTexts/18-12_c_E.pdf.

Greene, Owen, and Nicholas Marsh. 2012. "Introduction." In *Small Arms, Crime and Conflict: Global Governance and the Spread of Armed Violence,* edited by Owen Greene and Nicholas Marsh, 1–10. New York: Routledge.

Hall, Peter. 2014. "Products and Producers: A Global Business." In *Controlling Small Arms: Consolidation, Innovation and Relevance in Research and Policy,* edited by Peter Batchelor and Kai Michael Kenkel, 39–63. Small Arms Survey. New York: Routledge.

Holtom, Paul. 2012. *Prohibiting Arms Transfers to Non-State Actors and the Arms Trade Treaty.* Geneva: United Nations Institute for Disarmament Research. https://www.unidir.org/files/medias/pdfs/background-paper-prohibiting-arms-transfers-to-non-state-actors-and-the-arms-trade-treaty-paul-holtom-eng-0-259.pdf.

Hunter, Dean M. 2013. "Time to Reload: States Request More Time on the Arms Trade Treaty." *Saint Louis University Public Law Review* 33, no. 1: 227–54.

Hynek, Nik. 2018a. "Theorizing International Security Regimes: A Power-Analytical Approach." *International Politics* 55, no. 3–4 (May): 352–68.

———. 2018b. "Re-visioning Morality and Progress in the Security Domain: Insights from Humanitarian Prohibition Politics." *International Politics* 55, no. 3–4 (May): 421–40.

IANSA [International Action Network on Small Arms]. 2005. *International Action on Small Arms: Examining Implementation of the UN Programme of Action by Biting the Bullet.* https://www.files.ethz.ch/isn/20271/SW_red-book-2005_6.pdf.

———. 2017. *Civil Society Advocacy Guide: Implementation of the UN Program of Action (PoA) on Small Arms and Light Weapons.* https://92054894-4da4-47e4-9276-4b6cfef27021.filesusr.com/ugd/bb4a5b_25739bf94e2a44b4ab22b0212e7f19c9.pdf.

———. n.d. *Campaigns.* Accessed November 2, 2019. https://www.iansa.org/campaigns.

IPB [International Peace Bureau]. n.d. *Small Arms and Light Weapons.* Accessed November 2, 2019. http://www.ipb.org/small-arms-and-light-weapons/.

Kane, Angela. 2013. *Opening Remarks by High Representative for Disarmament Affairs.* New York: Side Event "Arms Transfers, Transparency, and the ATT," hosted by the United Nations Office for Disarmament Affairs, Stockholm International Peace Research Institute, Friedrich Ebert Stiftung, and the Permanent Missions of Sweden and Germany, March 18. https://unoda-web.s3-accelerate.amazonaws.com/wp-content/uploads/assets/HomePage/HR/docs/2013/2013-03-18_SIPRI_opener.pdf.

Klare, Michael. 1999/2018. "An Overview of the Global Trade in Small Arms and Light Weapons." In *Small Arms Control: Old Weapons, New Issues,* edited by Jayantha Dhanapala, Mitsuro Donowaki, Swadesh Rana, and Lora Lumpe, 3–10. United Nations Institute for Disarmament. New York: Routledge Revivals (Reissued 2018). First Published 1999 by Ashgate Publishing.

Krause, Keith. 1992. *Arms and the State: Patterns of Military Production and Trade.* Cambridge: Cambridge University Press.

———. 2001. *Norm-Building in Security Spaces: The Emergence of the Light Weapons Problematic.* Working Paper. https://depot.erudit.org/bitstream/000854dd/1/000257pp.pdf.

———. 2002. "Multilateral Diplomacy, Norm Building, and UN Conferences: The Case of Small Arms and Light Weapons." Review Essay. *Global Governance* 8, no. 2 (April–June): 247–63.

———. 2007. "Small Arms and Light Weapons: Towards Global Public Policy." *Coping with Crisis Working Paper Series.* New York: International Peace Academy, March.

————. 2010. "Instruments of Insecurity: Small Arms and Contemporary Violence." In *The Routledge Handbook of New Security Studies*, edited by J. Peter Burgess, 27–38. New York: Routledge.

————. 2011. "Leashing the Dogs of War: Arms Control from Sovereignty to Governmentality." *Contemporary Security Policy* 32, no. 1: 20–39.

Laurance, Edward J. 1999. "Monitoring the Flow, Availability and Misuse of Light Weapons: A New Tool for the Early Warning of Violent Conflict." In *Arms Watching: Integrating Small Arms and Light Weapons into the Early Warning of Violent Conflict*, edited by Edward J. Laurence, 5–18. London: International Alert. https://www.international-alert.org/sites/default/files/publications/lw_armswatching.pdf.

Lustgarten, Laurence. 2015. "The Arms Trade Treaty: Achievements, Failings, Future." *International and Comparative Law Quarterly* 64 (July): 569–600.

Macdonald, Anna, and Allison Pytlak. 2015. "The Banker, the Arms Dealer, and the Activist: Unlikely Allies for an Arms Trade Treaty." *Georgetown Journal of International Affairs* 16, no. 2 (Summer/Fall): 194–205.

MacFarquhar, Neil. 2013. "U.N. Treaty to Control Arms Sales Hits Snag." *The New York Times*, March 28. https://www.nytimes.com/2013/03/29/world/iran-and-north-korea-block-arms-trade-treaty.html.

Mehta, Sujata. 2013. "Why India Abstained on Arms Trade Treaty." Explanation of Vote by Permanent Representative of India to the Conference of Disarmament in Geneva. *The Hindu*, April 3. https://www.thehindu.com/opinion/op-ed/why-india-abstained-on-arms-trade-treaty/article4573882.ece.

Mutimer, David. 2000. *The Weapons State: Proliferation and the Framing of Security*. London: Lynne Rienner Publishers.

Nakamitsu, Izumi. 2019. *Remarks by High Representative for Disarmament Affairs: Building Peace through Effective Small Arms Control*. New York: ECOSOC Chamber, The Open Arria Formula Meeting of the United Nations Security Council, April 8. https://s3.amazonaws.com/unoda-web/wp-content/uploads/2019/04/Building-Peace-through-Effective-Small-Arms-Control-Final.pdf.

NRA-ILA [National Rifle Association Institute for Legislative Action]. 2012. "Disinformation Continues as U.N. Arms Treaty Takes Shape." July 20. https://www.nraila.org/articles/20120720/disinformation-continues-as-un-arms-treaty-takes-shape.

OAS [Organization of American States]. n.d. *Signatories and Ratifications: Inter-American Convention Against the Illicit Manufacturing of and Trafficking in Firearms, Ammunition, Explosives, and Other Related Material*. Accessed November 1, 2019. http://www.oas.org/juridico/english/sigs/a-63.html.

Olvera, Gustavo M. B. 2014. "The Security Council and the Illegal Transfer of Small Arms and Light Weapons to Non-State Actors." *Mexican Law Review* 6, no. 2 (January–June): 225–50.

Parker, Sarah. 2007. *Analysis of States' Views on an Arms Trade Treaty*. Geneva: United Nations Institute for Disarmament. https://www.unidir.org/files/publications/pdfs/analysis-of-states-views-on-an-arms-trade-treaty-332.pdf.

Peters, Rebecca. n.d. *Small Arms: No Single Solution. UN Chronicle*. Accessed November 15, 2019. https://www.un.org/en/chronicle/article/small-arms-no-single-solution.

PF-SALW [Parliamentary Forum on Small Arms and Light Weapons]. n.d. *The Organization*. Accessed October 25, 2019. http://parliamentaryforum.org/who-we-are/the-organisation/.

Price, Richard. 1998. "Reversing the Gun Sights: Transnational Civil Society Targets Land Mines." *International Organization* 52, no. 3 (Summer): 613–44.

Rapoport, David C. 2004. "The Four Waves of Modern Terrorism." In *Attacking Terrorism: Elements of a Grand Strategy*, edited by Audrey Kurth Cronin and James M. Ludes, 46–73. Washington, DC: Georgetown University Press.

Renner, Michael. 1997. "Small Arms, Big Impact: The Next Challenge of Disarmament." *World Watch Paper*, no. 137. DIANE Publishing, October.

Rogers, Damien. 2009. *Postinternationalism and Small Arms Control: Theory, Politics, Security.* Farnham, UK: Ashgate Publishing.

Ruhlman, Molly A. 2015. *Who Participates in Global Governance? States, Bureaucracies, and NGOs in the United Nations.* New York: Routledge.

SAS [Small Arms Survey]. 2010. *Transparency Counts: Assessing State Reporting on Small Arms Transfers, 2001–08,* authored by Jasna Lazarevic. Geneva: Graduate Institute of International and Development Studies, June. http://www.smallarmssurvey.org/fileadmin/docs/B-Occasional-papers/SAS-OP25-Barometer.pdf.

———. 2011. "Estimating Civilian Owned Firearms." *Research Notes: Armed Actors,* no. 9 (September). http://www.smallarmssurvey.org/fileadmin/docs/H-Research_Notes/SAS-Research-Note-9.pdf.

———. 2016. *A Guide to the UN Small Arms Process,* authored by Sarah Parker and Marcus Wilson. Geneva: Graduate Institute of International and Development Studies. http://www.smallarmssurvey.org/fileadmin/docs/Q-Handbooks/HB-02-Diplo-Guide/SAS-HB02-Guide-UN-Small-Arms-Process.pdf.

———. 2018a. *The 2018 Small Arms Trade Transparency Barometer,* authored by Paul Holtom and Irene Pavesi. Briefing Paper. Geneva, August. http://www.smallarmssurvey.org/fileadmin/docs/T-Briefing-Papers/SAS-BP-Transparency-Barometer-2018.pdf.

———. 2018b. *Trade Update 2018: Annexes A1 and A2—Major Exporters and Importers.* http://www.smallarmssurvey.org/fileadmin/docs/S-Trade-Update/SAS-Trade-Update-2018-Tables-A1-A2.pdf.

Sauer, Tom, and Mathias Reveraert. 2018. "The Potential Stigmatizing Effect of the Treaty on the Prohibition of Nuclear Weapons." *The Nonproliferation Review* 25, no. 5–6: 437–55.

Schroeder, Matthew. 2004. *Small Arms, Terrorism and the OAS Firearms Convention.* Occasional Paper, no. 1 (March). Washington, DC: Federation of American Scientists. https://fas.org/asmp/library/OAS/FullReport.pdf.

SIPRI [Stockholm International Peace Research Institute]. 2018. *Arms Transfer and SALW Controls in the Middle East and North Africa: Mapping Capacity-Building Efforts,* authored by Mark Bromley, Giovanna Maletta, and Kolja Brockmann. Background Paper, November. https://www.sipri.org/sites/default/files/2018-11/bp_1811_att_mena_1.pdf.

Strange, Susan. 1994. *States and Markets.* Second edition. London: Pinter.

Stroud, Angela. 2012. "Good Guys with Guns: Hegemonic Masculinity and Concealed Handguns." *Gender and Society* 26, no. 2 (April): 216–38.

UNGA [United Nations General Assembly]. 2006. *International Arms Trade Treaty Aim of Draft Resolution Approved by Disarmament Committee.* GA/DIS/3335. UNGA First Committee, 21st Meeting, October 26. https://www.un.org/press/en/2006/gadis3335.doc.htm.

UNODA [United Nations Office for Disarmament Affairs]. 2018. *Securing Our Common Future: An Agenda for Disarmament.* New York: United Nations. https://unoda-epub.s3.amazonaws.com/i/index.html?book=sg-disarmament-agenda.epub.

UNODC [United Nations Office on Drugs and Crime]. 2016. *The Firearms Protocol and the Arms Trade Treaty: Divergence or Complementarity?* Issue Paper. Vienna: United Nations, March. https://www.unodc.org/documents/firearms-protocol/Synergies-Paper.pdf.

———. 2019. "The Illicit Market in Firearms." *University Module Series:* Firearms, mod. 4. Vienna: United Nations, June. https://www.unodc.org/documents/e4j/Module_04_-_The_Illicit_Market_in_Firearms_FINAL.pdf.

UNSC [United Nations Security Council]. 2013. *Resolution 2117.* S/RES/2117. Adopted September 26, 2013 at the 7036th Meeting. https://undocs.org/S/Res/2117(2013).

———. 2015. *Resolution 2220.* S/RES/2220. Adopted May 22, 2015 at the 7447th Meeting. https://undocs.org/S/Res/2220(2015).

Whang, Cindy. 2015. "The Challenges of Enforcing International Military-Use Technology Export Control Regimes: An Analysis of the United Nations Arms Trade Treaty." *Wisconsin International Law Journal* 33, no. 1: 114–39.
Woolcott, Peter. 2014. *The Arms Trade Treaty*. United Nations Audiovisual Library of International Law. https://legal.un.org/avl/pdf/ha/att/att_e.pdf.

FIVE

Humanitarianism Meets Nuclear Arms Control

This chapter aims to trace power configurations with respect to the "hard core" of security practice: nuclear weapons. While there is no global prohibition regime formally banning the use or possession of nuclear weapons, a multifaceted international legal framework regulating nuclear technology has emerged. It has encompassed the general principles of international (humanitarian) law as well as various international, regional, bilateral, and unilateral efforts at regulating or outlawing the possession, transfer, testing, and use of nuclear (weapons) technology. While decomposing this assemblage, it is herein consistently demonstrated how the nuclear weapons regime borders the nuclear commerce regime. The ultimate goal is to show how this piecemeal regime defining the realm of (il)legitimacy with regard to atomic weapons has evolved, with its consequences and limits. Various efforts to regulate and proscribe nuclear weapons are systematically juxtaposed with the existing resistance in terms of their narratives, structural and institutional power, and leverage. In the first place, we offer a deep inquiry into conflicting interpretations of the Non-Proliferation Treaty and security that have defined the rift. The case is complemented by drawing parallels between nuclear weapons and the broader category of weapons of mass destruction (WMD). Afterward, a detailed power-analytical reading of related interactions between (variously inclined) states, IOs (UN agencies in particular), (I)NGOs and civil society groups, epistemic communities, and financial institutions is provided. A systematic consideration of the historical dimension of such interactions allows us to trace the transhistoricity of the nuclear disarmament campaign as well as the enduring nature of a relatively invariant resistant constellation. In doing so, all of the key developments and setbacks are interpreted in terms of their character and associated (un)favorable conditions of emergence. Inter alia, the proposed Nuclear Weapons Convenion is thoroughly analyzed and implications of this study for understanding its future prospects are flagged.

PIECEMEAL LEGAL REGULATION OF NUCLEAR WEAPONS

Although the use of nuclear weapons is not legally prohibited to date (Tannenwald 2005, 10), a multifaceted yet piecemeal international legal framework regulating nuclear technology has emerged. Its roots are traceable to the turn of the twentieth century, if one considers the broader framework of WMD. These are the Declaration of St. Petersburg (1868), the Hague Conventions (1899 and 1907), and the Geneva Protocol (1925) that have established an early basis for their illegality (Shamai 2015, 114–15). The adoption of the UN (United Nations) Charter and the Geneva Conventions (1949) further reinforced the case (Berry et al. 2010, 35–36). Although International Humanitarian Law (IHL) does not contain an explicit prohibition on nuclear weapons, it still features a crucial lens for assessing their (il)legitimate use in armed conflict (Maresca 2013, 137). Besides more general principles of international law and beyond the category of WMD, a specific issue-oriented regulatory regime has built up around nuclear technology. Over time, it has encompassed various multilateral, bilateral, and unilateral restraints with respect to nuclear weapons as well as supply-control mechanisms in the area of civil nuclear cooperation. Some clarification is in order.

The first resolution (1946) of the UN General Assembly (UNGA) calling for their elimination marked the dawn of international efforts to control atomic weapons (Berry et al. 2010, 39). Only in 1968, though, the first major international treaty, the Treaty on the Non-Proliferation of Nuclear Weapons (NPT), was adopted to contain proliferation and facilitate disarmament (Sauer and Reveraert 2018, 440). Tolerant of nuclear programs for energy purposes (Article IV), it obliged nonnuclear weapons states (NNWS) to forgo acquiring nuclear weapons (Article II) and nuclear weapons states (NWS) in turn to refrain from assisting in their spread (Article I) and get rid of their existing nuclear arsenals (Article VI) (Ruzicka and Wheeler 2016, 31–34). Pending complete disarmament, only the five declared states, namely Britain, China, France, Russia, and the United States were allowed to temporarily possess nuclear weapons (Tannenwald 2005, 9). This treaty features a cornerstone of the international nuclear weapons regime because it was extended indefinitely in 1995 and has spread globally, with the only exceptions of India, Israel, North Korea, and Pakistan (Ruzicka 2019, 53–56). Complementarily, multilateral efforts to regulate the testing of nuclear weapons led to the adoption of the Partial Test Ban Treaty (PTBT) in 1963 and the negotiation of the Comprehensive Test Ban Treaty (CTBT) (Berry et al. 2010, 39–40). Concluded in 1996, the latter is yet to be ratified by a number of countries, including the United States and China, to become a binding international treaty. The adoption of the Treaty on the Prohibition of Nuclear Weapons (TPNW) in July 2017 features the "crowning achievement" on the way toward nuclear disarmament (Ruzicka 2019, 53–54 and 57). Voted in favor by 122 states, it features an all-embracing prohibition on nuclear weapons, including their development, production, acquisition, possession, transfer, testing, use, and threat of use (Sauer and Reveraert 2018, 437). This treaty has, however, not entered into force due to a low number of ratifications. The two major traits of development have established the core issue-oriented institutional structure underlying or reinforcing these international agreements. The first was the establishment of the UN Atomic Energy Commission (AEC), the precursor of the International Atomic Energy Agency (IAEA). The second was the launch of the Eighteen Nation Committee that later transformed and expanded into the Conference of the Committee on Disarmament and the Conference on Disarmament, today's principal UN negotiating forum for the matter (Berry et al. 2010, 39; Tannenwald 2016, 109; Ruzicka 2019, 53–54 and 56).

Restraints on the regional presence of nuclear weapons, namely nuclear-weapons-free zones (NWFZs), feature a crucial facet of the global regulatory framework in relation to nuclear weapons (Ruzicka 2019, 59). Gradually spreading over Latin America, Africa, Central Asia, the South Pacific, or Southeast Asia, these significantly complement the NPT and strengthen the international nonproliferation regime (Cirincione, Wolfsthal, and Rajkumar 2005, 34). In addition, multiple rounds of bilateral reductions in and in relation to the US and Russian strategic nuclear arsenals have taken place (Hynek 2016, 100). These efforts gave rise to a number of milestone treaties, including the Strategic Arms Limitation Talks I (SALT-I) and the SALT-II, the Anti-Ballistic Missile Treaty (ABM Treaty), the Intermediate-Range Nuclear Forces Treaty (INF Treaty, remarkably eliminating a whole class of newly deployed weapons), the Strategic Arms Reduction Treaty I (START-I) and the START-II, as well as the New START (Berry et al. 2010, 40). Unilateral proposals or restraints voluntarily adhered to by NWS have historically featured another dimension of the international nuclear weapons regime. To mention a few, these included the "Atoms for Peace" initiative by President Dwight Eisenhower (1953), the no first use pledge by the Soviet Union (1982), the short-lived verbal statements by President Mikhail Gorbachev and President Ronald Reagan (1985), the Rajiv Gandhi Plan by India's prime minister (1988), the moratorium on nuclear weapons testing by President Jacques Chirac (1996), or the "Global Zero" proposal by President Barack Obama (2009) (BBC 1996; Whitney 1996; Shoumikhin 2011, 106; Paul 2016, 15–16; Ruzicka 2019, 56). What may also fall in this category is the landmark shift from the all-out nuclear war in favor of more flexible responses in the US and Soviet military doctrines (1960s) (Sagan

1989, 37–39; Scott 1992, 182–83; Paulsen 1994, 4–9). Significant in the same regard was, for example, the official post–Cold War commitment by Russia to sharply narrow down the role of its nuclear arsenal chiefly to deterring a nuclear war (1990s) (Herspring 2011, 4). Generally remarkable are also the Negative Security Assurances (NSAs) implying rigorous commitments by NWS not to use nuclear weapons against NNWS that are members of the NPT (Tannenwald 2005, 10). The norm of transparency is a particularly crucial aspect determining progress or its lack thereof with respect to nuclear disarmament. While the NPT forces it upon the NNWS, it has no legal capacity or mechanism to oversee progress toward nuclear disarmament on the part of NWS. Notable steps in the direction of increased transparency have however been made through voluntary declarations by individual NWS, in particular the United Kindom and France, and within the framework of the US-Soviet/Russian strategic arms control (Patton, Podvig, and Schell 2013, 1–5 and 17).

There is also a civil, or even explicitly commercial, dimension to this piecemeal international regime regulating nuclear weapons. The principle exercise and simultaneously a challenge in this regard has been the maintenance of the nuclear commerce regime alongside the nonproliferation regime. A part of the challenge is the dual-use nature of nuclear technology, and thus the blurred boundary between civilian atomic energy programs and weapons programs (Lynch 2013, 91; Bajrektarevic and Posega 2014, 52 and 55–56). The Nuclear Suppliers Group and the Zangger Committee are the two coalitions of nations that have served as a blueprint for the two to coexist (Cirincione, Wolfsthal, and Rajkumar 2005, 33; Ruzicka 2019, 59). Also falling to the category of export control mechanisms is the Wassenaar Arrangement. It is a multilateral regime set up in the area of civil nuclear cooperation to promote greater transparency and responsibility in transfers of dual-use technologies for the sake of international security (Bajrektarevic and Posega 2014, 56).

Although yet lacking a global prohibitionary regime, a multifaceted legal regulatory framework has gradually built up around nuclear weapons. This case echoes the nineteenth-century humanitarian arms control and disarmament regime and security regulation of SALW in that it also features an international *regime complex*. This is because it may similarly be characterized by "a number of elements, building blocks or agents capable of interacting with each other" (Alter and Meunier 2009, 13–14; Drezner 2009, 65). What follows is the inquiry into various related aspects, structures, and dynamics. In doing so, the goal is to dissect power configurations that have defined the development of this regime, with all its consequences and limits.

PRODUCTIVE POWER: STIGMATIZATION-DELEGITIMIZATION COMPLEX

Two complementary strategies have intertwined to frame atomic weapons as an illegitimate military instrument. These are stigmatization, emphasizing humanitarian and moral aspects and appealing to human sensibility, and delegitimization, stressing legal, political, and military aspects and appealing to human reasoning (Kurosawa 2018, 43 and 47). In addition, stigma imposition has systematically been facilitated through the development of international norms, even on the part of states not (immediately) joining the related endeavors (Fihn 2017, 44–47; Sauer and Reveraert 2018, 455; Tannenwald 2018, 20). Such efforts have coalesced into the three major waves. Antinuclear movements date back to the mid-1940s or, more explicitly, to the 1950s and the early 1960s (Tannenwald 2005, 14 and 21; Ruzicka 2019, 53). They revived in the 1980s to challenge the foundations of nuclear deterrence (Tannenwald 2005, 32). After the end of the Cold War and especially at the turn of the twenty-first century, the momentum has been restored with a more explicit reference to the framework of IHL (Evans and Kawaguchi 2009, 60; Tannenwald 2016, 113). More accurately, the overall trajectory of such developments may be termed the *stigmatization-delegitimization complex*. First, and rather intuitively, it merges the two strands, that is, stigmatization and delegitimization, making use of both a logic of appropriateness as well as a logic of consequences (Paul 2009, 3). Second, multiple perspectives are taken to condemn nuclear weapons. Importantly, such efforts concern the whole lifecycle chain of nuclear weapons, including their testing, maintenance, and use. Third, the collective stigmatization of WMD is a crucial point for consideration. Finally, it withal concerns not only atomic weapons but also their possessors as well as political and economic partners of the latter.

On general terms, nuclear weapons have been made incompatible with prestige, authority, and a good standing in the international community as well as with the principles of human rights, humanitarian, international and customary law, morality, ethics, and humanity (Tannenwald 2005, 14 and 22, 2016, 109; Berry et al. 2010, 35–36; RCW 2013a, 9; Kurosawa 2018, 36). This has been performed through the reexamination of prevailing discourses, ideas, and perceptions, notably those related to nuclear deterrence. The goal has been to redraw the approach to nuclear weapons by shifting the debate from national and military security to humanitarianism (Kurosawa 2018, 33 and 43; Tannenwald 2016, 113). Targets for criticism included the established deterrence practices, including that of extended deterrence, the instrumental necessity of nuclear weapons for peace, order, and stability as well as the imaginary of privilege and status attached to nuclear arsenals (Evans and Kawaguchi 2009, 61–71; Berry et al. 2010, 15–35; Sauer and Reveraert 2018, 442). The

humanitarian lens has instead been employed for accentuating the immediate and long-term devastating health, socioeconomic, and environmental consequences of the (un)authorized use of nuclear weapons and nuclear, especially atmospheric, tests (Chernobyl Forum 2003–2005; WHO
2005; UNSCEAR 2011; Bagshaw 2013, 121; Shamai 2015, 116; Tannenwald
2016, 113–14; Ware 2016, 123 and 133; Fihn 2017, 44; Kurosawa 2018, 34;
Sauer and Reveraert 2018, 439 and 442). One of the reports has particularly detailed the destructive repercursions of numerous episodes of nuclear
weapons testing in the Pacific sponsored by France, the United Kingdom,
and the United States (ICAN 2014a). Modernization programs, especially
aimed to make nuclear weapons more usable, have also been subject to
criticism (Fihn 2017, 47; Kristensen 2017, 33–34). Nuclear terrorism,
cyberattacks, false alarms, or spoofing and the aging of stockpiles have
been singled out as further sources of risk related to the maintenance of
nuclear arsenals (Borrie, Caughley, and Wan 2017). The most radical fear
has featured the ultimate destruction of human civilization or humankind (Tannenwald 2005, 22; Persbo 2016, 75). What has exacerbated the
case is distrust toward the existence of any credible defenses against
atomic weapons (Sauer and Reveraert 2018, 439). The aspiration for nuclear disarmament has thus been often framed through the prism of "the
moral imperative to preserve humanity" (Shamai 2015, 116). There has
ultimately developed a deeply entrenched image of nuclear weapons as
the most destructive, indiscriminate, inhuman, immoral, unethical, illegitimate, uncivilized, and unacceptable military tools (Tannenwald 2016,
109 and 113; Fihn 2017, 44; Kurosawa 2018, 33–36; Sauer and Reveraert
2018, 439 and 442). A broader perspective has even embedded the antinuclear sentiment into the global historical resistance to injustice, oppres-
sion, patriarchy, racism, or militarism (Acheson 2018, 249). All combined,
such a cognitive framing of nuclear weapons has been driven by an aspiration for the blanket global prohibition on and elimination of atomic
weapons (Tannenwald 2016, 113; Sauer and Reveraert 2018, 442).

The line beforehand drawn between conventional weapons and the
category of WMD features a crucial landmark paving the way for the
aforesaid discourse (Tannenwald 2005, 12 and 17). Associated with total
destruction and denounced as incompatible with humankind, such
weapons have been portrayed as unique and distinct (Shamai 2015, 104,
109, and 111–12). Such a categorical differentiation of weapons systems
has engendered a respective system of differentiation in the realm of
political subjects and generated certain "reputational effects" (Paul 2009,
2). This is the so-called discipline of civilization severely challenging the
perceived identities of actors possessing WMD (Price 1995, 95; Shamai
2015, 110; Hynek 2018a). Reflecting this more general rift, the image of
NWS as "civilized" states has also been called into question, while
NNWS have been defined as the "normals" (Tannenwald 2016, 113;
Sauer and Reveraert 2018, 440). The NPT has in this light been criticized

for formalizing the unequal division of states into two classes, namely the nuclear "haves" and "have nots" (Ruzicka and Wheeler 2016, 34). Aspiring to the remedy of this inequality, NNWS have condemned the failure of NWS to have lived up to their promise of nuclear disarmament codified in the NPT (Paul 2016, 17; Ruzicka 2019, 55). Exacerbating the gap, an atomic bomb has also been portrayed as a rich man's bomb (Price 1995, 98; Hynek 2018a). This is because nuclear arsenals require advanced financial and industrial capacities, complex know-how, and the access to related natural resources, even unlike chemical or biological weapons (Shamai 2015, 112). On top of this, it is important to articulate that the boundary delineating the outgroup has bolted out NWS together with their political and economic partners. Who has fallen to the abandoned cluster of actors are nuclear alliance states or allies of the nuclear-armed states as well as financial institutions associated with nuclear weapons production or stockpiling (Fihn 2017, 47; Sauer and Reveraert 2018, 452–53 and 455).

De facto, nuclear weapons have never been used in war again since the devastation of the two Japanese cities of Hiroshima and Nagasaki in 1945 (Løvold, Fihn, and Nash 2013, 146). It signifies that, over time, "the nuclear non-use norm" or "the tradition of non-use" has become deeply engrained despite the inadequacy of legal restraints (Paul 2009, 3–4). The conditions of emergence having allowed for the deep embeddedness of this discouse can be summarized as follows. Devastating operational precedents have been established by the notorious use of atomic weapons against Hiroshima and Nagasaki in 1945 and the "painful" history of nuclear weapons testing (BBC 1996; Whitney 1996; Tannenwald 2005, 14 and 21, 2016, 114; Paul 2016, 17; Ware 2016, 133). Strategic impetuses or episodes of nuclear brinkmanship have also spasmodically encouraged antinuclear sentiments. These included the placement of nuclear weapons in Europe as part of an extended deterrence by the North Atlantic Treaty Organization (NATO) in the late 1950s and early 1960s (Shamai 2015, 116). In the early 1980s, such an impulse was provided by the repudiation of arms control in favor of war-fighting strategies by President Ronald Reagan (Tannenwald 2005, 32). Expensive nuclear modernization programs recently launched by the United States and Russia fall under the same umbrella of provocative strategic developments (Cimbala 2017, 170). Aggravating the case, China, India, and Pakistan have also recently strived to expand and upgrade their nuclear arsenals (Tannenwald 2018, 16). Unauthorized activities as well as incidents of trafficking and malicious use have also been detected (IAEA 2019). Increasingly complex and interconnected, meaning dependent on digital technologies, nuclear weapons systems have additionally become ever more vulnerable to digital interference (Unal and Lewis 2017, 61). Numerous accidents, including the most severe one in Chernobyl (1986), have been reported at various nuclear (weapons) facilities (UNSCEAR 2011, 2–7). Exacerbating the

case with further safety repercussions, a great part of the currently in-
stalled nuclear power capacity has approached the end of its designed
life span (Brett 2009). Athwart such grave risks taken, there has been
repeatedly evidenced inadequacy on the part of nuclear weapons to prevent conventional, chemical, or biological attacks (Berry et al. 2010, 15–35;
Kurosawa 2018, 41). The antinuclear agenda has gained particular momentum after the end of the Cold War in light of a broader transformation in the security domain. Resonating the nineteenth-century humanitarian dispositif, security concepts centered on state sovereignty and
external threats have been overshadowed by human security, human
rights, and a humanitarian approach to nuclear disarmament (Krause
2002, 260; Caughley 2013, 22–23 and 27; Tannenwald 2016, 109; Hynek
2018b; Kurosawa 2018, 33–36). Inter alia, the final document of the NPT
Review Conference held in 2010 and the TPNW concluded in 2017 have
helped to reestablish the deep-seated centrality of IHL with respect to
atomic weapons (Fihn 2017, 43; Maresca 2013, 136). There has furthermore been observed an increasingly "impressive track record" of the
norms of IHL converging with the principles of international disarmament law (Berry et al. 2010, 37). It has been reinforced by the means of
legal grafting, that is, similar foundations of legal arguments, in particular humanitarian provisions, employed to frame various weapons regimes (Price 1998, 628; Hynek 2018a, 2018b). Such precedents for the case
of nuclear weapons have included the Biological Weapons Convention
(1972), the Chemical Weapons Convention (1993), the Mine Ban Convention (1997), the Convention on Cluster Munitions (2008), and the Arms
Trade Treaty (2013) (Berry et al. 2010, 37; Ritchie 2013, 63; Shamai 2015,
117). The evolving condemnation and subsequent legal prescription of
chemical and biological weapons have played a particularly crucial role
for outlawing nuclear weapons. This is because they all rest on the same
footing of the composite term of WMD legally constructed in 1948 (Shamai 2015, 106 and 114–16). Another attribute of the post–Cold War global
order, namely the "structural indeterminacy," has further contributed to
the condemnation of nuclear weapons. In particular, the aspiration for
atomic weapons by further states and terrorist groups, the escalation of
geopolitical tensions, and the regress in arms control have challenged the
foundations of conventional deterrence (Paul 2016, 17–21) as well as the
nuclear taboo (Tannenwald 2018, 16–18 and 24).

Despite the enormous constructive power and deep embeddedness of
the antinuclear weapons discourse, the central underlying ambition of a
global legal prohibition regime has not been satisfied. Progress has been
hindered by a divergence of attitudes in relation to the desirability for
such a regime as well as general concerns over its feasibility. In the first
place, there exists a different, even contradictory, interpretation of the
NPT. Having legally formalized the division between the nuclear
"haves" and "have nots," the treaty has rather been perceived by NWS as

a safeguard of their special status and superiority. In line with this interpretation, not NWS but those seeking to acquire atomic weapons have
instead been framed as outsiders or an outgroup (Shamai 2015, 117; Sauer
and Reveraert 2018, 440–41; Ruzicka 2019, 57). There may be observed a
similar dissonance in the interpretation of security. Proponents of nuclear
weapons have also referred to their notorious destructive potential,
though to highlight their unique deterrent quality for the sake of stability,
security, and peace. Not only nuclear weapons are thus still associated by
some with international security and national defense but, even more
importantly, the related world's history fairly allows us to draw such
associations (Colby 2016, 160–62; Persbo 2016, 75; Ware 2016, 134; Sauer
and Reveraert 2018, 439; Kmentt 2019). The recent deterioration of US-
Russian relations has contributed to cultivating such perceptions in the
post–Cold War age (Tannenwald 2016, 108). On top of this, nuclear umbrellas have long been seen as an essential nonproliferation tool (Cossa
and Glosserman 2011, 128). Beyond purely strategic considerations, nuclear weapons have also been associated by some with internal and external prestige, power, and superiority (Shamai 2015, 111; Acton 2016, 70;
Colby 2016, 160; Sauer and Reveraert 2018, 439). A number of more general concerns have further contributed to hindering nuclear disarmament. Among them is the lack of trust toward the NPT outflowing from
historical legacies and feelings of betrayal. What exacerbates the case is
the still nonuniversal nature of the treaty (Ruzicka and Wheeler 2016,
36–37 and 41). Furthermore, there has been little agreement among numerous approaches to nuclear disarmament proposed to date (Ware
2016, 122–25). The lack of a right authority to oversee the process, with
neither a single nation nor an international body having the necessary
competence or capability of obtaining it, has also curbed progress on this
front (Colby 2016, 165). Paradoxically enough, even if the agenda succeeded, the risk of nuclear rearmament would perennially persist because there is no chance of "un-inventing" the knowledge related to nuclear weapons (Schell 1984; Acton 2016, 62; Persbo 2016, 84).

STRUCTURAL POWER: HUMANITARIAN TRANSHISTORICAL
BLOC VERSUS EXCLUSIVE NUCLEAR CLUB

The movement against atomic weapons as we know it may be characterized as an *antinuclear humanitarian transhistorical bloc* traceable to the mid-
twentieth century. This section serves to carefully trace it by systematically highlighting its transhistorical character in terms of certain clusters of
actors consistently standing behind the agenda. This movement has progressively unified (international) nongovernmental organizations
(I)NGOs and their various umbrellas, including the International Committee of the Red Cross (ICRC), national Red Cross, and Red Crescent

societies as well as civil society groups. They have also joined forces with various elements of global and regional IOs as well as a committed group of (like-minded) states, particularly middle powers. Those who have generously favored the case include epistemic communities, city leaders and parliamentarians, church leaders and faith communities, Nobel Peace laureates and Peace laureate organizations, the private sector or financial institutions, the public, and the mass media. Political advocacy and grassroots movements against atomic weapons have historically formed a crucial part of the thrust. Traceable to the 1950s, they have firmly spread throughout the world (Tannenwald 2005, 20; Shamai 2015, 116). A good example to flag its subsequent transhistorical character is the Campaign to Ban the Bomb or the Campaign for Nuclear Disarmament (CND). Launched in the 1950s, it has continued to campaign to date (Shamai 2015, 116; CND n.d.-a). Such efforts have recently culminated in the International Campaign to Abolish Nuclear Weapons (ICAN). This is a massive civil society organization and transnational advocacy network featuring a coalition of nearly five hundred NGOs in more than a hundred states (Løvold, Fihn, and Nash 2013, 148; Ware 2016, 134; Sauer and Reveraert 2018, 453). Often in nexus with such groups and motivated by the desire to support the public interest, epistemic communities have also become crucial boosters of humanitarianism over time (Cross 2013, 150–55; Schneiker 2016, chap. 4). The letters by the physicist Niels Bohr to President Franklin D. Roosevelt (1944), the "Declaration of Conscience" by the renowned physician and humanitarian Albert Schweitzer (1957), and the formation of the transnational Pugwash group of scientists (1957) inter alia testify to scientists' deep-rooted involvement with the agenda (Tannenwald 2005, 15 and 21–22; Ruzicka 2019, 55–56). In the wake of early nuclear tests in the 1950s and early 1960s, prominent intellectuals and scientists notably contributed to facilitating antinuclear sentiments across broad portions of the globe. Among them were Bertrand Russell, Irène and Frédéric Joliot-Curie, Norman Cousins, Eugene Rabinowitch, and Joseph Rotblat (Tannenwald 2005, 21; Paul 2009, 33). In the 1980s and early 1990s, further professional communities such as the Physicians for Global Survival (PGS) or the International Physicians for the Prevention of Nuclear War (IPPNW), the International Association of Lawyers against Nuclear Arms (IALANA), the International Network of Engineers and Scientists for Global Responsibility (INES), and the International Peace Bureau (IPB) sided with the nuclear disarmament campaign (Bagshaw 2013, 121; IALANA n.d.; INES n.d.; IPB n.d.; IPPNW n.d.; PGS n.d.). Professional reports, for example *Nuclear Winter: Global Consequences of Multiple Nuclear Explosions* (1983) or *Effects of Nuclear War on Health and Health Services* (1987), simultaneously complemented the discourse (WHO 1987; Shamai 2015, 116). In the twenty-first century, in particular in the 2010s, scientists and experts have again stepped up warnings on the dangers and risks associated with nuclear weapons

(Tannenwald 2016, 114; Fihn 2017, 44). For example, the World Medical Association (WMA), the World Federation of Public Health Associations (WFPHA), and the International Council of Nurses (ICN) submitted a joint call for nuclear disarmament to the UN in 2016 (ICAN 2016). Among the key recent reports are *Eliminating Nuclear Threats: A Practical Agenda for Global Policy-Makers* (2009), *Delegitimizing Nuclear Weapons: Examining the Validity of Nuclear Deterrence* (2010), and *Unspeakable Suffering: The Humanitarian Impact of Nuclear Weapons* (2013) (ICAN 2013; RCW 2013b; Kurosawa 2018, 37 and 40). Another global network, namely Global Zero, was launched in 2008 to bring together engaged citizens, hundreds of political, military, and civic leaders, and disarmament experts (Ware 2016, 122–23; Global Zero n.d.). The involvement of the International Red Cross and Red Crescent Movement, especially the ICRC, can similarly be traced to the 1940s–1950s, in particular to its early calls for prohibition and disarmament and the renowned Draft Rules. With the focus increasingly shifted toward the humanitarian dimension of nuclear weapons after the end of the Cold War, its engagement has become even greater (Berry et al. 2010, 37; Maresca 2013, 139–40 and 143). A broader international movement, namely the Humanitarian Initiative, has ultimately grown to unify hundreds of professional and civil society (I)NGOs worldwide, including the CND, the ICAN, the IPPNW, and the ICRC as well as the National Red Cross and Red Crescent Societies (Fihn 2017, 48; Sauer and Reveraert 2018, 442; Ruzicka 2019, 57; ICAN n.d.-a).

Nonallied NNWS feature another cluster of actors constituting an essential part of the antinuclear movement. Their engagement with the agenda can be traced to the Non-Aligned Movement (NAM) but has principally gained momentum only upon the launch of the Humanitarian Initiative (Sauer and Reveraert 2018, 442–44). Driven by the aspiration to reshape the unequal nuclear order (temporarily) formalized by the NPT, they have long wished to force NWS to fulfill their part of the bargain (Paul 2016, 17; Ruzicka and Wheeler 2016, 31). In this light, the Humanitarian Initiative has gathered support of the majority of (NNW) states and has embedded their efforts within a broader coalition of international organizations and civil society groups. Middle powers such as Canada, Norway, Austria, Switzerland, Mexico, and Brazil have played a crucial role in advancing this agenda (Fihn 2017, 43; Sauer and Reveraert 2018, 443 and 437; MPI n.d.-a). The Middle Powers Initiative (MPI) has provided a complementary medium among (I)NGOs, including IALANA, INES, and IPB, and middle power governments as well as governments of both NWS and NNWS more generally (Ware 2016, 122–23; MPI n.d.-b). Having grown out of the 2014 "Austrian Pledge," the collective "Humanitarian Pledge" to prohibit and eliminate atomic weapons has reinforced intergovernmental solidarity. Joint statements on nuclear disarmament, drawing together increasingly more states since 2012, have also been repeatedly promoted at the NPT Review Conferences and the UNGA (Ware 2016, 133; Kurosawa 2018, 33–34).

Complementary channels for the disarmament agenda to even more governments globally have been provided by a committed group of city leaders and the parliamentary dimension of the campaign. Lobbying for nuclear disarmament since the 1980s, the Mayors for Peace have since 2003 contributed to promoting the agenda with their renowned "2020 Vision" (Ware 2016, 128–29; ICAN n.d.-b; MfP n.d.-a, n.d.-b). Parliamentarians for Nuclear Non-Proliferation and Disarmament (PNND) has long served as an international issue-oriented forum for parliamentarians (PNND n.d.). The European Parliament (EP) has repeatedly endorsed a ban, including in its 2005 and 2016 resolutions as well as by its support for "2020 Vision" articulated in 2004 (EP 2005, 2016; ICAN 2016b; MfP n.d.-c). The Inter-Parliamentary Union (IPU), bringing together 164 member parliaments, has facilitated the disarmament campaign with its landmark resolution *Toward a Nuclear Weapon Free World: The Contribution of Parliaments* (2011) (PNND 2014; Ware 2016, 128–29). A great number of individual parliamentarians across the globe has also pledged their commitment to nuclear disarmament (ICAN 2019a, n.d.-c).

Elements of IOs, particularly of the UN, have contributed to disseminating antinuclear weapons sentiments by endorsing nuclear disarmament or at least serving as negotiation fora for the cause. The UNGA engagement can be traced to 1946, when its first resolution established a commission to control the discovery of atomic energy and its peaceful use (UNODA n.d.-a). From 1959 to 1961, a number of UNGA resolutions focused on preventing the testing, acquisition, use, deployment, and proliferation of nuclear weapons (Johnson n.d.). Since the early 1960s, nonaligned states would actively sponsor UNGA resolutions in favor of a ban on the use of nuclear weapons (Tannenwald 2005, 28–30). The UNGA again called for nuclear disarmament and a nuclear-weapons-free world in its 2016 resolutions (Kurosawa 2018, 35). Key deliberation venues have included the traditional UNGA First Committee and the Preparatory Committees and Review Conferences of the NPT (Løvold, Fihn, and Nash 2013, 150). The latter, remarkably, dates back to 1975 (UNODA n.d.-b). The principal issue-oriented UN negotiating fora has evolved from the Ten-Nation Committee on Disarmament (1960), the Eighteen-Nation Committee on Disarmament (1962–1968), and the Conference of the Committee on Disarmament (1969–1978) to today's Conference on Disarmament (Tannenwald 2016, 109; UN n.d.). Disarmament conferences, for instance those held in 1978 and 1982, would greatly contribute to generating popular interest in disarmament (Tannenwald 2005, 33). Through action within the UN system, a new platform called UNFOLD ZERO has recently complemented, enhanced, and empowered the existing nuclear abolition networks and initiatives (UNFOLD ZERO n.d.-a). UN Secretary-Generals would repeatedly condemn nuclear weapons, inter alia, in

1969, 2008, and 2018 (Shamai 2015, 116; Guterres 2018; ICAN n.d.-d). The UN High Representatives for Disarmament would also systematically point at the importance of nuclear disarmament, inter alia, in 1998, 2001, 2013, and 2018 (Ware 2016, 139; Sauer and Reveraert 2018, 451; UNODA n.d.-c). Active since 1980, the United Nations Institute for Disarmament Research (UNIDIR) has consistently assessed various deleterious aspects of the nuclear dilemma (UNIDIR n.d.-a, n.d.-b). The UN humanitarian agencies such as the United Nations Office for the Coordination of Humanitarian Affairs (OCHA), the United Nations Development Programme (UNDP), the United Nations High Commissioner for Refugees (UNHCR), and the World Food Programme (WFP) have recently contributed to shifting attention to the humanitarian dimension of atomic weapons (Bagshaw 2013, 118 and 129). The International Court of Justice (ICJ) has favored the case with its renowned advisory opinion on the (il)legality of nuclear weapons (1996) and engagement with the Marshall Islands lawsuit since 2014 (Tannenwald 2016, 114; Ware 2016, 139; Kurosawa 2018, 37). Since the 1963 decision on the denuclearization by the Organisation of African Unity (OAU), the African Union (AU) has also been active in nuclear disarmament and among the key regional players advancing the TPNW (ICAN 2019b).

Numerous church leaders and pacifists as well as church and peace organizations have endorsed the antinuclear weapons agenda since the notorious recourse to atomic weapons in war and firmly throughout the 1950s–1960s. Inter alia, the US National Conference of Catholic Bishops voiced a moral critique also in the 1980s (Tannenwald 2005, 15, 21, and 32). A statement condemning atomic weapons was again made by the World Council of Churches in 2014 (ICAN 2014b). Similarly concerned, a coalition of faith communities also submitted a public statement to the UNGA First Committee in 2018 (Public Statement 2018). Joint statements or declarations by Nobel Peace laureates and Peace laureate organizations have also repeatedly endorsed the pursuit of nuclear disarmament for the sake of peace (Nobel Peace Summit 2002, 2006, 2013, 2014, 2017, 2019). It is interesting to recall that some core antinuclear campaigners, including the Pugwash Movement, the IPB, or the IPPNW, are the winners of the Nobel Peace Prize (Ruzicka 2019, 56; ICAN n.d.-e; IPB n.d.). Another cluster of actors underpinning the antinuclear weapons agenda is the public, especially as they are considered essential for framing security issues (Salter 2008; Emmers 2013, 134). Public anxieties about atomic weapons date back at least to the 1950s. In the 1980s, large antinuclear movements, drawing together millions of demonstrators, swept the United States and Europe (Tannenwald 2005, 21 and 32). More recent opinion polls, rallies, protests, and petitions have also showcased ample public support for nuclear nonproliferation and disarmament (Simons Foundation 2007; Sauer and Reveraert 2018, 451; ICAN 2016c, n.d.-b, n.d.-d; n.d.-f). The peace organization PAX has recently collected thousands of signatures against atomic weapons (Sauer and Reveraert 2018, 451). A petition with millions of signatures has been submitted to the UN by campaigners from Japan (ICAN n.d.-f). Featuring a crucial channel for disseminating and thus shaping various security-oriented agendas (Vultee 2011), the mass media have also generously favored the case. Concerns about nuclear weapons would consistently generate widespread media coverage, particularly remarkable in the 1950s and the 1970s–1980s, throughout the Cold War (Tannenwald 2005, 21; Shamai 2015, 116). The media and, newly, social networks around the world have greatly facilitated the agenda to date (Global Zero n.d.; ICNND n.d.). The case has also been supported by some private sector or financial institutions both in NWS and NNWS, for instance the Co-Operative Bank in the United Kingdom and the Government Pension Fund Global in Norway (Sauer and Reveraert 2018, 452; ICAN 2016d).

Nuclear weapon states and their allies, in particular states under extended nuclear deterrence, have always been at the core of the opposition to the blanket prohibition of nuclear weapons (Ware 2016, 133; Kurosawa 2018, 36). Voting for the TPNW has greatly illustrated the case, with the least enthusiastic being the United States, the United Kingdom, France, Russia, and China as well as members of NATO such as Germany and other nuclear umbrella states such as Japan. Alhough India and Pakistan have voted in its favor (Collina 2013), they have not ratified it afterward in line with the other NWS (ICAN n.d.-g). This may be explained by the deep-seated reliance on military options, including atomic weapons, for the sake of national interests and security on the part of NWS (Tannenwald 2016, 114; Ware 2016, 138). Little has changed to date. Russia still considers its nuclear arsenals as an alternative to its conventional backwardness in certain regards, a source of great power status and a bargaining instrument. Nuclear weapons are also still associated with security and status value by both the United States and the United Kingdom. Nuclear disarmament might not be attractive to France because of its propensity for strike force and independence in defense policy, as they are also driven by their aspiration for status and prestige. Territorial disputes and power rivalries among India, Pakistan, and China, with China furthermore seeking global power status, hold back the prospects of regional nuclear disarmament. The engrained sense of insecurity or concerns over regime survival have long driven strategic decisions, including those related to atomic weapons, by Israel, Pakistan, and North Korea (Paul 2016, 23–24; Tannenwald 2016, 108, 2018, 21). Nuclear weapons have generally compensated for asymmetries in conventional forces that are of particular importance for smaller states (Persbo 2016, 76; Ware 2016, 137). What has long been the core strategic framework and simultaneously the greatest barrier on the way toward a nuclear-weapons-free world is nuclear deterrence (Ware 2016, 137). Deterrence has become more complex and challenging after the end of the Cold War but is still considered viable by virtue of maintaining certain working modalities going beyond the traditional wisdom (Kapur 2009; Hynek 2010; Paul 2016, 18–21). Extended nuclear deterrence, including for the repeatedly stated purpose of nonproliferation, has long been perceived as a security-laden necessity by the United States and Russia as well as their allies (Evans and Kawaguchi 2009, 65; Tannenwald 2018, 21; Ruzicka 2019, 63–64). Under the regime of nonproliferation, nuclear umbrellas have generated certain political-strategic dependencies on the part of state recipients (Ruzicka 2019, 69). The realm of nuclear commerce features the other facet of structural interests and dependences within the nonproliferation regime (Bajrektarevic and Posega 2014, 52). Countries with greater supply capabilities, in particular the United States and Russia (the former Soviet Union), have long enjoyed strong advantages in the provision of civil nuclear energy (Aras and Ozbay 2006; Weiss 2007; Lynch 2013, 91; Bajrektarevic and Posega 2014; Ruzicka 2019, 66). However, a number of other nuclear supplier countries have also been recognized (NSG n.d.; Zangger Committee n.d.). With the world being progressively energy dependent, supplies of this sort have also given rise to certain external dependencies on the part of state recepients. What is crucial for comprehending the character of such dependencies is that related decisions have often been made on a (geo)political rather than purely economic or commercial basis (Bajrektarevic and Posega 2014, 6 and 52–57).

However, these are not only security and energy dependencies that have defined the lines of support for the nuclear-armed states. Their position has been backed by a good number of experts whose knowledge-based expertise or professional judgment may be thought of in terms of "authority" (Cross 2013, 150–55; Schneiker 2016, chap. 4). The debate around nuclear abolition has incidentally grown full fledged, with a variety of controversies brought to the fore for consideration (Perkovich and Acton 2009). These, for instance, include various challenges of maintaining stability at low numbers (Cimbala 2017). Having spotted the potential resultant menace to the world order and the inadequacy of alternatives to nuclear deterrence, some have also railed against nuclear disarmament (Perkovich and Acton 2009, 308; Boyd and Scouras 2013; Colby 2016). Many profit-driven private companies, including state-owned ones, have also been globally engaged in the production, development, and stockpiling of nuclear weapons (PAX 2019). For example, Lockheed Martin, Safran, and BWX Technologies have been condemned for their association with the nuclear arsenals of the United Kingdom, France, and the United States (Sauer and Reveraert 2018, 452). Public support for nuclear disarmament has also never been universal and absolute, especially with much of the public in the nuclear-armed states being confortable with the status quo (Simons Foundation 2007; Persbo 2016, 75).

To sum up, the humanitarian agenda has been set against nuclear weapons by a multifaceted and integrally intertwined group of disarmament adherents. As systematically discussed earlier, there is a strong transhistorical trend with regard to this antinuclear weapons movement. Same or at least categorically similar actors who would strive to outlaw atomic weapons in and around the 1950s stand by the same agenda in and around the 1980s and drive the same campaign in the post–Cold War era. Remarkably, a great portion of them, including the UN humanitarian agencies, the ICRC, and certain middle powers, have once stood against the antipersonnel landmines (APLs), cluster munitions (CMs), and chemical and biological weapons (Bagshaw 2013, 118; Maresca 2013, 134). This points at the existence of an even broader *humanitarian transnational historical bloc*. The 1970s were paramount for its structural empowerment, with an "effective and efficient" relationship between nongovernmental or civil society organizations and governments gradually set up in many liberal countries (Hynek 2018b). Throughout the whole history of the antinuclear movement, this bloc would consistently meet powerful resistance foremost from the nuclear-armed states. Their structural supremacy, having allowed them to withstand antinuclear sentiments, primarily lies with the exclusive nuclear club largely corresponding to veto-bearing members of the UNSC (Sauer and Reveraert 2018, 441). It is interesting to remark, as this book also systematically shows, that "the same few" weapons-dependent governments have also stood against severe restrictions on APLs, CMs, small arms, and "Killer Robots" (Krause 2002, 256; Marks 2008; Hynek 2018b; Bourne 2019; Johnson n.d.).

INSTITUTIONAL POWER: THE STRATEGIC UNDERBRUSH

As also depicted earlier, the antinuclear campaign of humanitarian disarmament has become progressively embedded, to varying degrees, in international institutions and agreements. What is particularly important is that this movement has successfully penetrated various UN bodies and fora to advance the agenda globally. In the first place, a nonaligned-country majority has emerged at the UNGA in pursuit of the agenda (Tannenwald 2005, 28–30, 33, and 46; Ware 2016, 139). Some of the committed nongovernmental associations such as the IALANA or Mayors for Peace have been granted a special consultative status with the UN (IALANA n.d.; MfP n.d.-a). The history of the ICRC and the UN working together is remarkably deep rooted (Fortin 2012). Alongside delegations representing governments, the UN, and other IOs, the International Conference on the Humanitarian Impact of Nuclear Weapons has also amply involved the ICRC and civil society (Ware 2016, 123; Kurosawa 2018, 34). What is also remarkable is that nuclear use/test survivors have also had a platform at the UN and thus a chance to steer the debate (ICAN 2017a).

The multiplication of deliberation fora has also repeatedly showcased how effective the campaigners have been in promoting nuclear disarmament (Ware 2016, 139; Tannenwald 2005, 10). A landmark expansion of institutional venues in this regard has been the organization of the Review Conferences designed to ponder the terms and future of the NPT (Ruzicka 2019, 67). One was, for instance, launched by Norway and Switzerland in 2010 as a joint effort by like-minded governments and civil society to further devalue atomic weapons (Tannenwald 2016, 113). The UNGA has also established an Open-Ended Working Group (OEWG) in order to facilitate the international dialogue on nuclear disarmament. Another contemporary platform allotted to generating UN-based initiatives and actions in pursuit of a nuclear-weapons-free world has been UNFOLD ZERO (Ware 2016, 139).

The institutionalization of the nuclear taboo began in the 1960s–1970s, and the realm of (il)legitimacy with respect to atomic weapons has been incrementally set up by the means of various treaties and regimes. These have principally encompassed NWFZs and bilateral and multilateral arms control agreements, including efforts to regulate and ban nuclear weapons testing, as well as agreements pertaining to the area of civil nuclear cooperation (Tannenwald 2005, 10 and 27; Ruzicka 2019, 59). However, one may fairly argue that, on par with normative considerations, also strategic or material/rationalist ones have driven the nuclear nonuse norm. The latter category includes mutual or extended deterrence, tactical or strategic unsuitability of nuclear weapons, their inadequacy in terms of military utility, power politics considerations, or the fear of retaliation (Paul 2009, 15–37). Similarly, (superpowers') strategic (self-)interests have defined the pattern of nuclear taboo formalization (Tannenwald 2005, 32 and 46). An insight into strategic baselines with respect to the core treaties and the principal deliberation fora is in order. Inter alia, the light is shed on the lines of institutional power and responsibility, decision-making rules, and the associated character of decisions. The main finding is the highly imbalanced institutionalization with respect to nonproliferation versus disarmament.

None of the existing treaties imposes severe pressure on the nuclear-armed states to disarm, possibly for the reason that none of them originally adopted with this intention. The cornerstone of the international regime in the realm of atomic weapons is the NPT because it formally distinguishes between their temporarily legitimate possessors and the rest (Sauer and Reveraert 2018, 440). Though designed to foster nuclear disarmament, it has ultimately become "an instrument for horizontal non-proliferation" (Paul 2016, 15). This is because the treaty stipulates a mechanism to ensure compliance by NNWS with their obligations, while not doing the same in relation to NWS (Patton, Podvig, and Schell 2013, 2). Especially through its near universality, it has thus stigmatized states that either disobey or evade the NPT on the grounds of nonproliferation rather than disarmament (Sauer and Reveraert 2018, 440). The explanation lies with this regime being driven by nuclear-armed states' military ambitions, rivalries, and shared determination to secure their unique global standing (Ruzicka 2019, 59–61; Johnson n.d.). A complementary element of this nonproliferation regime, serving certain structural interests, has been that of nuclear commerce. Both the Zangger Committee and the Nuclear Suppliers are voluntary coalitions, unbound by any legal requirements (Cirincione, Wolfsthal, and Rajkumar 2005, 33). Considering that the Wassenaar Arrangement is also not binding in legal terms, it is crucial to recall that the nuclear commerce regime has often been driven by (geo)political rather than purely economic or commercial decisions (Bajrektarevic and Posega 2014, 52–57). The nuclear deal between the United States and India, concluded in 2005 despite the latter's refusal to join the NPT, greatly illustrates the case (Ruzicka 2019, 67).

Strategic considerations have similarly driven most of the other nuclear weapons treaties. The strategic stalemate between the superpowers during the Cuban missile crisis feature the key drivers of arms control ventures during the Cold War (Tannenwald 2005, 28–30; Ruzicka 2019, 58). Since then, the SALT-I and the SALT-II, the ABM Treaty, the INF Treaty, the START-I and the START-II, as well as the New START have been spasmodically negotiated to shape the arms race rather than to disarm (Berry et al. 2010, 40; Persbo 2016, 83). What also testifies to the strategic underbrush of such endeavors is the history of their abandonment, including the US withdrawal from the ABM Treaty in 2002 and from the INF Treaty in 2019 (Berry et al. 2010, 40; Pompeo 2019). What virtually points at the same is the fact that blanket prohibition treaties have never yet generated enough support to enter into force. This momentum has not yet occurred in the case of the CTBT concluded in 1996 (Berry et al. 2010, 40). By the means of nonaligned NNWS utilizing the power of their number, an all-embracing ban has recently been adopted by virtue of the TPNW (Sauer and Reveraert 2018, 443). Inter alia opposed by China, France, Russia, the United Kingdom, and the United States as well as the latter's partners in deterrence within NATO and such as Australia, Japan, and South Korea, it has little chance of enforcing nuclear disarmament (Collina 2013; Fihn 2017, 45; Kurosawa 2018, 32). This is because the key actors in the nuclear realm would not be bound by the stipulated obligations (UNFOLD ZERO 2018). That said, the potency of multilateral disarmament pressure cannot be belittled, especially in the face of the INF Treaty (Johnson n.d.) and the PTBT (Berry et al. 2010, 39; Tannenwald 2005, 27).

An insight into the relevant institutional framework allows us to comprehend the roots of the aforesaid. While the institutional structure has vastly and continuously accommodated criticism, it has consistently favored the nonproliferation regime (Ruzicka 2019, 68). In particular, it has systematically fostered certain interests paving way for the (efficient) nonproliferation regime and the deadlock on nuclear disarmament. Progress on disarmament has been hindered by the principle of unanimous decision making (consensus) within the format of the Conference on Disarmament, the principal UN negotiating venue for the cause. The greatest limitation of the UN institutional framework more generally is also the veto power over any decisions held by the permanent members of the UNSC (China, France, Russia, the United Kingdom, and the United States) (Tannenwald 2016, 109; Ware 2016, 126 and 139). Although the UNGA can approve resolutions by majority vote, these have generally been nonbinding unless adopted by consensus or near consensus (UNFOLD ZERO 2018). At the same time, the IAEA has served the interests of powerful states within the nonproliferation regime. It has consistently monitored compliance with the NPT but, unable to enforce compliance, referred violators to the UNSC. The UN sanctions against Iran between 2006 and 2016 are a vivid illustration of this UNSC enforcement mechanism at work (Ruzicka 2019, 54 and 66). Generally capable of imposing legally binding rules (Bajrektarevic and Posega 2014, 57; Ruhlman 2015, 37–38; Persbo 2016, 81), the UNSC has used its resolutions to sustain and reinforce the nonproliferation regime (1540 Committee n.d.).

COMPULSORY POWER: DIRECT ENFORCEMENT AND STIGMA MANAGEMENT MECHANISMS

Various mechanisms have been deployed by the antinuclear weapons movement to alter the behavior of the nuclear-armed states and those who side with them. Tabooization of nuclear weapons has historically been performed via media outreach and news broadcasts, films and documentaries, knowledge-based argumentation, commemoration of atomic bombings, life stories of nuclear use/test survivors, court cases and their public boosting, and religious and peace norms (Tannenwald 2005, 21–22 and 32, 2016, 114–16; Shamai 2015, 111 and 116; Ware 2016, 133; Kurosawa 2018, 37 and 40; Ruzicka 2019, 55–56; ICAN 2014b, 2016a, 2016e, 2016f, 2019c, 2019d, 2019e, n.d.-d, n.d.-h; UNFOLD ZERO n.d.-b). The focal imagery featuring the most radical fear has been "the total elimination of human kind" (Shamai 2015, 116). Normative pressure has been put on resistant governments and financial institutions through the technique of naming and shaming. They primarily condemn the nuclear-armed states, including both the state parties to the NPT and those having remained outside of the framework, as well as their strategic allies (ICAN 2016g, 2016h, 2017b, 2018a, 2018b). The reputation of certain traditional leaders on disarmament such Sweden has also been questioned in light of their procrastination to ratify the TPNW (ICAN 2019f, 2019g). Normative pressure has also concerned the private sector by way of the annual *Don't Bank on the Bomb* report tracking investments by financial institutions in nuclear weapons production (Fihn 2017, 46; ICAN 2019h). Peer pressure has complemented this endeavor, with more banks, pension funds, and insurance agencies in both NWS and NNWS adopting antinuclear investment policies (Sauer and Reveraert 2018, 452; ICAN 2016i, 2019i). Similarly, like-minded governments have by various means exerted peer pressure on the decision makers in nuclear-armed states and their allies (Sauer and Reveraert 2018, 454). Their toolkit has included the "Humanitarian Pledge," joint statements at the NPT Review Conferences and the UNGA (Ware 2016, 133; Kurosawa 2018, 33–34), and the ratification of the TPNW (ICAN 2019j). Models of responsible behavior have been exemplified by South Africa, Belarus, Kazakhstan, and Ukraine having denounced their nuclear weapons, or Argentina and Brazil among the others having abandoned their nuclear weapons ambitions (Persbo 2016, 88; Sauer and Reveraert 2018, 449–50; Ruzicka 2019, 70; ICAN 2019k). What also falls to the category of such models but extends them to the regional level are NWFZs such as the 1995 African Pelindaba Treaty (ICAN 2019b). It features an important example because it has also built upon the success of nuclear disarmament by South Africa (Tannenwald 2016, 113). Bottom-up normative pressure on resistant national leaders and governments has jointly been generated by transnational advocacy networks and domestic activists (Tannenwald 2005, 12, 23 and 27; UNFOLD ZERO 2016; Sauer and Reveraert 2018, 453–54). In doing so, they have repeatedly resorted to the compilation of public opinion polls (ICAN 2016j, 2018c, 2019l, 2019m). Public support has also been mobilized through numerous rallies, demonstrations and protests, as well as via collective appeals and petitions (Tannenwald 2005, 21; ICAN 2016c, n.d.-b, n.d.-f). More recent examples of the latter have been the Hibakusha Appeal for a nuclear ban treaty (ICAN 2016k), the Global Zero petition to the UNSC (UNFOLD ZERO n.d.-c), and the Scrap Trident petition to the British government (CND n.d.-b). The #LetsTalkNukes hashtag has additionally been utilized as a social media platform to disseminate the agenda (UNFOLD ZERO n.d.-d). Top-down societal pressure on resistant decision makers has simultaneously been generated by some authoritative IOs. Multiple resolutions by the UNGA have urged states to prohibit the testing, acquisition, use, deployment, and proliferation of nuclear weapons and head for a nuclear-weapons-free world (Tannenwald 2005, 12 and 28–30; Kurosawa 2018, 35; Johnson n.d.). The ICJ has ruled out the legality of the threat or use of nuclear weapons by the means of its renowned decision (1996) (Ware 2016, 133). Its recent engagement with the cases brought by the Marshall Islands to charge the nuclear powers has also been essential for "agenda politics" (Tannenwald 2016, 114–15). On top of this, a formal resolution by the International Red Cross and Red Crescent Movement has also called on states to eliminate nuclear weapons (ICAN n.d.-a). The parliamentary dimension of the campaign has complemented the multidimensional societal pressure. By the means of the "Parliamentary Appeal," or later "Parliamentary Pledge," conscientious individual parliamentarians have committed to steer their governments' ambitions toward nuclear disarmament (ICAN 2017c, 2019a, n.d.-i, n.d.-j). On the regional level, the EP has in its resolutions repeatedly called on the EU and its member-states to pursue nuclear disarmament (EP 2005, 2016; ICAN 2016b). Going further, the declaration by OSCE parliamentarians has urged nuclear-armed and allied states to move forward with disarmament measures (PNND 2018). A landmark resolution unanimously adopted by the IPU has appealed to governments with a similar request (PNND 2014; Ware 2016, 128–29). Such parliamentary initiatives have had implications for individual governments, for example with both houses of the Swiss Parliament calling on their government to join the TPNW (ICAN 2018d).

The antinuclear weapons coalition has, however, been short of mechanisms of direct leverage over the resistant coalition. It signifies their relative impotence in regard to the already discernible nonsignatories of the TPNW. With structural dominance of the latter transmitted into actual policies, nonproliferation has solidified into a preeminent norm (Ruzicka 2019, 63). Capable of imposing legally binding rules on all UN member-states, the UNSC has repeatedly utilized this competence to sustain and reinforce the nonproliferation regime (Bajrektarevic and Posega 2014, 57; Persbo 2016, 81; 1540 Committee n.d.). It is structurally supreme compared to nonbinding resolutions long sponsored by the Non-Aligned Movement (NAM) at the UNGA (Sauer and Reveraert 2018, 443–44), the EP's nonbinding resolutions in regard to the EU foreign policy matters (ICAN 2016b), as well as the nonbinding legal status of the OSCE (OSCE n.d.). Additional support-generating grip has been ensured by certain degrees of dependencies within the frames of extended nuclear deterrence (Ruzicka 2019, 69) and within the nuclear commerce regime (Bajrektarevic and Posega 2014, 52). This regime has additionally normalized the use of force or other forms of compulsory power to be set against violators. Besides mere deterrence, coercive diplomacy, including diplomatic isolation, bilateral and unilateral sanctions, as well as the use of force have been performed for this cause. Among the examples are coercive diplomacy and the military intervention in Iraq, the Israeli air strike aimed to destroy a clandestine nuclear facility in Syria, repeated threats of the use of force, and coercive diplomacy with several rounds of sanctions by the UNSC, the United States, and its allies in the Iranian case (Nader 2012; Haggard and Noland 2012; Palkki and Smith 2012; Ruzicka 2019, 59, 62–64, and 68). Various means have also been utilized by the governments in resistance to sustain their controversial stance toward nuclear weapons. As already discussed earlier, they have in the first place regularly engaged in counter-stigmatization of nuclear weapons by virtue of stressing their indispensability for state survival and international order (Sauer and Reveraert 2018, 447–48). A good illustration of this strategy in action from a different perspective is how the Eisenhower admin-istration was, by virtue of tactical or small nuclear weapons, "convention-alizing" them. The development of new generations of "mini-nukes," blurring the line between conventional and nuclear weapons, increasing-ly paves the way for the same nowadays (Tannenwald 2005, 24 and 43). However, under the weight of heavy and continuous criticism, nuclear-armed states have often avoided stigma by "concealing the deviant at-tribute, or by refraining from situations in which the stigma can be im-posed." The examples include the Israeli strategy of opacity regarding nuclear weapons or repeated refusals by NWS to attend the humanitar-ian conferences and the TPNW negotiations (Sauer and Reveraert 2018, 445). What also falls to the same catogory is the engrained "tradition of non-use," even in the face of the most severe Cold War crises (Paul 2009, 1). As a qualitative extension of this strategy, the nuclear-armed states have also repeatedly resorted to "virtual abolition schemes." Among them have been increases in transparency, narrowing circumstances and the scale of use, voluntary nuclear restraints, no-first-use declarations, legally binding NSAs, and the "taboo talk" (Tannenwald 2016, 109–12). Such initiatives would, though, feature virtual efforts because nuclear arsenals have still been perceived on their part as compulsory prudence at least (Colby 2016, 160). For instance, the 1940s–1950s Soviet disarma-ment calls were undertaken alongside their own nuclear weapons accel-eration, the 1982 Soviet no-first-use pledge was no more than "a symbolic gesture," and President Obama's vision of a nuclear-weapons-free world was promoted alongside a huge nuclear modernization program by the United States (Tannenwald 2005, 19, 2018, 22; Shoumikhin 2011, 101, 106, and 111–12; Arbatov 2017, 40). A complementary strategy of reconciling such contradictory ambitions has often been stigma evasion, with stigma-tized parties assigning responsibility for their possession of atomic weap-ons to some third parties or external circumstances (Sauer and Reveraert 2018, 447–48). For example, NATO has reassured its commitment to dis-armament though indicated its intention to remain a nuclear alliance as long as atomic weapons would exist (NATO n.d.).

CONCLUSION

This chapter provided insight into power configurations with regard to international regulatory/prohibition politics evolving around the security issue of nuclear weapons. It opened with a legally oriented analysis of the emerging nuclear weapons *regime complex*. This complex was decom-posed into a set of multiple international, regional, bilateral, and unilater-al formative steps. A multifaceted regulatory framework coupling the nuclear weapons regime and the nuclear commerce regime was ultimate-ly portrayed. However, attention was drawn to its incompleteness and piecemeal character in that the renowned proposals for blanket prohibition, primarily the CTBT and the TPNW, have not succeeded.

The power-analytical approach, with its four conceptions of power, was then utilized to reflect on dynamics and conditions that have defined triumphs and limitations of the regime under consideration. Keeping in mind the deep-rooted history of push and pull factors with respect to nuclear weapons regulation/prohibition and related efforts, a longue durée perspective was taken. The section on productive power introduced a notion of the stigmatization-delegitimization complex and, through its prism, anatomized the antinuclear humanitarian discourse. The latter's favorable structural conditions of emergence were then extensively discussed to show how it has evolved into the de facto nuclear taboo. However, to reflect on the inadequacy of legal constraints in this regard, conflicting interpretations of the NPT and security (counter-discourse) and various practical barriers were discussed. An inquiry into the complex working of structural power followed. This part relied on the notion of the *antinuclear humanitarian transhistorical bloc*. This is because it helped accurately depict the transhistorical character of the antinuclear campaign in terms of the same or categorically similar actors involved in advancing it since the mid-twentieth century to date. A broader concept of the *transnational historical bloc*, introduced and referred to in the previous chapters, was also found pertinent on the basis of the presented campaign composition and a cross-case comparision. However, an insight into the systemic distribution of power and associated interests made it plain that there has been a nearly irreconcilable clash of interests with the nuclear-armed states. What is even more important, it showed how their superior structural standing has long steered the progress in their favor and sustained steadfast resistance to a blanket ban on nuclear weapons.

Next, complex operations of institutional power were put under the microscope, starting with reiterated remarkable achievements by the antinuclear weapons movements in the realm of institutional loci. What followed was a nuanced review of the core agreements and deliberation venues related to atomic weapons regulation and nuclear disarmament. In doing so, strategic underpinnings were pointed out with respect to all of these, even including an analogous remark on the nuclear nonuse norm as such. The core finding of this investigation was that the institutional structure has long served the interests of the great powers and eventually favored the nonproliferation regime to nuclear disarmament. Finally, attention was drawn to mutual mechanisms of direct leverage defining the conception of compulsory power. Through its lenses, we demonstrated how the nuclear disarmament campaign has consistently employed a broad range of tools to stigmatize both atomic weapons and identities of their endorsers. Through the same prism, it was discovered that such efforts have not been inadequate in terms of taking a firm grip on the resistant bloc. From their structural position, not much can legitimately be done to force the nuclear-armed states to change their position on the security issue of nuclear weapons. Simultaneously, counterleverage mechanisms of the dominant players have regularly prevailed both in terms of enforcing compliance with their favored principles and justifying their controversial stance.

As this chapter comprehensively showcased, leaps forward with respect to nuclear weapons regulation/prohibition have truly been striking and their culmination has recently manifested as the TPNW. The prospects of this crowning global agreement being universally ratified remain grim, however, especially because political tensions have increased and arms races have intensified. The key obstruction in this regard is a deep rift that has traditionally divided preferences by the two clusters of governments, primarily those of NWS and those of NNWS. A nonuniversal ratification of the TPNW seems more promising, though it does not really pave the way for nuclear disarmament.

REFERENCES

1540 Committee [Security Council Committee established pursuant to resolution 1540/2004]. n.d. *About 1540 Committee: General Information.* Accessed November 5, 2019. https://www.un.org/en/sc/1540/about-1540-committee/general-information.shtml.

Acheson, Ray. 2018. "Impacts of the Nuclear Ban: How Outlawing Nuclear Weapons Is Changing the World." *Global Change, Peace and Security* 30, no. 2: 243–50.

Acton, James M. 2016. "Virtual Nuclear Deterrence and Strategic Stability." In *Global Nuclear Disarmament: Strategic, Political, and Regional Perspectives,* edited by Nik Hynek and Michal Smetana, 61–74. New York: Routledge.

Alter, Karen J., and Sophie Meunier. 2009. "The Politics of International Regime Complexity." *Symposium* 7, no. 1 (March): 13–24.

Aras, Bulent, and Fatih Ozbay. 2006. "Dances with Wolves: Russia, Iran and the Nuclear Issue." *Middle East Policy* 13, no. 4 (Winter): 132–47.

Arbatov, Alexey. 2017. "Understanding the US–Russia Nuclear Schism." *Survival* 59, no. 2: 33–66.

Bagshaw, Simon. 2013. "Responding to the Detonation of Nuclear Weapons: A United Nations Humanitarian Perspective." In *Viewing Nuclear Weapons through a Humanitarian Lens,* edited by John Borrie and Tim Caughley, 118–30. Geneva: United Nations Institute for Disarmament Research (UNIDIR), United Nations Publications.

Bajrektarevic, Anis H., and Petra Posega. 2014. "Nuclear Commerce: Security, Politico-Military, Legal and Socio-Economic Aspects." *Modern Diplomacy: International Edition,* Special Reports, no. 6 (December).

BBC. 1996. *France Halts Nuclear Testing.* January 29. http://news.bbc.co.uk/onthisday/hi/dates/stories/january/29/newsid_4665000/4665676.stm.

Berry, Ken, Patricia Lewis, Benoît Pélopidas, Nikolai Sokov, and Ward Wilson. 2010. *Delegitimizing Nuclear Weapons: Examining the Validity of Nuclear Deterrence.* Monterey, CA: James Martin Center for Nonproliferation Studies, Monterey Institute of International Studies.

Borrie, John, Tim Caughley, and Wilfred Wan, eds. 2017. *Understanding Nuclear Weapon Risks.* Geneva: United Nations Institute for Disarmament Research (UNIDIR), UNIDIR Resources.

Bourne, Mike. 2019. "Powers of the Gun: Process and Possibility in Global Small Arms Control." In *Regulating Global Security: Insights from Conventional and Unconventional*

Regimes, edited by Nik Hynek, Ondrej Ditrych, and Vit Stritecky, 143–68. Cham: Palgrave Macmillan.

Boyd, Dallas, and James Scouras. 2013. "Escape from Nuclear Deterrence: Lessons for Global Zero from the Strategic Defense Initiative." *Nonproliferation Review* 20, no. 2: 339–60.

Brett, Patricia. 2009. "The Dilemma of Aging Nuclear Plants." *New York Times*, October 19. https://www.nytimes.com/2009/10/20/business/global/20renuke.html.

Caughley, Tim. 2013. "Tracing Notions about Humanitarian Consequences." In *Viewing Nuclear Weapons through a Humanitarian Lens*, edited by John Borrie and Tim Caughley, 14–28. Geneva: United Nations Institute for Disarmament Research (UNIDIR), United Nations Publications.

Chernobyl Forum. 2003–2005. *Chernobyl's Legacy: Health, Environmental and Socio-Economic Impacts and Recommendations to the Governments of Belarus, the Russian Federation and Ukraine.* Second revised version. https://www.iaea.org/sites/default/files/chernobyl.pdf.

Cimbala, Stephen J. 2017. "Nuclear Arms Control under Trump and Putin: End of the Road?" *The Journal of Slavic Military Studies* 30, no. 2: 170–86.

Cirincione, Joseph, Jon B. Wolfsthal, and Miriam Rajkumar. 2005. *Deadly Arsenals: Nuclear, Biological, and Chemical Threats.* Second edition. Washington, DC: Carnegie Endowment for International Peace.

CND [Campaign for Nuclear Disarmament]. n.d.-a. *Who We Are.* Accessed November 10, 2019. https://cnduk.org/who/.

———. n.d.-b. *Scrap Trident Petition: Time to Stop Trident.* Accessed November 2, 2019. https://cnduk.org/actions/time-stop-trident/.

Colby, Elbridge. 2016. "A World Order Critique of Nuclear Abolition." In *Global Nuclear Disarmament: Strategic, Political, and Regional Perspectives*, edited by Nik Hynek and Michal Smetana, 159–73. New York: Routledge.

Collina, Tom Z. 2013. "UN Vote Backs Talks on Nuclear Arms Ban." *Arms Control Association.* December. https://www.armscontrol.org/act/2013_12/UN-Vote-Backs-Talks-on-Nuclear-Arms-Ban.

Cossa, Ralph A., and Brad Glosserman. 2011. "Extended Deterrence and Disarmament." *Nonproliferation Review* 18, no. 1: 125–45.

Cross, Mai'a K. Davis. 2013. "Rethinking Epistemic Communities Twenty Years Later." *Review of International Studies* 39: 137–60.

Daryl Kimball. n.d. "The Nuclear Testing Tally." *Arms Control Association.* Fact Sheets and Briefs. Last updated February 2019. https://www.armscontrol.org/factsheets/nucleartesttally.

Drezner, Daniel W. 2009. "The Power and Peril of International Regime Complexity." *Perspectives on Politics* 7, no. 1 (March): 65–70.

Emmers, Ralf. 2013. "Securitization." In *Contemporary Security Studies*, third edition, edited by Alan Collins, 131–45. Oxford: Oxford University Press.

EP [European Parliament]. 2005. *European Parliament Resolution on the Non-Proliferation Treaty 2005 Review Conference—Nuclear Arms in North Korea and Iran.* (2005/2518(RSP)). Texts adopted, March 10, 2005. https://www.europarl.europa.eu/sides/getDoc.do?type=TA&reference=P6-TA-2005-0075&language=EN.

———. 2016. *European Parliament Resolution on Nuclear Security and Non-Proliferation.* (2016/2936(RSP)). Joint Motion for a Resolution, October 25. https://www.europarl.europa.eu/doceo/document/RC-8-2016-1122_EN.html.

Evans, Gareth, and Yoriko Kawaguchi (cochairs). 2009. *Eliminating Nuclear Threats: A Practical Agenda for Global Policymakers.* Report of the International Commission on Nuclear Non-Proliferation and Disarmament. Canberra: International Commission on Nuclear Non-Proliferation and Disarmament.

Fihn, Beatrice. 2017. "The Logic of Banning Nuclear Weapons." *Survival* 59, no. 1 (February–March): 43–50.

Fortin, Katharine. 2012. "Complementarity between the ICRC and the United Nations and International Humanitarian Law and International Human Rights Law, 1948–1968." *International Review of the Red Cross* 94, no. 888 (Winter): 1433–54.

Global Zero. n.d. *About Global Zero.* Accessed November 4, 2019. https://www.globalzero.org.

Guterres, António. 2018. "Foreword." May 24. In *Securing Our Common Future. An Agenda for Disarmament.* New York: United Nations Office for Disarmament Affairs (UNODA). https://s3.amazonaws.com/unoda-web/wp-content/uploads/2018/06/sg-disarmament-agenda-pubs-page.pdf#view=Fit.

Haggard, Stephan, and Marcus Noland. 2012. "Engaging North Korea: The Efficacy of Sanctions and Inducements." In *Sanctions, Statecraft, and Nuclear Proliferation*, edited by Etel Solingen, 232–60. Cambridge: Cambridge University Press.

Herspring, Dale R. 2011. "Russian Nuclear and Conventional Weapons: The Broken Relationship." In *Russian Nuclear Weapons: Past, Present, and Future*, edited by Stephen J. Blank, 1–31. Carlisle, PA: US Army War College, Strategic Studies Institute.

Hynek, Nik. 2010. "Missile Defence Discourses and Practices in Relevant Modalities of 21st-Century Deterrence." *Security Dialogue* 41, no. 4: 435–59.

———. 2016. "Missile Defense, Deterrence, and Denuclearization Prospects." In *Global Nuclear Disarmament: Strategic, Political, and Regional Perspectives*, edited by Nik Hynek and Michal Smetana, 94–103. New York: Routledge.

———. 2018a. "Theorizing International Security Regimes: A Power-Analytical Approach." *International Politics* 55, no. 3–4 (May): 352–68.

———. 2018b. "Re-Visioning Morality and Progress in the Security Domain: Insights from Humanitarian Prohibition Politics." *International Politics* 55, no. 3–4 (May): 421–40.

IAEA [International Atomic Energy Agency]. 2019. "Incidents of Nuclear and Other Radioactive Material Out of Regulatory Control." *IAEA Incident and Trafficking Database (ITDB).* Fact Sheet, April 19. https://www.iaea.org/sites/default/files/19/04/itdb-factsheet-2019.pdf.

IALANA [International Association of Lawyers Against Nuclear Arms]. n.d. *Who We Are.* Accessed November 10, 2019. https://www.ialana.info/about-us/who-we-are/.

ICAN [International Campaign to Abolish Nuclear Weapons]. 2013. *Unspeakable Suffering.* February 28. http://www.icanw.org/campaign-news/global/unspeakable-suffering-a-comprehensive-report-on-devastating-impact-of-nuclear-weapons/.

———. 2014a. *Banning Nuclear Weapons: A Pacific Islands Perspective.* January. http://www.icanw.org/wp-content/uploads/2014/01/ICAN-PacificReport-FINAL-email.pdf.

———. 2014b. *The World Council of Churches Pushes for a Prohibition on Nuclear Weapons.* July 10. http://www.icanw.org/campaign-news/the-world-council-of-churches-pushes-for-a-prohibition-on-nuclear-weapons/.

———. 2016a. *Four Leading Health Federations Warn: Nuclear Weapons Must Be Prohibited.* May 2. http://www.icanw.org/campaign-news/four-leading-health-federations-warn-nuclear-weapons-must-be-prohibited/.

———. 2016b. *European Parliament Votes in Favour of a Ban.* October 27. http://www.icanw.org/campaign-news/european-parliament-calls-on-eu-member-states-to-prohibit-nuclear-weapons/.

———. 2016c. *UK's Biggest Anti-Nuclear March in a Generation.* March 2. http://www.icanw.org/campaign-news/britains-biggest-anti-nuclear-march-in-a-generation/.

———. 2016d. *Is Your Bank Ready for the Ban?* December 7. http://www.icanw.org/action/is-your-bank-ready-for-the-ban/.

———. 2016e. *Indigenous Women Call for Ban on Nuclear Weapons.* April 4. http://www.icanw.org/campaign-news/indigenous-women-call-for-a-nuclear-weapon-ban/.

———. 2016f. *Nobel Laureates Urge Nations to Support a Ban.* October 24. http://www.icanw.org/campaign-news/nobel-laureates-urge-nations-to-support-a-ban/.

———. 2016g. *Britain Renews Commitment to Nuclear Weapons*. July 19. http://www.icanw.org/campaign-news/britain-renews-commitment-to-nuclear-weapons/
.

———. 2016h. *The United States Tests New, Smaller Nuclear Weapons*. January 18. http://www.icanw.org/campaign-news/the-united-states-tests-new-smaller-nuclear-weapons/.

———. 2016i. *Cambridge, Massachusetts Divests from Nuclear Weapons Production*. April 3. http://www.icanw.org/campaign-news/cambridge-massachusetts-divests-from-nuclear-weapons-production/.

———. 2016j. *German Public Rejects Nuclear Weapons*. March 23. http://www.icanw.org/campaign-news/german-public-rejects-nuclear-weapons/.

———. 2016k. *Hibakusha Appeal for a Nuclear Ban Treaty*. December 8. http://www.icanw.org/campaign-news/hibakusha-appeal-for-a-nuclear-ban-treaty/.

———. 2017a. *Australian Nuclear Test Survivor Speaks at UN*. March 28. http://www.icanw.org/campaign-news/australia/australian-nuclear-test-survivor-speaks-up-at-the-un-ban-negotiations/.

———. 2017b. *North Korea Carries Out New Missile Test*. September 15. http://www.icanw.org/campaign-news/north-korea-carries-out-new-missile-test/.

———. 2017c. *Italy's Parliamentarians Spearhead Efforts to Ratify Ban Treaty*. October 25. http://www.icanw.org/campaign-news/italys-parliamentarians-spearhead-efforts-to-ratify-ban-treaty/.

———. 2018a. *India and Russia Are Testing Nuclear Missiles: Where Is the Global Outcry?* June 6. http://www.icanw.org/campaign-news/india-and-russia-test-nuclear-missiles/.

———. 2018b. *New Research: 35 States Are Sabotaging the NPT*. April 23. http://www.icanw.org/campaign-news/new-research-35-states-are-sabotaging-the-npt/.

———. 2018c. *New Poll: Europeans Reject US Nuclear Weapons on Own Soil*. July 6. http://www.icanw.org/campaign-news/yougov-poll-europeans-reject-us-nuclear-weapons-support-tpnw-nuclearba/.

———. 2018d. *Both Houses of Swiss Parliament Call on Government to Join the Nuclear Ban Treaty Immediately*. December 12. http://www.icanw.org/campaign-news/both-houses-of-swiss-parliament-call-on-government-to-sign-the-nuclear-ban-treaty/.

———. 2019a. *EU Elections: ICAN Urges MEPs to Join the ICAN Parliamentary Pledge*. May 21. http://www.icanw.org/campaign-news/eu-elections-ican-urges-meps-to-join-the-ican-parliamentary-pledge/.

———. 2019b. *Advancing the TPNW: African States Leading the Process*. June. http://www.icanw.org/wp-content/uploads/2019/06/ICAN-briefing-note-on-African-Adherence-to-TPNW-EN-A4.pdf.

———. 2019c. *The Story of a Nuclear Test Veteran*. May 29. http://www.icanw.org/campaign-news/the-story-of-a-nuclear-test-veteran/.

———. 2019d. *New Study on US-Russia Nuclear War: 91.5 Million Casualties in First Few Hours*. September 18. http://www.icanw.org/campaign-news/new-study-on-us-russia-nuclear-war-91-5-million-casualties-in-first-few-hours/.

———. 2019e. *Climate Disruption: New Study Highlights the Devastating Global Impact of Regional Nuclear Conflict Between India and Pakistan*. October 2. http://www.icanw.org/campaign-news/climate-disruption-new-study-highlights-the-devastating-global-impact-of-regional-nuclear-conflict-between-india-and-pakistan/.

———. 2019f. *Disappointing Report from the Swedish Inquiry into Joining Nuclear Ban Treaty*. January 18. http://www.icanw.org/campaign-news/sweden-inquiry-into-joining-nuclear-ban-treaty/.

———. 2019g. *A Big Step Backwards: Why Sweden's Decision not to Sign TPNW Damages Its Reputation as a Leader on Disarmament*. July 14. http://www.icanw.org/campaign-news/a-big-step-backwards-why-swedens-decision-not-to-sign-tpnw-damages-its-reputation-as-a-leader-on-disarmament/.

————. 2019h. *These Are the Banks and Financial Institutions Investing $748 Billion in Nuclear Weapon Producers.* June 5. http://www.icanw.org/action/these-are-the-banks-and-financial-institutions-investing-748-billion-in-nuclear-weapon-producers/.

————. 2019i. *These Are the 36 Banks, Pension Funds and Insurers Taking a Stand Against Nuclear Weapons.* October 17. http://www.icanw.org/campaign-news/these-are-the-36-banks-pension-funds-and-insurers-taking-a-stand-against-nuclear-weapons/.

————. 2019j. *12 States Join the Nuclear Ban Treaty on International Day for the Total Elimination of Nuclear Weapons 2019.* September 27. http://www.icanw.org/campaign-news/12-states-join-the-nuclear-ban-treaty-on-international-day-for-the-total-elimination-of-nuclear-weapons-2019/.

————. 2019k. *South Africa: From Nuclear Armed State to Disarmament Hero.* February 25. http://www.icanw.org/campaign-news/south-africa-from-nuclear-armed-state-to-disarmament-hero/.

————. 2019l. *Polls: Public Opinion in EU Host States Firmly Opposes Nuclear Weapons.* April 24. http://www.icanw.org/campaign-news/polls-public-opinion-in-eu-host-states-firmly-opposes-nuclear-weapons/.

————. 2019m. *84% of Finns Want the Government to Join the TPNW.* November 8. http://www.icanw.org/campaign-news/84-of-finns-want-the-government-to-join-the-tpnw/.

————. n.d.-a. *Humanitarian Initiative: Timeline.* Accessed November 1, 2019. http://www.icanw.org/campaign/humanitarian-initiative/.

————. n.d.-b. *Campaign Milestones 2007.* Accessed November 3, 2019. http://www.icanw.org/campaign/campaign-overview/campaign-milestones-2007/.

————. n.d.-c. *Parliamentary Pledge.* Accessed November 6, 2019. http://www.icanw.org/projects/pledge/.

————. n.d.-d. *Campaign Milestones 2008.* Accessed November 3, 2019. http://www.icanw.org/campaign/campaign-overview/campaign-milestones-2008/.

————. n.d.-e. *Campaign Milestones 2006.* Accessed November 1, 2019. http://www.icanw.org/campaign/campaign-overview/campaign-timeline/.

————. n.d.-f. *Campaign Milestones 2010.* Accessed November 1, 2019. http://www.icanw.org/campaign/campaign-overview/campaign-milestones-2010/.

————. n.d.-g. *Signature/Ratification Status of the Treaty on the Prohibition of Nuclear Weapons.* Accessed November 1, 2019. http://www.icanw.org/status-of-the-treaty-on-the-prohibition-of-nuclear-weapons/.

————. n.d.-h. *Setsuko Thurlow: Hiroshima Survivor and ICAN Campaigner.* Accessed November 3, 2019. http://www.icanw.org/setsuko-thurlow/.

————. n.d.-i. *Parliamentary Appeal.* Accessed November 10, 2019. http://www.icanw.org/projects/appeal/.

————. n.d.-j. *ICAN Parliamentary Pledge.* Accessed November 1, 2019. http://www.icanw.org/projects/pledge/.

ICNND [International Commission on Nuclear Non-proliferation and Disarmament]. n.d. *ICNND Research Papers Now Available Online in Social Networks.* Accessed November 2, 2019. http://www.icnnd.org.

INES [International Network of Engineers and Scientists for Global Responsibility]. n.d. *About INES.* Accessed November 15, 2019. http://inesglobal.net/ineshome/about-ines/.

IPB [International Peace Bureau]. n.d. *Who We Are.* Accessed November 10, 2019. http://www.ipb.org/who-we-are/.

IPPNW [International Physicians for the Prevention of Nuclear War]. n.d. *IPPNW: A Brief History.* Accessed November 15, 2019. https://www.ippnw.org/history.html.

Johnson, Rebecca. n.d. "The United Nations and Disarmament Treaties." *UN Chronicle.* Accessed November 11, 2019. https://www.un.org/en/chronicle/article/united-nations-and-disarmament-treaties.

Kapur, S. Paul. 2009. "Deterring Nuclear Terrorists." In *Complex Deterrence: Strategy in the Global Age*, edited by T. V. Paul, Patrick M. Morgan, and James J. Wirtz, 109–32. Chicago: University of Chicago Press.

Kmentt, Alexander. 2019. "Can the NPT and the TPNW Co-Exist?" *Beyond Nuclear International*. May 4. https://beyondnuclearinternational.org/2019/05/04/can-the-npt-and-the-tpnw-co-exist/.

Krause, Keith. 2002. "Multilateral Diplomacy, Norm Building, and UN Conferences: The Case of Small Arms and Light Weapons." Review Essay. *Global Governance* 8, no. 2 (April–June): 247–63.

Kristensen, Hans M. 2017. "The Quest for More Useable Nuclear Weapons." In *Understanding Nuclear Weapon Risks*, edited by John Borrie, Tim Caughley, and Wilfred Wan, 33–44. Geneva: United Nations Institute for Disarmament Research (UNIDIR), UNIDIR Resources.

Kurosawa, Mitsuru. 2018. "Stigmatizing and Delegitimizing Nuclear Weapons." *Journal for Peace and Nuclear Disarmament* 1, no. 1: 32–48.

Løvold, Magnus, Beatrice Fihn, and Thomas Nash. 2013. "Humanitarian Perspectives and the Campaign for an International Ban on Nuclear Weapons." In *Viewing Nuclear Weapons through a Humanitarian Lens*, edited by John Borrie and Tim Caughley, 145–56. Geneva: United Nations Institute for Disarmament Research (UNIDIR), United Nations Publications.

Lynch, Timothy J., ed. 2013. *The Oxford Encyclopedia of American Military and Diplomatic History*—"Nuclear Weapons and Strategy: Nuclear Counter-Proliferation after the Cold War." Oxford: Oxford University Press.

Maresca, Lou. 2013. "The Catastrophic Humanitarian Consequences of Nuclear Weapons: The Key Issues and Perspective of the International Committee of the Red Cross." In *Viewing Nuclear Weapons through a Humanitarian Lens*, edited by John Borrie and Tim Caughley, 131–44. Geneva: United Nations Institute for Disarmament Research (UNIDIR), United Nations Publications.

Marks, Paul. 2008. "Anti-Landmine Campaigners Turn Sights on War Robots." *New Scientist*, March 28. https://www.newscientist.com/article/dn13550-anti-landmine-campaigners-turn-sights-on-war-robots/.

MfP [Mayors for Peace]. n.d.-a. *About Us: Outline, Mission, Structure*. Accessed November 4, 2019. http://www.mayorsforpeace.org/english/outlines/index.html.

———. n.d.-b. *2020 Vision: An Emergency Campaign to Ban Nuclear Weapons—Outline*. Accessed November 7, 2019. http://www.mayorsforpeace.org/english/ecbn/index.html.

———. n.d.-c. *2020 Vision: An Emergency Campaign to Ban Nuclear Weapons—Resolutions of Support*. Accessed November 7, 2019. http://www.mayorsforpeace.org/english/ecbn/resolution.html.

MPI [Middle Powers Initiative]. n.d.-a. *History and Achievements*. Accessed November 3, 2019. http://www.middlepowers.org/history-achievements/.

———. n.d.-b. *Home Page*. Accessed November 1, 2019. http://www.middlepowers.org.

Nader, Alireza. 2012. "Influencing Iran's Decisions on the Nuclear Program." In *Sanctions, Statecraft, and Nuclear Proliferation*, edited by Etel Solingen, 211–31. Cambridge: Cambridge University Press.

NATO [North Atlantic Treaty Organization]. n.d. *NATO's Nuclear Deterrence Policy and Forces*. Last updated October 25, 2019. https://www.nato.int/cps/en/natohq/topics_50068.htm?selectedLocale=en.

Nobel Peace Summit. 2002. *Water Emergency and Other Emergencies of the Planet: Final Statement*. The 3rd World Summit of Nobel Peace Laureates, Rome, October 18–21. http://www.nobelpeacesummit.com/wp-content/uploads/2017/02/2002-Final-Declaration.pdf.

———. 2006. *Atom for Peace or Atom for War? Final Statement*. The 7th World Summit of Nobel Peace Laureates, Rome, November 17–19. http://

www.nobelpeacesummit.com/wp-content/uploads/2017/02/2006-Final-Declaration.pdf.

———. 2013. *Human Solidarity— A Foundation of Peace and Stability: Final Statement*. The 13th World Summit of Nobel Peace Laureates, Warsaw, October 23. http://www.nobelpeacesummit.com/wp-content/uploads/2017/02/2013-Final-Declaration.pdf.

———. 2014. *Living Peace: Final Statement*. The 14th World Summit of Nobel Peace Laureates, Rome, December 12–14. http://www.nobelpeacesummit.com/wp-content/uploads/2017/02/2014-Final-Declaration.pdf.

———. 2017. *Building Roads to Peace: Final Statement*. The 16th Nobel Peace Laureates Summit, Bogotá, February 4. http://www.nobelpeacesummit.com/wp-content/uploads/2017/02/2017-Final-Statement-XVI-Nobel-ENGLISH.pdf.

———. 2019. *Make Your Mark For Peace: Final Declaration*. The 17th Nobel Peace Laureates Summit, Mérida, September 22. http://www.nobelpeacesummit.com/make-your-mark-for-peace-final-declaration-of-the-17th-nobel-peace-summit/.

NSG [Nuclear Suppliers Group]. n.d. *Participants*. Accessed November 4, 2019. https://www.nuclearsuppliersgroup.org/en/about-nsg/participants1.

OSCE [Organization for Security and Co-Operation in Europe]. n.d. *Who We Are*. Accessed November 14, 2019. https://www.osce.org/whatistheosce.

Palkki, David D., and Shane Smith. 2012. "Contrasting Causal Mechanisms: Iraq and Lybia." In *Sanctions, Statecraft, and Nuclear Proliferation*, edited by Etel Solingen, 261–96. Cambridge: Cambridge University Press.

Patton, Tamara, Pavel Podvig, and Phillip Schell. 2013. *A New START Model for Transparency in Nuclear Disarmament*. Geneva: United Nations Institute for Disarmament Research (UNIDIR), United Nations Publications.

Paul, T. V. 2009. *The Tradition of Non-Use of Nuclear Weapons*. Stanford, CA: Stanford University Press.

———. 2016. "Nuclear Abolition: Strategic Context and Constraints." In *Global Nuclear Disarmament: Strategic, Political, and Regional Perspectives*, edited by Nik Hynek and Michal Smetana, 15–30. New York: Routledge.

Paulsen, Richard A. 1994. *The Role of US Nuclear Weapons in the Post-Cold War Era*. Maxwell AFB, AL: Maxwell Airforce Base, Air University Press.

PAX. 2019. "Producing Mass Destruction: Private Companies and the Nuclear Weapon Industry," authored by Susi Snyder. *Don't Bank on the Bomb*. Utrecht, May. https://www.dontbankonthebomb.com/wp-content/uploads/2019/05/2019_Producers-Report-FINAL.pdf.

Perkovich, George, and James M. Acton, eds. 2009. *Abolishing Nuclear Weapons: A Debate*. Washington, DC: Carnegie Endowment for International Peace.

Persbo, Andreas. 2016. "Verification and Nuclear Disarmament." In *Global Nuclear Disarmament: Strategic, Political, and Regional Perspectives*, edited by Nik Hynek and Michal Smetana, 75–93. New York: Routledge.

PGS [Physicians for Global Survival]. n.d. *About PGS*. Accessed November 12, 2019. https://pgs.ca/?page_id=2.

PNND [Parliamentarians for Nuclear Non-Proliferation and Disarmament]. 2014. *World Body of Parliaments Calls for Negotiations to Abolish Nuclear Weapons*. March 23. http://pnnd.org/article/world-body-parliaments-calls-negotiations-abolish-nuclear-weapons.

———. 2018. *OSCE Parliamentarians Call for Confidence Building Measures Including No-First-Use of Nuclear Weapons*. July 11. http://www.pnnd.org/article/osce-parliamentarians-call-confidence-building-measures-including-no-first-use-nuclear.

———. n.d. *What Is PNND?* Accessed November 2, 2019. http://www.pnnd.org/what-pnnd-0.

Pompeo, Michael R. 2019. "U.S. Withdrawal from the INF Treaty on August 2, 2019." *US Department of State*. Press Statement, August 2. https://www.state.gov/u-s-withdrawal-from-the-inf-treaty-on-august-2-2019/.

Price, Richard. 1995. "A Genealogy of the Chemical Weapons Taboo." *International Organization* 49, no. 1: 73–103.

———. 1998. "Reversing the Gun Sights: Transnational Civil Society Targets Land Mines." *International Organization* 52, no. 3 (Summer): 613–44.

Public Statement. 2018. *Public Statement by Faith Communities Concerned about Nuclear Weapons.* Submitted to the 2018 UN General Assembly First Committee, October. https://20561860-86b7-4801-a5d6-af3a3b4e6a59.filesusr.com/ugd/dca5da_cd7626f7eb784339bededc9d29854f53.pdf.

RCW [Reaching Critical Will]. 2013a. *Preventing Collapse: The NPT and A Ban on Nuclear Weapons,* authored by Ray Acheson and Beatrice Fihn. October. http://www.reachingcriticalwill.org/images/documents/Publications/npt-ban.pdf.

———. 2013b. *Unspeakable Suffering: The Humanitarian Impact of Nuclear Weapons,* edited by Beatrice Fihn. February. http://www.reachingcriticalwill.org/resources/publications-and-research/publications/7422-unspeakable-suffering-the-humanitarian-impact-of-nuclear-weapons.

Ritchie, Nick. 2013. "Legitimizing and Delegitimizing Nuclear Weapons." In *Viewing Nuclear Weapons through a Humanitarian Lens,* edited by John Borrie and Tim Caughley, 44–77. Geneva: United Nations Institute for Disarmament Research (UNIDIR), United Nations Publications.

Ruhlman, Molly A. 2015. *Who Participates in Global Governance? States, Bureaucracies, and NGOs in the United Nations.* New York: Routledge.

Ruzicka, Jan. 2019. "Nuclear Non-Proliferation Regime: Between Prevention and Prohibition." In *Regulating Global Security: Insights from Conventional and Unconventional Regimes,* edited by Nik Hynek, Ondrej Ditrych, and Vit Stritecky, 53–76. Cham: Palgrave Macmillan.

Ruzicka, Jan, and Nicholas J. Wheeler. 2016. "Trust Building in Nuclear Disarmament." In *Global Nuclear Disarmament: Strategic, Political, and Regional Perspectives,* edited by Nik Hynek and Michal Smetana, 31–43. New York: Routledge.

Sagan, Scott D. 1989. *Moving Targets: Nuclear Strategy and National Security.* Princeton, NJ: Princeton University Press.

Salter, Mark B. 2008. "Securitization and Desecuritization: A Dramaturgical Analysis of the Canadian Air Transport Security Authority." *Journal of International Relations and Development* 11: 321–49.

Sauer, Tom, and Mathias Reveraert. 2018. "The Potential Stigmatizing Effect of the Treaty on the Prohibition of Nuclear Weapons." *The Nonproliferation Review* 25, no. 5–6: 437–55.

Schell, J. 1984. *The Abolition.* New York: Alfred A. Knopf.

Schneiker, Andrea. 2016. *Humanitarian NGOs, (In)Security and Identity: Epistemic Communities and Security Governance.* New York: Routledge.

Scott, Harriet Fast. 1992. "Soviet Military Doctrine in the Nuclear Age, 1945–1985." In *Soviet Military Doctrine from Lenin to Gorbachev: 1915–1991,* edited by Willard C. Frank and Philip S. Gillette, 175–92. Westport, CT: Greenwood Press.

Shamai, Patricia. 2015. "Name and Shame: Unravelling the Stigmatization of Weapons of Mass Destruction." *Contemporary Security Policy* 36, no. 1: 104–22.

Shoumikhin, Andrei. 2011. "Nuclear Weapons in Russian Strategy and Doctrine." In *Russian Nuclear Weapons: Past, Present, and Future,* edited by Stephen J. Blank, 99–160. Carlisle, PA: US Army War College, Strategic Studies Institute.

Simons Foundation. 2007. *Global Public Opinion on Nuclear Weapons.* Vancouver, September. http://www.thesimonsfoundation.ca/sites/default/files/2007%20Poll%20on%20Global%20Public%20Opinion%20on%20Attitudes%20Towards%20Nuclear%20Weapons_0.pdf.

Tannenwald, Nina. 2005. "Stigmatizing the Bomb: Origins of the Nuclear Taboo." *International Security* 29, no. 4 (Spring): 5–49.

———. 2016. "Normative Strategies for Disarmament." In *Global Nuclear Disarmament: Strategic, Political, and Regional Perspectives,* edited by Nik Hynek and Michal Smetana, 107–21. New York: Routledge.

———. 2018. "The Vanishing Nuclear Taboo? How Disarmament Fell Apart." *Foreign Affairs* 97, no. 6 (November/December): 16–24.

UN [United Nations]. n.d. *Conference on Disarmament: An Introduction to the Conference.* Accessed November 1, 2019. https://www.unog.ch/80256EE600585943/(httpPages)/BF18ABFEFE5D344DC1256F3100311CE9?OpenDocument.

Unal, Beyza, and Patricia Lewis. 2017. "Cyber Threats and Nuclear Weapons Systems." In *Understanding Nuclear Weapon Risks,* edited by John Borrie, Tim Caughley, and Wilfred Wan, 61–72. Geneva: United Nations Institute for Disarmament Research (UNIDIR), UNIDIR Resources.

UNFOLD ZERO. 2016. *Chain Reaction: A Global Action for Nuclear Disarmament.* July 8–October 2. http://www.unfoldzero.org/get-involved/chain-reaction-2016/.

———. 2018. *A Divided UN General Assembly Votes on Nuclear Disarmament Resolutions.* November 7. http://www.unfoldzero.org/a-divided-un-general-assembly-votes-on-nuclear-disarmament-resolutions/.

———. n.d.-a. *About Us.* Accessed November 3, 2019. http://www.unfoldzero.org/about-us/.

———. n.d.-b. *Nuclear Zero World Court Case—Take Action: Sign the Petition. Ask Your Government to Join the Lawsuit.* Accessed November 3, 2019. http://www.unfoldzero.org/get-involved/nuclear-zero-world-court-case/.

———. n.d.-c. *Take Action: Sign the Global Zero Petition.* Accessed November 1, 2019. http://www.unfoldzero.org/get-involved/un-security-council/.

———. n.d.-d. *Take Action: #LetsTalkNukes.* Accessed November 2, 2019. http://www.unfoldzero.org/get-involved/oewg-2016/.

UNIDIR [United Nations Institute for Disarmament Research]. n.d.-a. *For a More Stable and Secure World.* Accessed November 1, 2019. https://www.unidir.org/about.

———. n.d.-b. *Weapons of Mass Destruction and Other Strategic Weapons.* Accessed November 13, 2019. https://www.unidir.org/programmes/weapons-mass-destruction-and-other-strategic-weapons.

UNODA [United Nations Office for Disarmament Affairs]. n.d.-a. *Nuclear Weapons.* Accessed November 15, 2019. https://www.un.org/disarmament/wmd/nuclear/.

———. n.d.-b. *NPT Review Conferences and Preparatory Committees.* Accessed November 13, 2019. https://www.un.org/disarmament/wmd/nuclear/npt-review-conferences/.

———. n.d.-c. *High Representative's Statements.* Accessed November 1, 2019. https://www.un.org/disarmament/hrstatement/.

UNSCEAR [United Nations Scientific Committee on the Effects of Atomic Radiation]. 2011. *Sources and Effects of Ionizing Radiation.* UNSCEAR 2008 Report to the General Assembly with Scientific Annexes, Vol. II, Scientific Annexes C, D, and E. Vienna: United Nations Office, United Nations Publication. http://www.unscear.org/docs/reports/2008/11-80076_Report_2008_Annex_C.pdf.

Vultee, Fred. 2011. "Securitization as a Media Frame: What Happens When the Media 'Speak Security.'" In *Understanding Securitisation Theory: How Security Problems Emerge and Dissolve,* edited by Thierry Balzacq, 77–93. New York: Routledge.

Ware, Alyn. 2016. "Advocacy Networks and A World Free of Nuclear Weapons." In *Global Nuclear Disarmament: Strategic, Political, and Regional Perspectives,* edited by Nik Hynek and Michal Smetana, 122–44. New York: Routledge.

Weiss, Leonard. 2007. "U.S.-India Nuclear Cooperation." *Nonproliferation Review* 14, no. 3: 429–57.

Whitney, Craig R. 1996. "France Ending Nuclear Tests that Caused Broad Protests." *New York Times.* January 30. https://www.nytimes.com/1996/01/30/world/france-ending-nuclear-tests-that-caused-broad-protests.html.

WHO [World Health Organization]. 1987. *Effects of Nuclear War on Health and Health Services.* Second edition. Report of the WHO Management Group on Follow-Up of Resolution WHA 36.28. Geneva: World Health Organization. https://apps.who.int/iris/bitstream/handle/10665/39199/9241561092_%28p1-p82%29.pdf?sequence=1&isAllowed=y.

———. 2005. *Chernobyl: The True Scale of the Accident—20 Years Later a UN Report Provides Definitive Answers and Ways to Repair Lives.* Joint News Release WHO/IAEA/UNDP, September 5. https://www.who.int/mediacentre/news/releases/2005/pr38/en/.

Zangger Committee. n.d. *Members.* Accessed November 13, 2019. http://www.zanggercommittee.org/members.html.

SIX

On the Verge of Change?

"Killer Robots" and Security Regulation

This chapter aims to tailor the power-analytical approach to international regulatory/prohibition politics evolving around the security issue of Killer Robots. Currently in development, Killer Robots, or better still autonomous weapon systems (AWS), can be differentiated from all other weapon categories by a unique combination of attributes. First, they are fully autonomous. This presupposes their ability to engage in autonomous (lethal) decision making, autonomous (lethal) targeting, and autonomous (lethal) force. A crucial part of this autonomy is their ability to operate without human control or supervision in dynamic, unstructured, and open environments. Second, they could be used as offensive autonomous weapons. Third, these are advances in artificial intelligence (AI)—particularly in machine learning and artificial neural networks—that pave the way for and characterize fully autonomous (lethal) weapon systems (Solovyeva and Hynek 2018, 171). The so-called Campaign to Stop Killer Robots, though yet working preventively, features "the latest in a series of transnational advocacy campaigns in the area of humanitarian disarmament" (Carpenter 2016, 58). It has united more than a hundred nongovernmental organizations (NGOs) based in various countries, gained broad public support and successfully dragged into its agenda a good number of state governments, thousands of experts, over twenty Nobel Peace laureates, as well as elements of the United Nations (UN) and the European Union (EU) (CSKR n.d.-a, n.d.-b). The Convention on Certain Conventional Weapons (CCW) in Geneva has become the core global intergovernmental deliberation forum (Altmann and Sauer 2017, 132). The most hotly debated attribute of these technologies is machine autonomy with respect to life-and-death decisions. Given potential humanitar-

ian risks, critics call for a blanket preventive global ban on their development, production, and use (HRW 2012, 2014, 2016; Sharkey 2012, 799;
Asaro 2012, 709; Johnson and Axinn 2013, 137; Garcia 2015, 57; FLI 2015;
ICRAC n.d.). Others conversely argue that such risks might rather be
associated with a blanket prohibition on advanced autonomy in weapon
systems (Anderson and Waxman 2012, 39–45; Arkin 2018, 321). Individual governments' preferences are divided by a deep rift. Some of them
have either endorsed a full-fledged ban or considered a limited ban at the
most, while others have been either skeptical to such restrictions or explicitly opposed them altogether (CSKR 2019a). We seek to understand and
dissect the nature of the dynamics and conditions that have determined
the prospects and limitations of AWS security regulation. While there is
no global prohibition regime banning AWS, this chapter traces power
configurations related to attempts at establishing one and the articulated
resistance against it. Inter alia, multiple discursive, normative, legal, cultural, humanitarian, institutional, political, economic, strategic, and technological dynamics as well as various interstices between them are taken
into consideration. In doing so, we repeatedly draw parallels between the
selected case and other regulatory/prohibition precedents, including respective efforts.

TOWARD SECURITY REGULATION: LEGAL UNDERBRUSH AND "SEVERE" POLITICIZATION

There is currently no global security regime for fully autonomous (lethal)
weapon systems. However, two tightly intertwined strands of developments are relevant for interpreting the advancement on this front. First,
this chapter sheds light on the legal underbrush concerning AWS security
regulation. Second, the success of what might be termed the "severe politicization" (Emmers 2013, 137) of Killer Robots is put under the microscope. With regard to the former, two aspects are of importance. It is
certainly expected that AWS should fit with the readily established legal
framework. Primarily, these are International Humanitarian Law (IHL),
International Human Rights Law (IHRL), and the Charter of the United
Nations (UN) that regulate the use of force, the principle of political
responsibility, and the legality of weapons (Liu 2012, 638; Garcia 2015, 60;
Brehm 2017). Also falling to this category are the Draft Rules proposed by
the ICRC, which have proposed the prohibition of weapons with harmful, including uncontrollable and unforeseen, effects to the civilian population (ICRC 1956/1957; Mathews 2001, 992). The other relevant dimension of the legal backdrop is an emerging framework regulating the use
of cyberweapons and its implications for AWS. Such key international
mechanisms involve the Wassenaar Arrangement on Export Controls for
Conventional Arms and Dual-Use Goods and Technologies as well as the

Council of Europe Convention on Cybercrime (Stevens 2019, 271). Both, inter alia, concern digital information, software, computers, computer networks, and telecommunications (CoE 2001; WA 2018). AWS are often discussed with reference to cyberspace, cybervulnerability, cyberwarfare, cybercrime, or cyberterrorism (Liu 2012, 648; Schmitt 2013; Noone and Noone 2015, 33; Klincewicz 2015, 163 and 169–70; Sharkey 2017, 183). This is because AWS similarly feature (networks of) computers or software-controlled systems operating across the digital and the physical (Dehuri, Cho, and Ghosh 2011, 2; McFarland 2015, 1326–28; Altmann and Sauer 2017, 122–23; Hallaq et al. 2017; Gadiyar, Zhang, and Sankaranarayanan 2019; Um 2019, 1–3). Going beyond the legal background, the principal driving force of AWS international regulatory/prohibition politics is the Campaign to Stop Killer Robots. Formed in 2012 as a coalition of nongovernmental organizations, it has grown into a transnational political advocacy network, or a "global coalition," as per their self-designation (CSKR n.d.-a). Cutting through the thicket of legal, ethical, moral, philosophical, political-strategic, scientific, and military discourses, their agenda has deeply penetrated the political scene and the domain of security regulation. Their thrust has spread across global, regional, and local levels. Issue-specific and ad hoc calls, pledges, reports, open letters, directives, resolutions, and declarations have been produced by (groups of) individuals with diverse expertise, NGOs, technology companies, segments of global and regional intergovernmental organizations (IOs), and certain governments (Bolton, Nash, and Moyes 2012; HRW 2012; DoD 2012/2017; Heyns 2013, 2014; EP 2014; NWI 2014; Hennessey 2014; Nobel Peace Summit 2014; PAX 2014a; FLI 2015, n.d.; Kerr et al. 2017; Open Letter 2017a; Open Letter 2017b; Guterres 2018; Conn 2018; EP 2018a; OSCEPA 2019; CSKR n.d.-a, n.d.-b). Since 2013, systematic deliberations between nation-states have unfolded at the United Nations (CSKR 2013a; Altmann and Sauer 2017, 132).

All of the previously mentioned legal and political elements represent mere steps toward AWS security regulation but do not furnish one. As Stevens (2019, 271) concluded, the legal framework regulating cyberweapons is fragmented and only features piecemeal measures. Given the lessons from the case of cyberweapons, the applicability of more general international laws to regulate a "weaponized code" might also be severely contested (Stevens 2019, 287–88). At the same time, despite the great success of giving AWS a political footing, the issue has not become truly "securitized." This is evident with securitizing actors having not been granted a right to adopt extraordinary issue-specific measures beyond standard political procedures (Emmers 2013, 133–35). The inquiry into various related aspects and a systematic explanation of these shadowy dynamics of AWS legal and political governance are in order. Some analogies between the development and deficiency of a global cyberweapons regime and the case of AWS are drawn.

PRODUCTIVE POWER: STIGMATIZATION OF A "POLITICIZED" CONCEPT

This section focuses on the discursive and cognitive framing of AWS with a regulatory effect. Particular attention is paid to the related system of differentiation of political subjects into an ingroup or an outgroup. The goal is to assess the constructive power and prominence of this complex generated system of meanings with respect to AWS security regulation. Light is shed on the constitutive role of technologies and differences in their interpretation, legal conditions, production and transfer peculiarities, economic disparities, intellectual traditions and habitual practices, ethics, and culture.

Stigmatized under this speculative term by opponents, Killer Robots are "a historical imaginary of the twenty-first century" (Karppi, Böhlen, and Granata 2016, 120). This section concerns the construction of AWS as illegitimate military instruments. Proponents of their prohibition build up the case upon the convergence of deontology and consequentialism. From the perspective of the former, they denounce the automation of lethal decision making as by definition unacceptable in moral and ethical terms (Asaro 2012, 708–9; Zawieska 2017, 49). This deontological viewpoint is reinforced by multidimensional consequentialist reasoning. Such technologies are condemned by critics to "operate in a lawless zone" (Kastan 2013, 47). In the first place, they reputedly threaten to breach IHL and IHRL, including the principle of individual and state political responsibility and accountability for violations (Asaro 2008, 2012, 692–93). Similar and closely related concerns are raised with respect to the UN Charter norm of (non)use of force, the principle of legal review of (new) weapons codified in the additional protocol to the Geneva Convention, as well as the Martens Clause introduced in the second Hague Convention and the Geneva Convention additional protocols (Gubrud 2014, 40). As also discussed in the previous chapters, there is a repeated practice of employing similar foundations of legal arguments and humanitarian language in framing successive security regimes (Hynek 2018a). This is what Price (1998, 628) termed a tradition of legal "grafting." This conception conforms to the AWS case. Roughly the same legal set, in particular with its humanitarian provisions, served as the basis for previous weapons treaties such as the Chemical Weapons Convention, the Mine Ban Treaty, or the Convention on Cluster Munitions (Hynek 2018b). Though failing to score a global security regime, similar concerns have also been raised with respect to regulating cyberweapons (Stevens 2019). The premise of noncompliance in the case of AWS particularly lies with what is termed the "dehumanization of killing" (Wagner 2014, 1410) and "depersonalization of war" (Klincewicz 2015, 163). The former implies depriving combat of healthy human emotions and judgment (HRW 2012; Asaro 2012, 701; Johnson and Axinn 2013, 136; Wagner 2014, 1415; Sharkey 2017, 180). The latter stands for both the depersonalization of responsibility (Heyns 2016, 12) and the objectification of enemy (non)combatants (Sharkey 2012, 788; Korać 2018, 54). All of this is condemned as a threat to the fundamental values of human dignity and human life (Sparrow 2007, 68; Heyns 2013, 6; Johnson and Axinn 2013, 134; HRW 2014; Garcia 2015, 58–61; Heyns 2016, 3). The inability to conform to legal standards is often attributed to the unpredictable character of such technologies. It derives from the impossibility to code full-fledged intelligence in the first place, inherent software imperfections, and vulnerability to cyberattacks (Lin, Bekey, and Abney 2008, 20 and 78; Asaro 2012, 691; Klincewicz 2015, 167–70; Noone and Noone 2015, 33; Solovyeva and Hynek 2018, 172–76). What exacerbates the case is a warning that autonomous weapons might evolve into a mass product or "the Kalashnikovs of tomorrow" (FLI 2015). All combined, this technological turn is described with a reference to a revolution in warfare (FLI 2015). The alarm is given that this one is different from earlier military revolutions (Heyns 2013, 5) and represents a radical departure in strategic affairs (Payne 2018, 218). The most radical fears feature robots "running amok" and "destroying humankind" (Lin, Bekey, and Abney 2008, 63 and 78) and a "robot revolution" (Asaro 2008, 55). Elon Musk even denounced AI as "the biggest risk we face as a civilisation" (cited in *The Telegraph* 2017). Given all the risks, "do-gooders," that is, those working to ban AWS (CSKR n.d.-a), have drawn a sharp dividing line between themselves and the resistance. Having portrayed the removal of meaningful human control over the use of lethal force portrayed as unethical, irresponsible, immoral, and illegal (Asaro 2012, 695 and 708–9), they have particularly called this one a moral red line (CSKR 2019b) or a moral threshold (HRW 2016). While discussing the precedent of a preemptive ban, namely the one on blinding lasers, Human Rights Watch (2018) has recalled the notions of "civilized nations" or "civilization" and, on balance, that of "barbarity." Resembling the fate of nuclear and chemical weapons, this discursively (re)produced rift thus again delineates the ingroup of "normals" or the "civilized" (Price 1995, 95; Sauer and Reveraert 2018, 438; Hynek 2018a). Portrayed as an attribute of rich and elaborate economies, AWS technology further supports the implied stigmatization of the outgroup via fears of imbalanced and asymmetric warfare (Asaro 2008, 62–63; Garcia 2018, 339).

Structural conditions of emergence paved the way for the deep embeddedness of this discourse. The general condition of possibility was the traditional distinction between human and machine with respect to control over life and death (Karppi, Böhlen, and Granata 2016, 111–12). The deeply rooted history of technological advance produced a strong imaginary of weapons as "passive tools" (Bourne 2012, 142). It thus consolidated the dominant logic that "guns don't kill people, people do" (Latour 1999, 174). This contributed to the stigmatization of Killer Robots by contravening the hypothetically reversed logic that "guns don't kill people, cyborgs do" (Bourne 2012, 141). After the end of the Cold War, there also occurred a macroshift in the systemic ethical force. It was the replacement of *sovereignty* by *human rights* as the central force of compassion. This implies the concept of security having concentrated on a human dimension previously resting within the sovereign purview of states (Krause 2002, 260). Echoing the nineteenth-century humanitarian dispositif, this change featured the (re)constitution of an individual—be it soldier (earlier) or civilian (later)—as a referent object of security (Hynek 2018b). The established international legal framework(s) detailed earlier and, in particular, the principle of human dignity and the right to life facilitated the case (HRW 2014; Garcia 2015, 60–61; Heyns 2016, 8–10). A crucial challenge in this regard is that laws are generally imperfect, incomplete, and require human interpretation and judgment to apply to real-world situations (Asaro 2012, 700 and 705). Besides giving the key means for the cognitive framing of Killer Robots, these developments helped safely divert attention from the military utility of AWS. What is more, they unfolded against the background of a general rise of the economic within the political (Hynek 2018b). This transformation also had a formative impact for the Killer Robots discourse. It brought to the fore the interaction between this broader change in ethics and the typification of security and other structural forces, namely conflict and economy (Hynek 2018b). Of particular importance in this regard is the *stratified* global arms business/transfer system, involving domestic sales from companies to governments, (illicit) trade, and coproduction arrangements (Krause 1992, 205–15; Stavrianakis 2010, chap. 2). Regardless, it is crucial to note that civilian technologies are increasingly in the lead and the military often finds it preferable to adopt operating technologies from the commercial sector (Smith and Udis 2003, 102–3). Being a dual-use and easy-to-acquire technology, AWS have raised an enormous amount of related concerns (FLI 2015; Altmann and Sauer 2017, 132). What further contributed to this resistance was the increasing prominence of the concept of revolution in military affairs (RMA). Often associated with the notion of a radical shift (Krepinevich 1994; Cohen 1996, 43–51, 2004, 403; Gray 1996, 8–10, 2002, 67–68; Hundley 1999, 9; Sloan 2002, 3; Shimko 2010, 9–11; Horowitz 2010, 22–23, 2018, 46), it intellectually assisted in framing the revolutionary nature of Killer Robots. Their prohibitionary character was also coconstituted by deeply rooted science fiction and popular culture images and stereotypes (Carpenter 2016). Countless sci-fi films and novels played a remarkable role in creating the image of the robot that could potentially become self-aware and disobey its programming (Krishnan 2009, 7–8). This imaginary particularly reflected Western cultural representations of automata, as depicted in movies such as *The Terminator* (1984) or *I, Robot* (2004) (Karppi, Böhlen, and Granata 2016, 111). On top of this, security regulation precedents are of particular importance. Complete bans previously imposed upon certain military instruments such as biological and chemical weapons, antipersonnel landmines (APLs), and cluster munitions (CMs) encourage uncompromising ambitions in the case under consideration (Hynek 2018b). The "preemptive" ban on blinding lasers still features the key precedent (HRW 2018). The limited advancement of legal control of cyberweapons, as detailed earlier, in turn provides a starting point and precursor principles for AWS security regulation. What is even more important, the advocacy underwriting the case of cyberweapons embeds and complements the same polemic on AWS. Because existing international laws are barely applicable to the (insecure) nature of code and internet architecture, an issue-oriented global regime is considered indispensable to address such transnational challenges (Stevens 2019, 272, 280, and 287).

Well thought through, coherent, and deeply embedded, the Killer Robots discourse has gained a strong foothold. This is fair to claim that "a stigma is already becoming attached to the prospect of removing meaningful human control from weapons systems and the use of force" (CSKR 2019b). The central underlying goal of a global prohibition regime for (lethal) autonomous weapons has, however, not been achieved. Which explanations might already be discerned at the stage of scrutinizing the discourse? Though grounded in materiality and often likened to the cases of biological, chemical, gunpowder, and nuclear weapons (Heyns 2013, 5; FLI 2015; Singer 2009, 179 and 203), Killer Robots are less a physical entity than a "politicized" concept (Karppi, Böhlen, and Granata 2016, 111). Fully autonomous (lethal) weapons do not yet exist, barring the exception of precursor systems of various complexity (Walsh 2015, 2; Noone and Noone 2015, 28; Sauer 2016). Advocacy has apparently overrun practice. This controversy accounts for the failure to properly define and delineate the object of stigmatization (Horowitz 2016). A related concern is also that true autonomous weapons might severely challenge the distinction between weapons, methods of warfare, and warriors (Liu 2012, 628–29 and 636–37; Heyns 2013, 6). The situation echoes and exacerbates the setback of cyberweapons governance. The dual-use, digital, and unconventional (physical) nature of such technologies make their global prohibition or overregulation neither desirable nor possible in terms of verification, compliance, and enforcement (Stevens 2019, 272, 280, and 288; Denning 2000). Stigma politics apparently lack a meaningful practical basis within the AWS security issue area. Besides that, the Killer Robots discourse has grown essentially radical and exclusive. In attempts to push forward stigmatization of noncompliance and its performers, the exaggeration of the real state of affairs sometimes borders misinterpretation of reality. For example, there are warnings that Russia and the United States "attempt to legitimize killer robots" (CSKR 2019c). In reality, both states informally adhere to the principle of meaningful human control, to which their recent technological developments also testify (DoD 2012/2017; TASS 2018a, 2018b; Freedberg 2019; BBC 2019). This adherence

also goes in line with the generally affirmed principle of the human element in the use of (lethal) force, one of the ten common conclusions
within the CCW (CCW 2018, 4, 2019a, 4–5). Marginalizing or confronting
advantages of AWS in the military domain more generally, the Killer
Robots discourse meets a thrust of firmly grounded skepticism or sometimes even resistance. The latter also draws attention to the military utility and positive strategic implications of AWS as well as illusions and
biases guiding the prohibition discourse (Arkin 2010, 2017, 2018; Anderson and Waxman 2012, 2013; Schmitt 2013; Noone and Noone 2015, 33;
McFarland 2015, 1326–27 and 1338; Birnbacher 2016, 118–21; Solovyeva
and Hynek 2018). All these nuances, including differences in interpreting
AWS, have prevented the assembled discourse from becoming a dominant "regime of truth" (Foucault 1980, 131; Hynek 2018a).

STRUCTURAL POWER: FRAGMENTED SOCIAL STANCE AND TRANSNATIONAL HISTORICAL BLOC

The following lines analyze the power hierarchy and associated interests
defining the key stakeholders in the (emerging) domain of AWS. In doing
so, the structural position of the "do-gooders," that is, advocators and
endorsers of the preemptive ban on AWS, is carefully delineated. Based
on the discovered distribution of benefits, obligations, and objectives,
inferences are made with regard to their regulatory weight. The coalition
working to ban Killer Robots is composed of (international) nongovernmental organizations (I)NGOs and their various umbrellas, elements of
global and regional IOs, (like-minded) states, epistemic communities of
scientists, Nobel Peace laureates and Peace laureate organizations, faith
leaders, hi-tech business companies, and the mass media (CSKR 2017a,
n.d.-b). Multiple power heterarchies, with all of the actors in different
roles and capacities, are apparently involved. Each in exercise of the function—be it oriented on human rights, international peace or security,
non(armed)violence, nonproliferation or arms control, etc.—international, regional, and national (I)NGOs have flocked together under the umbrella of the Campaign to Stop Killer Robots for transnational political
advocacy work (CSKR n.d.-c). Structurally, an "effective and efficient"
relationship between nongovernmental or civil society organizations and
governments has been gradually set up in many liberal countries (Flora
1986; Gidron, Kramer, and Salamon 1992; Hynek 2018b). Such agencies
have even been considered better than governments in much of what
they do, including the promotion of a greater public awareness of international issues (Chrétien 1995; Hynek 2018b). With their functions limited mainly to consultation or observation, nongovernmental entities have
also penetrated the global (UN) system of governance via either formal or
informal mechanisms (Ruhlman 2015, 37–40). Recalling the small arms

case, for example, there is also a practice by states to include nongovernmental representatives on their national delegations (Krause 2002, 256). In this sense, (I)NGOs may potentially influence policy outcomes directly (bargaining power) or indirectly (agenda setting) (Krause 2002, 256). With converging agenda—inter alia, oriented on international peace and security, conflict prevention, arms control, and human rights (UNHRC n.d.; UNSG n.d.; EP n.d.; OSCEPA n.d.; OSCE n.d.-a)—some elements of global and regional IOs have expressed support for the prohibition of Killer Robots. Others have at least served as negotiation fora for the cause. Among them are the UN Secretary General (UNSG), the UN Security Council (UNSC), the UN General Assembly (UNGA), the UN Human Rights Council (UNHRC), the European Parliament (EP), the European Commission (EC), and the OSCE Parliamentary Assembly (OSCEPA) (UNGA 2018; EC 2018; AI HLEG 2019; HRW 2019c; EC n.d.; CSKR 2018b, n.d.-b). Acknowledged to be an important frame of securitization (Vultee 2011), media around the world have generously favored the case. Among those having covered the agenda are high-profile outlets such as the BBC, *The Independent, Forbes, The Guardian, The New York Times, The Washington Post, The Telegraph,* and the Thomson Reuters Foundation (CSKR 2014a, 2014b, 2015, 2017b, 2018a). It has also been intertwined with science fiction and fantasy, assumed to be increasingly "invoked by policy elites in service of arguments about the real world" (Carpenter 2016, 53).

However, the main venue for global (UN) deliberations, particularly for intergovernmental negotiations, has become the CCW in Geneva (Altmann and Sauer 2017, 132). Blocked by some treaty members or particularly great power interests, the CCW format has previously failed to ban APLs and CMs (Abramson 2017; Hynek 2018b). This is because political elites are the main actors in the global (UN) decision-making process (Basu 2004, 139). From the theoretical perspective, they are also believed to have an advantage over other actors in seeking to influence audiences and calling for the implementation of extraordinary measures (Emmers 2013, 134). Almost thirty states, including Algeria, Austria, Brazil, Costa Rica, Ghana, Guatemala, Jordan, Morocco, Nicaragua, Pakistan, Uganda, and Zimbabwe, have already objected to AWS (CSKR 2019a). Because this does not even constitute the majority, a political-economic insight is offered into their relative structural weight with respect to AWS regulatory politics. The global arms transfer and production system is stratified (Krause 1992, 206–10). The barriers to movement between tiers in such a system remain relatively high (Krause 1992, 206), whereby dominant actors concentrate on the pursuit of power in their arms exports (Krause 1992, 98). Possibly for these reasons, less technologically developed states have endorsed the ban while dominant producers and suppliers such as the United States or Russia (former Soviet Union) have opposed it (CSKR 2019a). It is worth underlining that the United States has been particularly influential in software-based weapons research, innovation, and market stimulus (Stevens 2019, 275 and 280). A circuit of "arms transfer dependence" on the part of recipients helps conceive the opposition to the ban by other less technologically developed states (Kinsella 1998, 19). Those economically dominant actors concurrently command the UN Security Council, which has the primary responsibility of maintaining international peace and security (Ruhlman 2015, 37–38). Tailored upon the contours of business logic, their political domination recalls the destiny of cyberweapons and heralds that "decisive political will supporting prohibition is unlikely" (Stevens 2019, 289).

Though significant for a country's economic competitiveness and export success, information technologies are among those primarily driven by commercial interests and private funds, often within transnational companies (Smith and Udis 2003, 102–3). There are clear indications that the commercial sector actively detaches itself from military robotics or so-called Killer Robots. For example, Tesla and DeepMind took part in the open letter; Google pledged to not develop AI for use in weapons, having also sold the respectively controversial Boston Dynamics; Clearpath Robotics pledged its endorsement of the preemptive ban on AWS; and Silicon Valley voices have underlined the importance of meaningful human control over the use of lethal force (Altmann and Sauer 2017, 132–33; Google 2018; HRW 2019c; CSKR n.d.-d). While the discourse is settling, the practical commercial-military bond has become entrenched in the process of AI development. Though well known at the time for its close ties to the US military, Boston Dynamics was acquired by Google for commercial purposes (Altmann and Sauer 2017, 132–33; Diakogiannis 2019). Google's AI has also supported the US military drone program (Gibbs 2018). While committed to its pledge, ClearPath Robotics has continued to work with its military clients (CSKR n.d.-d). The Russian government, particularly the Ministry of Defense, has joined forces in AI development with key national corporations and companies such as Sberbank, Yandex, Rostelecom, Gazprom Neft, and Rosatom (President of Russia 2019a, 2019b). More generally, robotics as well as automation and complex analytics have deeply penetrated the profit-driven manufacturing industry, including tech giants such as GE, Siemens, Intel, Funac, Kuka, Bosch, NVIDIA, and Microsoft (Walker 2019). What is of particular importance across all these cases is the dual-use character of both robotics and AI having jointly paved the way for AWS (Altmann and Sauer 2017, 124).

Often tightly interlinked with the previous cluster of actors, epistemic communities have also engaged in deliberations over AWS security regulation across both global and regional scenes (CCW 2015, 2–4; EC n.d.). They are usually motivated by knowledge-based expertise and a desire to support the public interest or improve human welfare (Cross 2013, 150–55). This category combines scientists, technicians, defense experts, military officials, international lawyers, and even faith leaders (Cross

2013, 154–58). The recognition of their field expertise or more general professional judgment may be thought of in terms of "authority" (Schneiker 2016, chap. 4). Framing a particular issue or problem and/or its context from various perspectives, they influence both governments and nonstate actors (Cross 2013, 138; Schneiker 2016, chap. 4). They have also become crucial boosters of humanitarianism (Schneiker 2016, chap. 4). In this sense, they feature "a major means by which knowledge translates into power" (Cross 2013, 138). Especially with transnational processes and transnational global governance evolving, epistemic communities are becoming ever more significant (Cross 2013, 139). What is crucial is that members of such groups are also driven by their particular professional self-understanding (Schneiker 2016, chap. 4). It potentially implies variation in internal cohesion within epistemic communities as well as coexisting or conflicting epistemic communities (Cross 2013, 147–48). This hypothetical setup well depicts the case of AWS. Some experts have articulated support for the ban (Sharkey 2012, 2017; Asaro 2012; Garcia 2015; Klincewicz 2015). Others have simultaneously pointed out either biases or weaknesses of their approach or positive facets of AWS (Arkin 2010, 2018; Anderson and Waxman 2012, 2013; Schmitt 2013). There is a risk of their concerns being silenced because internal cohesion within an epistemic community is essential for exercising influence on policy outcomes (Cross 2013, 138).

The International Committee of the Red Cross (ICRC) deserves special attention. This neutral INGO with a legal personality and an IO-equivalent status engages in humanitarian diplomacy and occasionally prohibition-oriented policy advocacy to which the cases of APLs, CMs, and Killer Robots testify (Price 1998, 632; ICRC 2016a, 2018a, n.d.-a, n.d.-b; Hynek 2018b). It also seeks to establish and strengthen ties with the private sector (ICRC 2018b). At the same time, it may be thought of in terms of a humanitarian epistemic community with its multidimensional humanitarian agenda (Schneiker 2016, chap. 4; ICRC n.d.-a). It withal possesses legal expertise in the field of international humanitarian law and international human rights law, the progressive convergence of which has also entailed the convergence of their respective "guardian institutions," namely the ICRC and the UN. This implies that they have repeatedly taken an active interest in each other's work and legal mandates, including assistance provided to the UN by the ICRC on issues of mutual competence (Fortin 2012). Diplomatic facilitation of opposition to Killer Robots by the ICRC is thus of particular importance (ICRC 2016b). Admitted to have an impact on securitization processes (Salter 2008; Emmers 2013, 134), the public also gets retracted into AWS-oriented regulatory politics. Their stance, however, remains fragmented, with only 61 percent clearly endorsing the ban (HRW 2019a).

Overall, while opposition to Killer Robots might be broken down into (I)NGO advocacy, state and audience support, expert blessing, and commercial sector endorsement, opposition to their prohibition can be broken down into roughly the same categories. This signifies a fragmented social stance in relation to AWS security regulation. In terms of the structural distribution of power and associated interests, the current state of affairs does not favor the coalition working to ban Killer Robots. The three key clusters of stakeholders are crucial for consideration in this regard. States, epistemic communities, and the commercial sector are those that primarily exercise control over the sphere of security, knowledge production, as well as finance and material production (Strange 1994, 24–32; Hynek 2018a). The most powerful states oppose the ban on AWS. They particularly do so under the umbrella of a knowledge-based rationale provided by experts and in collaboration with commercial players. This testifies to a disadvantageous structural position of the anti–Killer Robots coalition. Importantly, many of its participants have been involved with successful APLs and CMs prohibition campaigns and with regulatory efforts in the case of small arms and light weapons (Marks 2008; Krause 2002, 256; Hynek 2018b). This once again reaffirms the notion of what we term the *humanitarian transnational historical bloc*, dating back to the 1970s and evidently gaining momentum after the end of the Cold War (Hynek 2018b). Despite its apparent resurgence and the campaigners now turning their sights on Killer Robots, the recent past has shown their prospects of success are indeterminate. As the previous chapters demonstrated in detail, opposition to such humanitarian endeavors has in most cases also principally lied with "a handful of weapons-dependent governments" (Johnson n.d.). To specify, "the same few" have also stood against severe restrictions on APLs, CMs, small arms, and nuclear weapons (Krause 2002, 256; Marks 2008; Hynek 2018b; Bourne 2019; Johnson n.d.).

INSTITUTIONAL POWER: MULTIVOICE DECISION-MAKING DEADLOCK

In this part, we offer an insight into the mediatory power of involved institutions and the nature of indirect interactions among the aforesaid key stakeholders therein. Decisional rules, lines of involvement and responsibility, configurations of path dependence, and associated indirect consequences are taken into consideration (Hynek 2018a). Particular attention is paid to whether and how "do-gooders" influence or control other actors via institutional loci with respect to the security governance of Killer Robots. Among the key involved global and regional IO platforms are the UN CCW, the UNGA, the UNSC, the UNSG, the UNHRC, the OSCEPA, the EP, and the EC (EC 2018; UNGA 2018; CSKR 2018b, n.d.-b). In the surge of lethal autonomous robotics, the report of the UNHRC's Special Rapporteur on extrajudicial, summary, or arbitrary executions has brought human rights and ethics to the fore (Heyns 2013;

CCW 2015, 16). Endorsing the ban on Killer Robots, the UNSG has posed a challenge to the opposition (Guterres 2018). The OSCEPA and the EP have also supported the ban on the parliamentary level (EP 2014, 2018b; OSCEPA 2019). In reaction to the CCW process, the statement on behalf of the EU has similarly underlined the importance of human control on life and death decisions (EEAS 2018, 2019). The EC and the proposed EU Coordinated Plan on Artificial Intelligence have also promoted a "human-centric approach to AI" (EC 2018).

The CCW has firmly established itself as an international humanitarian law instrument (UNODA 2014). The practice of successfully adopted protocols on blinding laser weapons, explosive remnants of war, nondetectable fragments, and other devices has set procedural and path-dependence characteristics of this negotiation format (Hynek 2018b; UN n.d.). Such prohibitive practices have a standard-setting function going far beyond a particular treaty (Rappert 2008; Acheson and Fihn 2013). Having broadened its scope to include Killer Robots, the CCW has brought together its state parties and other states, UN agencies, (regional) IOs, the ICRC, and other registered (I)NGOs, including the Campaign to Stop Killer Robots (UNODA 2014; CSKR 2018b). Campaigners acknowledge that it has been a twenty-year practice of meaningful (I)NGO participation in such sessions (CSKR n.d.-d). The history of the ICRC and the UN working together is even more deeply rooted (Fortin 2012). To clarify the position by the ICRC, it has underlined the importance of human responsibility over decisions to kill, thereby granting diplomatic support to the campaign within the UN (ICRC 2016a). Informal meetings between representatives of the campaign and diplomats have additionally been arranged under UN auspices (CSKR n.d.-d). Over a hundred nations are state parties to the CCW, including all five permanent members of the UNSC (CSKR 2018b). Regular issue-oriented deliberations at the UNGA First Committee on Disarmament and International Security have complemented the CCW procedure (CSKR n.d.-e). A close relationship between the UNHRC and the CCW is admitted in view of the linkage between IHRL and IHL (Bieri and Dickow 2014, 3; CCW 2015, 19). Experts, academics, researchers, and analysts have also gained a firm seat in the CCW negotiation format, two which recent reports also testify (CCW 2015, 2–4, 2018, 3, 2019a, 2019b). Scientists, academics, and political, military, legal, economic, and technical specialists have also appeared among governmental representatives along with ministers, secretaries, ambassadors, counselors, and attachés (CCW 2019b).

Deeply embedded within such a multivoice and multilevel institutional composition, the security issue of AWS has not become institutionalized via a working international regulatory/prohibition regime. In line with the cases of APLs and CMs, as Hynek (2018b) showcased, dominant powers have again blocked the regime proposal through exercises of their structural power. There are few barriers to this because the established institutional limits do not stand sufficient to restrain their interests and statutory authority. Though enjoying the right of interference in internal affairs of states with humanitarian services and a broad right of initiative, the ICRC lacks credible enforcement mechanisms, particularly outside of conflict and crisis zones (ICRC 2011, n.d.-b, n.d.-c). The OSCE, the EU (in the domain of security and defence policy), as well as the CCW all build upon the principle of consensual decision making (CSKR 2013b; Abramson 2017; EP 2019; OSCE n.d.-a). The EU's political stance is fragmented, with Austria calling for a ban while France, Germany, and the United Kingdom remain either skeptical toward the ban or opposing it (CSKR 2019a). While the UNGA upholds the principle of equality as well, the five permanent member-states of the Security Council maintain the right to veto decisions concerning international peace and security (Ruhlman 2015, 37–38). With only China inclining toward a limited ban at the most, all of the five oppose the all-embracing ban on the use, development, and production of AWS (CSKR 2019a). With the exception of Peru, state endorsers of the AWS ban barely have any influence within the current Security Council (CSKR 2019a; UNSC n.d.). All of this indicates the fragility of institutional prowess and the powerlessness of AWS prohibition advocates in the face of great powers' interests.

COMPULSORY POWER: HYBRID THRUST VERSUS GREAT POWER POLITICS

This section examines attempts by prohibition proponents to alter the behavior of resistant actors outside of the working institutional framework. In particular, the discursive and practical confrontation between the hybrid thrust generated by the campaign and the resistance produced by great power interests and politics is put under the microscope.

The hybrid nature of the thrust might be evident, for example, with one of the UNGA First Committee side events held on October 18, 2016 (CSKR 2016a). It brought together a person chiefly pertaining to the CCW context, a well-known scientist and representatives of the Campaign to Stop Killer Robots, Human Rights Watch, and the International Committee for Robot Arms Control. Various sources of power constituted this hybrid force, as interpreted earlier. They, inter alia, include field knowledge and expert authority, informal or formal (legal) standing, and moral or political authority of (I)NGOs, especially the ICRC, and IOs, particularly the UN and its bodies. The recognized history of security regulation practice, most importantly within the CCW format, also plays a constructive role (Hynek 2018b). Harnessing this leverage, the hybrid force deployed various mechanisms to alter the behavior of the outgroup. To stigmatize opponents of their agenda and simultaneously put pressure on them, they named and shamed such countries as Russia, China, Israel,

South Korea, the United Kingdom, and the United States (CSKR 2019a, 2019b, 2019c, n.d.-f; HRW 2019b). Tabooization of AWS is also performed via imaginaries of urgency, consequential and deontological arguments, emotional appeals, and speculative fantasies (Carpenter 2016, 53; CSKR n.d.-f). To give an example of the latter, photos from *The Terminator* and *Battlestar Galactica* have been featured in their media coverage (Carpenter 2016, 53). Imitating the course of nuclear weapons stigmatization (Tannenwald 2016, 115), religious norms are also harnessed (PAX 2014b). For the sake of advancing tabooization, "do-gooders" often emphasize certain attributes while ignoring other relevant traits (Sauer and Reveraert 2018, 438). Persuasion through normative and peer pressure on multiple fronts is also in their toolkit. They bring their agenda to various conferences and events organized by governments, (I)NGOs, Ios, and groups of individuals with various expertise (CSKR n.d.-d). Open letters initiated by AI/robotics research communities have been broadly circulated for further signatures both globally and locally (FLI 2015; Kerr et al. 2017; Open Letter 2017a; Open Letter 2017b). Another open letter, particularly targeting the CCW, has been produced by tech companies (FLI 2017). With a majority vote of participants at one of the specialized workshops, experts have issued a statement calling for a ban on AWS (ICRAC n.d.). Audiences also get increasingly dragged into the process because documents of this sort often call for their endorsement via signatures (FLI 2015, n.d.). Statistics on favorable public opinion are collected and reported in the form of opinion polls as a complementary mechanism of support stimulation (IPSOS 2019; CSKR 2019d). In line with its traditional mission of urging governments to adapt IHL to changing circumstances, the ICRC has also called on states to set limits on autonomy in weapon systems (ICRC 2016a, 2016b). It has considered its position having also collaborated with the campaign in issuing one of its *International Review of the Red Cross* journal editions (CSKR 2013c). Elements of global and regional IOs also play a crucial role in steering national ambitions in the desired direction. The declaration by the OSCEPA and resolutions by the EP have urged their member-states to work toward a legally binding ban on AWS (EP 2014, 2018b; OSCEPA 2019). Some states such as Austria, Cuba, Costa Rica, Pakistan, and Guatemala incline toward AWS prohibition, thereby generating peer pressure on other states, especially within IOs (CSKR 2016b, 2018c; UNGA 2018). Actor-oriented letters and reports have also been used to put or increase normative pressure on both commercial entities (Wareham 2018a, 2018b) and individual governments (Wareham 2017, 2018c, 2018d, 2019; Amoroso et al. 2018). Certain reactive guarantees on the part of both (private) economic actors and states broaden the scope of peer pressure (Google 2018; Maas 2018; Peters 2019). More generally, campaigners regularly undertake media outreach to draw public attention (CSKR 2014a, 2014b, 2015, 2017b, 2018a).

The resistance generated by great power interests and politics prevails. Leverage that politically and economically dominant states maintain over all other actors in the equation is unparalleled. The legal status of the OSCE in relation to participating states is nonbinding (OSCE n.d.-a) and the CCW also lacks enforcement mechanisms (CSKR 2013b; Abramson 2017). Despite its increasing prominence, the EP has little influence over member-states in the domain of EU security and defence policy (EP 2019). Within the global (UN) system of governance, the Security Council stands out as "the most structurally unequal body" (Ruhlman 2015, 37–38). The stratified global arms transfer and production system enables dominant producers and suppliers such as the United States or Russia (former Soviet Union) to manipulate arms transfers and dependences for political ends (Kinsella 1998, 19; Krause 1992, 206–10 and 99–126). With minor exceptions, strategic partnerships run through the Shanghai Cooperation Organization, the Gulf Cooperation Council, the North-Atlantic Treaty Organization, the OSCE, the EU, and beyond also account for certain degrees of dependence and followership, particularly between smaller and greater states (Cooper, Higgott, and Nossal 1991; SCO n.d.; GCC n.d.; NATO n.d.; OSCE n.d.-b; EU n.d.). As the experience with nuclear weapons has shown and as now evident with Killer Robots, nonallied states tend to join humanitarian disarmament or prohibition agendas (Sauer and Reveraert 2018, 442). Besides making use of their almost uncompromised preponderance, dominant actors have also resorted to discursive mechanisms. The latter is performed in order to warrant and sustain their controversial stance on the AWS security issue. The (informal) discourse endorsing norm compliance, as also supported by relevant technological developments, is utilized to accommodate the normative pressure. For example, both Russia and the United States (informally) highlight the preservation of a meaningful human element in their AI-oriented military projects (TASS 2018a, 2018b; Freedberg 2019; BBC 2019). It was furthermore stressed that, even in the event of degraded or lost communications, tele-operated systems should not be capable of autonomously selecting and engaging targets (DoD 2012/2017). Following the same course, the United Kingdom has also underlined the significance of human direction for the application of lethal force (UK 2018). Often backed by knowledge-based expertise, such actors concurrently try to shift attention to the positive value of AWS (Pellerin 2016; McKay 2018; USA 2018; UK 2018; Russia 2019; Gronlund 2019). A clear indication of expert support is, for example, that the Berlin Statement was not endorsed unanimously at the experts' workshop in Berlin (ICRAC n.d.). The aforesaid implies that these actors simultaneously engage both in "stigma rejection," meaning they recognize the stigma but detach themselves from it, and "counter-stigmatization" (Sauer and Reveraert 2018, 446–47).

Despite the broad reach and thriving appeal of the hybrid humanitarian thrust, their discourses and practices cannot withstand that of politically and economically dominant states. Recalling the Ottawa (APLs) and Oslo (CMs) Processes, there is a real possibility for lesser powers led by patrons (typically middle powers) to bypass conventional arms control for an ad hoc and self-selecting regime (Hynek 2018b). In line, campaigners insist on the development of the ban on Killer Robots outside of the traditional framework, unless one is adopted within the CCW format (Bieri and Dickow 2014, 3). The prospects of assembling a meaningful prohibition regime in this way remain yet blurred, but other successful treaties have demonstrated that the UNSC resistance is not necessarily decisive (Johnson n.d.).

CONCLUSION

The presented chapter shed light on the complex workings of power around the security issue of Killer Robots and their prospective global prohibition. For a start, attention was drawn to the legal backdrop and political advancements that jointly point toward international security regulation of AWS. We discerned that the legal underbrush applicable for managing AWS is restricted. This is because it principally features general international laws of war, in particular humanitarian principles, and a piecemeal emerging framework regulating cyberweapons. It was then shown how, given these limitations, the issue-oriented prohibitionary agenda has deeply penetrated the political scene and the domain of security governance cutting across global, regional, and local levels. The opening section concluded that, despite the success of "severe politicization," Killer Robots have not become truly "securitized." What testifies to this is the deficiency of extraordinary reactive measures and the standstill on the way toward a global regime banning or at least regulating AWS.

The power-analytical approach was then utilized to reflect on dynamics and conditions having determined promises of and impediments to AWS security regulation. Attempts at establishing a global prohibition regime banning AWS and existing resistance to this were brought into sharp focus. The first part of this scrutiny relied on the notion of productive power and dissected (counter-)discourses related to the stigmatization of Killer Robots and proponents of AWS. Multiple enabling and constraining conditions to the construction of AWS as an illegitimate military instrument were extensively discussed. The core finding of this investigation was that a strong stigma is already being attached to Killer Robots, despite them being a "politicized" concept rather than a technological category. Next, attention was directed toward the working of structural power. Through its lens, we demonstrated how the structural position of ban endorsers is disadvantaged in the prevailing systemic distribution of power and associated interests. To emphasize a very high caliber of their composition still, heterarchies of power governing a multilevel political movement to ban Killer Robots were comprehensively depicted. Particular attention was devoted to reviewing structural statuses as well as general and issue-oriented motivations of (I)NGOs, IOs, nation-states, hi-tech business companies, epistemic communities, the media, and audience. The concept of the transnational historical bloc introduced and referred to in the previous chapters was found pertinent to tracing related advocacy efforts. Once again detected convergences between the selected case and precedents in this regard testify to the relevance of this notion not only for the case of Killer Robots but also for analyzing regulatory/prohibition advocacy more generally.

What followed was the application of institutional power. Having examined decisional rules, lines of responsibility, and path-dependence characteristics with respect to key involved intergovernmental platforms, we discovered a multivoice decision-making deadlock. This is the one that makes AWS prohibition advocates, though deeply embedded within relevant institutional structures, powerless in the face of great powers' interests. Given the circumstances, the former have indicated their interest in developing a ban on Killer Robots outside of conventional arms control fora. In this light, there followed an inquiry into mechanisms of compulsory power that ban advocates possess to steer the behavior of resistant actors outside of institutional frames. As the examples demonstrating related dynamics showed, they engage in naming and shaming, tabooization or stigmatization, as well as persuasion via normative and peer pressure on multiple fronts. Having portrayed this powerful hybrid humanitarian thrust, we showcased how their discourses and practices still concede to those wielded by resistant great powers.

Enormous leaps forward, especially in stigmatizing the removal of human control from (lethal) weapons systems, have been made on the way toward AWS security regulation. However, chances for a global ban on AWS to be adopted within the traditional institutional fora are miserably low given the predominance of great power interests and politics. Prospects of an ad hoc and self-selecting prohibition regime also remain shrouded in the mist of the future. What might hamper such efforts are the unfavorable structural and institutional standing of ban advocates as well as their shortage of direct leverage over potential nonsignatories.

REFERENCES

Abramson, Jeff. 2017. "Convention on Certain Conventional Weapons (CCW) at a Glance." *Arms Control Association*, Fact Sheets and Briefs, September. https://www.armscontrol.org/factsheets/CCW.

Acheson, Ray, and Beatrice Fihn. 2013. *Preventing Collapse: The NPT and a Ban on Nuclear Weapons*. New York: Reaching Critical Will, October. http://www.reachingcriticalwill.org/images/documents/Publications/npt-ban.pdf.

AI HLEG [the High-Level Expert Group on AI]. 2019. *Ethics Guidelines for Trustworthy AI: Building Trust in Human-Centric AI*. Brussels: European Commission, April 8. https://ec.europa.eu/futurium/en/ai-alliance-consultation/guidelines#Top.

Altmann, Jürgen, and Frank Sauer. 2017. "Autonomous Weapon Systems and Strategic Stability." *Survival* 59, no. 5 (October–November): 117–42.

Amoroso, Daniele, Frank Sauer, Noel Sharkey, Lucy Suchman, and Guglielmo Tamburrini. 2018. "Autonomy in Weapon Systems: The Military Application of Artificial Intelligence as a Litmus Test for Germany's New Foreign and Security Policy." *Heinrich Böll Stiftung Publication Series on Democracy* 49, edited by the Heinrich Böll Foundation. Großbeeren: ARNOLD group. https://www.boell.de/sites/default/files/boell_autonomy-in-weapon-systems_1.pdf?dimension1=division_oen.

Anderson, Kenneth, and Matthew Waxman. 2012. "Law and Ethics for Robot Soldiers." *Policy Review*, no. 176: 35–49.

———. 2013. *Law and Ethics for Autonomous Weapon Systems: Why a Ban Won't Work and How the Laws of War Can*. Stanford University, The Hoover Institution Jean Perkins Task Force on National Security & Law Essay Series; American University Washington College of Law Research Paper 2013–11; Columbia Public Law Research Paper 13-351.

Arkin, Ronald C. 2010. "The Case for Ethical Autonomy in Unmanned Systems." *Journal of Military Ethics* 9, no. 4: 332–41.

———. 2017. "A Roboticist's Perspective on Lethal Autonomous Weapon Systems." In *Perspectives on Lethal Autonomous Weapon Systems*, UNODA Occasional Papers, no. 30, 35–48. New York: United Nations Publication.

———. 2018. "Lethal Autonomous Systems and the Plight of the Non-combatant." In *The Political Economy of Robots*, edited by Ryan Kiggins, 317–26. Switzerland: Palgrave Macmillan.

Asaro, Peter. 2008. "How Just could a Robot War Be?" In *Current Issues in Computing and Philosophy*, edited by Adam Briggle, Katinka Waelbers, and Philip A. E. Brey, 50–64. Amsterdam: IOS Press.

———. 2012. "On Banning Autonomous Weapon Systems: Human Rights, Automation, and the Dehumanization of Lethal Decision-Making." *International Review of the Red Cross* 94, no. 886: 687–709.

Basu, Rumki. 2004. *The United Nations: Structure and Functions of an International Organisation*. New Delhi: Sterling Publishers Private Limited.

BBC. 2019. *US Seeks to Allay Fears Over Killer Robots*. March 11. https://www.bbc.com/news/technology-47524768.

Bieri, Matthias, and Marcel Dickow. 2014. "Lethal Autonomous Weapons Systems: Future Challenges." *CSS Analyses in Security Policy*, no. 164 (November), edited by Christian Nünlist. Zurich: Center for Security Studies (CSS). https://css.ethz.ch/content/dam/ethz/special-interest/gess/cis/center-for-securities-studies/pdfs/CSSAnalyse164-EN.pdf.

Birnbacher, Dieter. 2016. "Are Autonomous Weapons Systems a Threat to Human Dignity?" In *Autonomous Weapons Systems: Law, Ethics, Policy*, edited by Nehal Bhuta et al., 105–21. Cambridge: Cambridge University Press.

Bolton, Matthew, Thomas Nash, and Richard Moyes. 2012. "Ban Autonomous Armed Robots." *Article 36*, March 5. http://www.article36.org/statements/ban-autonomous-armed-robots/.

Bourne, Mike. 2012. "Guns Don't Kill People, Cyborgs Do: A Latourian Provocation for Transformatory Arms Control and Disarmament." *Global Change, Peace and Security* 24, no. 1: 141–63.

———. 2019. "Powers of the Gun: Process and Possibility in Global Small Arms Control." In *Regulating Global Security: Insights from Conventional and Unconventional*

Regimes, edited by Nik Hynek, Ondrej Ditrych, and Vit Stritecky, 143–68. Cham: Palgrave Macmillan.

Brehm, Maya. 2017. *Defending the Boundary: Constraints and Requirements on the Use of Autonomous Weapons Systems under International Humanitarian and Human Rights Law*. Academy Briefing No. 9, May. Geneva: Geneva Academy.

Carpenter, Charli. 2016. "Rethinking the Political/-Science-/Fiction Nexus: Global Policy Making and the Campaign to Stop Killer Robots." *American Political Science Association* 14, no. 1 (March): 53–69.

CCW [The Convention on Certain Conventional Weapons]. 2015. *Report of the 2015 Informal Meeting of Experts on Lethal Autonomous Weapons Systems*. CCW/MSP/2015/3, June 2, 2015. Meeting of the High Contracting Parties to the Convention on Prohibitions or Restrictions on the Use of Certain Conventional Weapons Which May Be Deemed to Be Excessively Injurious. Geneva, November 12–13, 2015. https://undocs.org/pdf?symbol=en/ccw/msp/2015/3.

———. 2018. *Report of the 2018 Session of the Group of Governmental Experts on Emerging Technologies in the Area of Lethal Autonomous Weapons Systems*. CCW/GGE.1/2018/3, October 23, 2018. Group of Governmental Experts of the High Contracting Parties to the Convention on Prohibitions or Restrictions on the Use of Certain Conventional Weapons Which May Be Deemed to Be Excessively Injurious or to Have Indiscriminate Effects. Geneva, April 9–13, 2018, and August 27–31, 2018. https://undocs.org/en/CCW/GGE.1/2018/3.

———. 2019a. *Report of the 2019 Session of the Group of Governmental Experts on Emerging Technologies in the Area of Lethal Autonomous Weapons Systems*. Draft. CCW/GGE.1/2019/CRP.1/Rev.2, August 21, 2019. Group of Governmental Experts of the High Contracting Parties to the Convention on Prohibitions or Restrictions on the Use of Certain Conventional Weapons Which May Be Deemed to Be Excessively Injurious or to Have Indiscriminate Effects. Geneva, March 25–29, 2019, and August 20–21, 2019. https://www.unog.ch/80256EDD006B8954/(httpAssets)/5497DF9B01E5D9CFC125845E00308E44/$file/CCW_GGE.1_2019_CRP.1_Rev2.pdf.

———. 2019b. *Provisional List of Participants*. CCW/GGE.1/2019/MISC.1, March 26, 2019. Group of Governmental Experts on Emerging Technologies in the Area of Lethal Autonomous Weapons Systems. Geneva, March 25–29. Convention on Prohibitions or Restrictions on the Use of Certain Conventional Weapons Which May Be Deemed to Be Excessively Injurious or to Have Indiscriminate Effects. https://undocs.org/ccw/gge.1/2019/misc.1.

Chrétien, Jean. 1995. *Speech by Prime Minister Jean Chrétien to the National Forum on Canada's International Relations*. Toronto, September 11.

CoE [Council of Europe]. 2001. *Convention on Cybercrime*. European Treaty Series, no. 185. Signed November 23, 2001 in Budapest, Hungary. https://www.europarl.europa.eu/meetdocs/2014_2019/documents/libe/dv/7_conv_budapest_/7_conv_budapest_en.pdf.

Coeckelbergh, Mark. 2011. "From Killer Machines to Doctrines and Swarms, or Why Ethics of Military Robotics Is Not (Necessarily) About Robots." *Philosophy and Technology*, Special Issue.

Cohen, Eliot A. 1996. "A Revolution in Warfare." *Foreign Affairs* 75, no. 2 (March/April): 37–54.

———. 2004. "Change and Transformation in Military Affairs." *Journal of Strategic Studies* 27, no. 3: 395–407.

Conn, Ariel. 2018. "AI Companies, Researchers, Engineers, Scientists, Entrepreneurs, and Others Sign Pledge Promising Not to Develop Lethal Autonomous Weapons." *Future of Life Institute*, July 18. https://futureoflife.org/2018/07/18/ai-companies-researchers-engineers-scientists-entrepreneurs-and-others-sign-pledge-promising-not-to-develop-lethal-autonomous-weapons/.

Cooper, Andrew, Richard Higgott, and Kim Nossal. 1991. "Bound to Follow? Leadership and Followership in the Gulf Conflict." *Political Science Quarterly* 106, no. 3: 391–410.

Cross, Mai'a K. Davis. 2013. "Rethinking Epistemic Communities Twenty Years Later." *Review of International Studies* 39: 137–60.

CSKR [Campaign to Stop Killer Robots]. 2013a. *Consensus: Killer Robots Must Be Addressed.* May 28. https://www.stopkillerrobots.org/2013/05/nations-to-debate-killer-robots-at-un/.

———. 2013b. *The Convention on Conventional Weapons and Fully Autonomous Weapons.* Background Paper, September 26. https://stopkillerrobots.org/wp-content/uploads/2013/09/KRC_BackgrounderCCW_26Sep2013.pdf.

———. 2013c. *ICRC on New Technologies and Warfare.* August 6. https://www.stopkillerrobots.org/2013/08/icrc-on-new-technologies-and-warfare/.

———. 2014a. *Convention on Conventional Weapons Meeting of High Contracting Parties Geneva 11–15 November 2013.* Report on Activities, March 4. https://www.stopkillerrobots.org/wp-content/uploads/2013/03/KRC_ReportCCW2013_final-1.pdf.

———. 2014b. *Convention on Conventional Weapons Annual Meeting of High Contracting Parties United Nations Geneva 13–14 November 2014.* Report on Activities, December 22. https://www.stopkillerrobots.org/wp-content/uploads/2013/03/KRC_ReportCCW2014_22Dec20141.pdf.

———. 2015. *Convention on Conventional Weapons Annual Meeting of High Contracting Parties United Nations Geneva 12–13 November 2015.* Report on Activities, December 16. https://www.stopkillerrobots.org/wp-content/uploads/2013/03/KRC_ReportCCWannual16Dec2015_uploaded-1.pdf.

———. 2016a. *Fully Autonomous Weapons and the CCW Review Conference.* Side Event Briefing, Tuesday, October 18, 2016. United Nations General Assembly. First Committee on Disarmament and International Security. https://www.stopkillerrobots.org/wp-content/uploads/2013/03/KRC_UNGAFlyer_18Oct2016-1.pdf.

———. 2016b. *Extracts on Killer Robots from Statements to 2016 UNGA First Committee on Disarmament and International Security.* October. https://www.stopkillerrobots.org/wp-content/uploads/2016/10/KRC_UNGA2016_Statements.pdf.

———. 2017a. *Who Supports the Call to Ban Killer Robots?* June 27. https://www.stopkillerrobots.org/wp-content/uploads/2013/03/KRC_ListBanEndorsers_27June2017.pdf.

———. 2017b. *Convention on Conventional Weapons Fifth Review Conference United Nations Geneva 12–16 December 2016.* Report on Activities, February 1. https://www.stopkillerrobots.org/wp-content/uploads/2013/03/CCW_ReportRC_Feb2017.pdf.

———. 2018a. *Convention on Conventional Weapons Group of Governmental Experts Meeting on Lethal Autonomous Weapons Systems & Meeting of High Contracting Parties United Nations Geneva November 2017.* Report on Activities, February 26. https://www.stopkillerrobots.org/wp-content/uploads/2018/02/CCW_Report_Nov2017_posted.pdf.

———. 2018b. *Five Years of Campaigning, CCW Continues.* March 18. https://www.stopkillerrobots.org/2018/03/fiveyears/.

———. 2018c. *UN Head Calls for a Ban.* November 12. https://www.stopkillerrobots.org/2018/11/unban/.

———. 2019a. *Country Views on Killer Robots.* August 21. https://www.stopkillerrobots.org/wp-content/uploads/2019/08/KRC_CountryViews21Aug2019.pdf.

———. 2019b. *Minority of States Delay Effort to Ban Killer Robots.* March 29. https://www.stopkillerrobots.org/2019/03/minority-of-states-delay-effort-to-ban-killer-robots/.

———. 2019c. *Russia, United States Attempt to Legitimize Killer Robots.* August 22. https://www.stopkillerrobots.org/2019/08/russia-united-states-attempt-to-legitimize-killer-robots/.

————. 2019d. *Global Poll Shows 61% Oppose Killer Robots.* January 22. https://www.stopkillerrobots.org/2019/01/global-poll-61-oppose-killer-robots/.

————. n.d.-a. *A Growing Global Coalition.* Accessed October 1, 2019. https://www.stopkillerrobots.org/about/.

————. n.d.-b. *Who Wants to Ban Fully Autonomous Weapons.* Video. Accessed October 1, 2019. https://www.stopkillerrobots.org.

————. n.d.-c. *Membership List.* Accessed October 2, 2019. https://www.stopkillerrobots.org/members/

————. n.d.-d. *All Actions and Achievements.* Accessed October 23, 2019. https://www.stopkillerrobots.org/action-and-achievements/.

————. n.d.-e. *Publications: Statements, Reports and Other Publications.* Accessed October 15, 2019. https://www.stopkillerrobots.org/publications/.

————. n.d.-f. *The Problem.* Accessed October 12, 2019. https://www.stopkillerrobots.org/learn/#problem.

Dehuri, Satchidananda, Sung-Bae Cho, and Susmita Ghosh. 2011. "Swarm Intelligence and Neural Networks." In *Integration of Swarm Intelligence and Artificial Neural Network,* edited by Sung-Bae Cho et al. Singapore: World Scientific.

Denning, D. 2000. "Reflections on Cyberweapons Controls." *Computer Security Journal* 16, no. 4: 43–53.

Diakogiannis, Agapitos. 2019. "The Future of Manufacturing Technology." *Forbes,* August 6. https://www.forbes.com/sites/columbiabusinessschool/2019/08/06/the-future-of-manufacturing-technology/#400b25e8774c.

DoD [Department of Defense]. 2012/2017. *Department of Defense Directive 3000.09.* Adopted November 21, 2012; Modified May 8, 2017. United States of America. https://fas.org/irp/doddir/dod/d3000_09.pdf.

EC [European Commission]. 2018. *Communication from the Commission to the European Parliament, the European Council, the Council, the European Economic and Social Committee and the Committee of the Regions—Coordinated Plan on Artificial Intelligence (COM(2018) 795 Final).* Announced December 7. https://ec.europa.eu/digital-single-market/en/news/coordinated-plan-artificial-intelligence.

————. n.d. *High-Level Expert Group on Artificial Intelligence.* Last updated October 4, 2019. https://ec.europa.eu/digital-single-market/en/high-level-expert-group-artificial-intelligence.

EEAS [European External Action Service]. 2018. *Statements on Behalf of the EU: EU Statement, Group of Governmental Experts Lethal Autonomous Weapons Systems Convention on Certain Conventional Weapons Geneva, 27–31 August 2018.* August 27. https://eeas.europa.eu/headquarters/headquarters-homepage/49763/convention-certain-conventional-weapons-group-governmental-experts-lethal-autonomous-weapons_en.

————. 2019. *Statements on Behalf of the EU: EU Statement, Group of Governmental Experts on Lethal Autonomous Weapons Systems Convention on Certain Conventional Weapons Geneva, 20–21 August 2019.* August 20. https://eeas.europa.eu/headquarters/headquarters-homepage/66584/group-governmental-experts-lethal-autonomous-weapons-systems-convention-certain-conventional_en.

Emmers, Ralf. 2013. "Securitization." In *Contemporary Security Studies,* third edition, edited by Alan Collins, 131–45. Oxford: Oxford University Press.

EP [European Parliament]. 2014. *European Parliament Resolution on the Use of Armed Drones.* (2014/2567(RSP)). Joint Motion for a Resolution, February 25, 2014. https://www.europarl.europa.eu/sides/getDoc.do?type=MOTION&reference=P7-RC-2014-0201&language=EN.

————. 2018a. *Draft Recommendation to the Council on the 73rd session of the United Nations General Assembly.* (2018/2040(INI)). Reported June 27. https://www.europarl.europa.eu/doceo/document/A-8-2018-0230_EN.html?redirect.

————. 2018b. *European Parliament Resolution on Autonomous Weapon Systems.* (2018/2752(RSP)). Texts Adopted, September 12, 2018. https://www.europarl.europa.eu/doceo/document/TA-8-2018-0341_EN.pdf?redirect.

———. 2019. *Common Security and Defence Policy*. Fact Sheets on the European Union. https://www.europarl.europa.eu/ftu/pdf/en/FTU_5.1.2.pdf.

———. n.d. *Democracy and Human Rights*. Accessed October 1, 2019. https://www.europarl.europa.eu/about-parliament/en/democracy-and-human-rights.

EU [European Union]. n.d. *The 28 Member Countries of the EU*. Accessed October 1, 2019. https://europa.eu/european-union/about-eu/countries_en.

FLI [Future of Life Institute]. 2015. *Autonomous Weapons: An Open Letter from AI and Robotics Researchers*. July 28. https://futureoflife.org/open-letter-autonomous-weapons/.

———. 2017. *Open Letter to the United Nations Convention on Certain Conventional Weapons*. August 21. https://futureoflife.org/autonomous-weapons-open-letter-2017/.

———. n.d. *Lethal Autonomous Weapons Pledge*. Accessed October 1, 2019. https://futureoflife.org/lethal-autonomous-weapons-%20pledge/.

Flora, P., ed. 1986. *Growth to Limits: The Western European Welfare States Since World War II. Vol. 1: Sweden, Norway, Finland, Denmark*. Berlin: Walter de Gruyter and Co.

Fortin, Katharine. 2012. "Complementarity between the ICRC and the United Nations and International Humanitarian Law and International Human Rights Law, 1948–1968." *International Review of the Red Cross* 94, no. 888 (Winter): 1433–54.

Foucault, Michel. 1980. *Power/Knowledge: Selected Interviews and Other Writings 1972–1977*. Brighton: Harvester Press.

Freedberg, Sydney J. 2019. "ATLAS: Killer Robot? No. Virtual Crewman? Yes." *Breaking Defense*, March 4. https://breakingdefense.com/2019/03/atlas-killer-robot-no-virtual-crewman-yes/.

Gadiyar, Rajesh, Tong Zhang, and Ananth Sankaranarayanan. 2019. "Artificial Intelligence Software and Hardware Platforms." In *Artificial Intelligence for Autonomous Networks*, edited by Mazin Gilbert. Boca Raton, FL: CRC Press.

Garcia, Denise. 2015. "Killer Robots: Why the US Should Lead the Ban." *Global Policy* 6, no. 1: 57–63.

———. 2018. "Lethal Artificial Intelligence and Change: The Future of International Peace and Security." *International Studies Review* 20, no. 2: 334–41.

GCC [The Gulf Cooperation Council]. n.d. *Member States*. Accessed October 3, 2019. https://www.gcc-sg.org/en-us/AboutGCC/MemberStates/Pages/Home.aspx.

Gibbs, Samuel. 2018. "Google's AI Is Being Used by US Military Drone Programme." *The Guardian*, March 7. https://www.theguardian.com/technology/2018/mar/07/google-ai-us-department-of-defense-military-drone-project-maven-tensorflow.

Gidron, B., R. M. Kramer, and L. M. Salamon. 1992. "Government and the Third Sector in Comparative Perspective: Allies or Adversaries?" In *Government and the Third Sector: Emerging Relationship in Welfare States*, edited by B. Gidron, R. M. Kramer, and L. M. Salamon, 1–30. San Francisco: Jossey-Bass Publishers.

Google. 2018. *AI at Google: Our Principles*. June 7. https://blog.google/technology/ai/ai-principles/.

Gray, Colin S. 1996. "The Changing Nature of Warfare?" *Naval War College Review* 49, no. 2: 7–22.

———. 2002. *Strategy for Chaos: Revolutions in Military Affairs and the Evidence of History*. London: Frank Cass.

Gronlund, Kirsten. 2019. "State of AI: Artificial Intelligence, the Military and Increasingly Autonomous Weapons." *Future of Life Institute*, May 9. https://futureoflife.org/2019/05/09/state-of-ai/.

Gubrud, Mark. 2014. "Stopping Killer Robots." *Bulletin of the Atomic Scientists* 70, no. 1: 32–42.

Guterres, António. 2018. *Remarks at "Web Summit" by United Nations Secretary-General*. Lisbon, November 5. https://www.un.org/sg/en/content/sg/speeches/2018-11-05/remarks-web-summit.

Hallaq, Bilal, Tiia Somer, Anna-Maria Osula, Kim Ngo, and Timothy Mitchener-Nissen. 2017. "Artificial Intelligence within the Military Domain and Cyber Warfare."

In *Proceedings of 16th European Conference on Cyber Warfare and Security*, edited by Mark Scanlon and Nhien-An Le-Khac. Dublin: University College Dublin.

Hennessey, Meghan. 2014. "ClearPath Robotics Takes Stance Against 'Killer Robots' [An Open Letter to the Public]." *ClearPath Robotics*, August 13. https://clearpathrobotics.com/blog/2014/08/clearpath-takes-stance-against-killer-robots/.

Heyns, Christof. 2013. *Report of the Special Rapporteur on Extrajudicial, Summary or Arbitrary Executions.* A/HRC/23/47, April 9. Human Rights Council. United Nations General Assembly. https://www.ohchr.org/Documents/HRBodies/HRCouncil/RegularSession/Session23/A-HRC-23-47_en.pdf.

——. 2014. *Report of the Special Rapporteur on Extrajudicial, Summary or Arbitrary Executions.* A/HRC/26/36, April 1. Human Rights Council. United Nations General Assembly. https://documents-dds-ny.un.org/doc/UNDOC/GEN/G14/128/20/PDF/G1412820.pdf?OpenElement.

——. 2016. "Autonomous Weapons Systems: Living a Dignified Life and Dying a Dignified Death." In *Autonomous Weapons Systems: Law, Ethics, Policy*, edited by Nehal Bhuta et al., 3–20. Cambridge: Cambridge University Press.

Horowitz, Michael C. 2010. *The Diffusion of Military Power: Causes and Consequences for International Politics.* Princeton, NJ: Princeton University Press.

——. 2016. "Why Words Matter: The Real World Consequences of Defining Autonomous Weapons Systems," *Temple International and Comparative Law Journal* 30, no. 1: 85–98.

——. 2018. "Artificial Intelligence, International Competition, and the Balance of Power." *Texas National Security Review* 1, no. 3: 36–57.

HRW [Human Rights Watch]. 2012. *Losing Humanity: The Case against Killer Robots.* November 19. https://www.hrw.org/sites/default/files/reports/arms1112ForUpload_0_0.pdf.

——. 2014. *Shaking the Foundations: The Human Rights Implications of Killer Robots.* May. https://www.hrw.org/sites/default/files/reports/arms0514_ForUpload_0.pdf.

——. 2016. *Making the Case: The Dangers of Killer Robots and the Need for a Preemptive Ban.* December 9. https://www.hrw.org/sites/default/files/report_pdf/arms1216_web.pdf.

——. 2018. *Heed the Call: A Moral and Legal Imperative to Ban Killer Robots.* August 21. https://www.hrw.org/report/2018/08/21/heed-call/moral-and-legal-imperative-ban-killer-robots.

——. 2019a. *Poll Shows Strong Opposition to "Killer Robots": Urgent Need for Treaty Banning Fully Autonomous Weapons.* January 22. https://www.hrw.org/news/2019/01/22/poll-shows-strong-opposition-killer-robots.

——. 2019b. *"Killer Robots": Russia, US Oppose Treaty Negotiations: New Law Needed to Retain Meaningful Human Control Over the Use of Force.* August 19. https://www.hrw.org/news/2019/08/19/killer-robots-russia-us-oppose-treaty-negotiations.

——. 2019c. *Statement by the Campaign to Stop Killer Robots, UN General Assembly First Committee on Disarmament and International Security, Delivered by Marta Kosmyna,* Campaign to Stop Killer Robots. October 18. https://www.hrw.org/news/2019/10/18/statement-campaign-stop-killer-robots-un-general-assembly-first-committee.

Hundley, Richard O. 1999. *Past Revolutions, Future Transformations: What Can the History of Revolutions in Military Affairs Tell Us about Transforming the U.S. Military?* Santa Monica, CA: RAND, National Defense Research Institute.

Hynek, Nik. 2018a. "Theorizing International Security Regimes: A Power-Analytical Approach." *International Politics* 55, no. 3–4 (May): 352–68.

——. 2018b. "Re-Visioning Morality and Progress in the Security Domain: Insights from Humanitarian Prohibition Politics." *International Politics* 55, no. 3–4 (May): 421–40.

ICRAC [International Committee for Robot Arms Control]. n.d. *Statements: Mission Statement, Berlin Statement.* Accessed October 15, 2019. http://icrac.net/ statements/.

ICRC [International Committee of the Red Cross]. 1956/1957. *Draft Rules for the Limitation of the Dangers Incurred by the Civilian Population in Time of War.* Second edition.

ICRC: Geneva, September. XIXth International Red Cross Conference: New Delhi, January. Printed in Switzerland.

———. 2011. *Building Respect for the Law.* May 1. https://www.icrc.org/en/doc/what-we-do/building-respect-ihl/overview-building-respect-ihl.htm.

———. 2016a. *Autonomous Weapons: Decisions to Kill and Destroy Are a Human Responsibility.* Statement, April 11. Read at the Meeting of Experts on Lethal Autonomous Weapons Systems, Convention on Certain Conventional Weapons, Geneva, April 11–16. https://www.icrc.org/en/document/statement-icrc-lethal-autonomous-weapons-systems.

———. 2016b. *Views of the International Committee of the Red Cross (ICRC) on Autonomous Weapon Systems.* Paper, April 11. Circulated at the Meeting of Experts on Lethal Autonomous Weapons Systems, Convention on Certain Conventional Weapons, Geneva, April 11–15, 2016. https://www.icrc.org/en/document/views-icrc-autonomous-weapon-system.

———. 2018a. *Statutes of the International Committee of the Red Cross.* January 1. https://www.icrc.org/en/document/statutes-international-committee-red-cross-0.

———. 2018b. *Ethical Principles Guiding the ICRC's Partnerships with the Private Sector.* March 1. https://www.icrc.org/en/document/ethical-principles-guiding-icrc-partnerships-private-sector.

———. n.d.-a. *What We Do.* Accessed October 15, 2019. https://www.icrc.org/en/what-we-do.

———. n.d.-b. *The ICRC's Mandate and Mission.* Accessed October 15, 2019. https://www.icrc.org/en/mandate-and-mission.

———. n.d.-c. *Treaties, States Parties and Commentaries.* Accessed October 22, 2019. https://ihl-databases.icrc.org/ihl/WebART/375-590006.

IPSOS [Institut de Publique Sondage d'Opinion Secteur]. 2019. *Six in Ten (61%) Respondents Across 26 Countries Oppose the Use of Lethal Autonomous Weapons Systems.* January 22. https://www.ipsos.com/sites/default/files/ct/news/documents/2019-01/human-rights-watch-autonomous-weapons-pr-01-22-2019_0.pdf.

Johnson, Aaron M., and Sidney Axinn. 2013. "The Morality of Autonomous Robots." *Journal of Military Ethics* 12, no. 2: 129–41.

Johnson, Rebecca. n.d. "The United Nations and Disarmament Treaties." *UN Chronicle.* Accessed November 11, 2019. https://www.un.org/en/chronicle/article/united-nations-and-disarmament-treaties.

Karppi, Tero, Marc Böhlen, and Yvette Granata. 2016. "Killer Robots as Cultural Techniques." *International Journal of Cultural Studies* 21, no. 2: 107–23.

Kastan, Benjamin. 2013. "Autonomous Weapons Systems: A Coming Legal 'Singularity'?" *University of Illinois Journal of Law, Technology and Policy,* no. 1: 45–82.

Kerr, Ian, Yoshua Bengio, Geoffrey Hinton, Rich Sutton, and Doina Precup. 2017. *Open Letter to the Prime Minister of Canada by Canadian AI Research Community.* Announced November 2. https://techlaw.uottawa.ca/bankillerai.

Kinsella, David. 1998. "Arms Transfer Dependence and Foreign Policy Conflict." *Journal of Peace Research* 35, no. 1: 7–23.

Klincewicz, Michal. 2015. "Autonomous Weapons Systems, the Frame Problem and Computer Security." *Journal of Military Ethics* 14, no. 2: 162–76.

Korać, Srđan T. 2018. "Depersonalisation of Killing: Towards A 21st Century Use of Force 'Beyond Good And Evil?'" *Philosophy and Society* 29, no. 1: 49–64.

Krause, Keith. 1992. *Arms and the State: Patterns of Military Production and Trade.* Cambridge: Cambridge University Press.

———. 2002. "Multilateral Diplomacy, Norm Building, and UN Conferences: The Case of Small Arms and Light Weapons." Review Essay. *Global Governance* 8, no. 2 (April–June): 247–63.

Krepinevich, Andrew F. 1994. "Cavalry to Computer: The Pattern of Military Revolutions." *The National Interest,* no. 37 (September). https://nationalinterest.org/article/cavalry-to-computer-the-pattern-of-military-revolutions-848.

Krishnan, Armin. 2009. *Killer Robots: Legality and Ethicality of Autonomous Weapons.* Farnham, UK: Ashgate Publishing.

Latour, Bruno. 1999. *Pandora's Hope: Essays on the Reality of Science Studies.* Cambridge, MA: Harvard University Press.

Lin, Patrick, George Bekey, and Keith Abney. 2008. *Autonomous Military Robotics: Risk, Ethics, and Design.* US Department of Navy. San Luis Obispo: California Polytechnic State University.

Liu, Hin-Yan. 2012. "Categorization and Legality of Autonomous and Remote Weapons Systems." *International Review of the Red Cross* 94, no. 886: 627–52.

Maas, Heiko. 2018. *Speech by Foreign Minister of Germany at the General Debate of the 73rd General Assembly of the United Nations.* September 28. https://new-york-un.diplo.de/un-de/20180928-maas-general-assembly/2142290.

Marks, Paul. 2008. "Anti-Landmine Campaigners Turn Sights on War Robots." *New Scientist,* March 28. https://www.newscientist.com/article/dn13550-anti-landmine-campaigners-turn-sights-on-war-robots/.

Mathews, Robert J. 2001. "The 1980 Convention on Certain Conventional Weapons: A Useful Framework Despite Earlier Disappointments." *International Review of the Red Cross* 83, no. 844 (December): 991–1012.

McFarland, Tim. 2015. "Factors Shaping the Legal Implications of Increasingly Autonomous Military Systems." *International Review of the Red Cross* 97, no. 900: 1313–39.

McKay, Ian R. 2018. *U.S. Statement on Possible Options for Addressing the Humanitarian and International Security Challenges Posed by Emerging Technologies.* Geneva, Convention on Certain Conventional Weapons Group of Government Experts on Lethal Autonomous Weapons, April 13. US Mission to International Organizations in Geneva. https://geneva.usmission.gov/2018/04/13/u-s-statement-on-possible-options-for-addressing-the-humanitarian-and-international-security-challenges-posed-by-emerging-technologies-in-the-area-of/.

NATO [North Atlantic Treaty Organization]. n.d. *NATO Member Countries.* Accessed October 1, 2019. https://www.nato.int/cps/en/natohq/nato_countries.htm.

Nobel Peace Summit. 2014. *Living Peace: Final Statement.* 14th World Summit of Nobel Peace Laureates and Peace Laureate Organizations, Rome, December 12–14. http://www.nobelpeacesummit.com/wp-content/uploads/2017/02/2014-Final-Declaration.pdf.

Noone, Gregory P., and Diana C. Noone. 2015. "Debate Over Autonomous Weapons Systems." *Case Western Reserve Journal of International Law* 47, no. 1: 25–35.

NWI [Nobel Women's Initiative]. 2014. *Nobel Peace Laureates Call for Preemptive Ban on Autonomous Weapons.* May 12. https://nobelwomensinitiative.org/nobel-peace-laureates-call-for-preemptive-ban-on-killer-robots/?ref=204.

Open Letter. 2017a. *Belgian Scientists Letter on Autonomous Weapons by Belgian AI and Robotics Research Community.* Announced December. https://docs.google.com/document/u/1/d/e/2PACX-1vQU8W-mpdjBqLHlA4Xgbe1BhKI4scm2UyQg3cPpylpjnOVF81OmPSE7QmzaXNDfqBeLGrNFS4ozRL8-/pub.

Open Letter. 2017b. *Open Letter to the Prime Minister of Australia by Australian AI Research Community.* Announced November 2. https://www.dropbox.com/sh/ujslcvq7224c1gw/AADADLoJV_NCbwcOsfI9n6wba?dl=0&preview=7+Nov+AI+Letter.pdf.

OSCE [Organization for Security and Co-operation in Europe]. n.d.-a. *Who We Are.* Accessed October 20, 2019. https://www.osce.org/whatistheosce.

———. n.d.-b. *Participating States.* Accessed October 20, 2019. https://www.osce.org/participating-states.

OSCEPA [Organization for Security and Co-Operation in Europe Parliamentary Assembly]. 2019. *Luxembourg Declaration.* Adopted July 4–8, 2019, in Luxembourg at The Twenty-Eighth Annual Session. https://www.oscepa.org/documents/annual-sessions/2019-luxembourg/3882-luxembourg-declaration-eng/file.

———. n.d. *Parliamentary Dimension of the OSCE.* Accessed October 5, 2019.

PAX [PAX for Peace]. 2014a. *Interfaith Declaration*. February 1. https://www.paxforpeace.nl/stay-informed/news/interfaith-declaration.

———. 2014b. *Religious Leaders Call for a Ban on Killer Robots*. November 12, https://www.paxforpeace.nl/stay-informed/news/religious-leaders-call-for-a-ban-on-killer-robots.

Payne, Kenneth. 2018. *Strategy, Evolution, and War: Apes to Artificial Intelligence*. Washington, DC: Georgetown University Press.

Pellerin, Cheryl. 2016. "Deputy Secretary: Third Offset Strategy Bolsters America's Military Deterrence." *US Department of Defense*, October 31. https://www.defense.gov/Newsroom/News/Article/Article/991434/deputy-secretary-third-offset-strategy-bolsters-americas-military-deterrence/.

Peters, Rt. Hon. Winston. 2019. *Letter to Mary Wareham, Coordinator of Campaign to Stop Killer Robots*. May 1. https://www.stopkillerrobots.org/wp-content/uploads/2019/05/NZ-Peters-Response.pdf.

President of Russia [President's Website]. 2019a. *Excerpts from Transcript of Meeting on the Development of Artificial Intelligence Technologies*. Presidential Executive Office. Events, May 30. http://en.kremlin.ru/events/president/news/60630.

———. 2019b. *Instructions Following Meeting on Artificial Intelligence Technology Development*. Presidential Executive Office. Documents, June 12. http://en.kremlin.ru/acts/news/60748.

Price, Richard. 1995. "A Genealogy of the Chemical Weapons Taboo." *International Organization* 49, no. 1: 73–103.

———. 1998. "Reversing the Gun Sights: Transnational Civil Society Targets Land Mines." *International Organization* 52, no. 3 (Summer): 613–44.

Rappert, Brian. 2008. *A Convention beyond the Convention: Stigma, Humanitarian Standards and the Oslo Process*. London: Land-Mine Action, May. https://brianrappert.net/images/downloads/publications/Rappert2008-A_convention_beyond.pdf.

Ruhlman, Molly A. 2015. *Who Participates in Global Governance? States, Bureaucracies, and NGOs in the United Nations*. New York: Routledge.

Russia [Russian Federation]. 2019. Потенциальные Возможности и Ограничения Военного Применения Смертоносных Автономных Систем Вооружений [*Potential Opportunities and Limitation of Military Uses of Lethal Autonomous Weapons Systems*]. CCW/GGE.1/2019/WP.1. Working Paper Submitted to Group of Governmental Experts of the High Contracting Parties to the Convention on Prohibitions or Restrictions on the Use of Certain Conventional Weapons Which May Be Deemed to Be Excessively Injurious or to Have Indiscriminate Effects. Geneva, 8 March. https://www.unog.ch/80256EDD006B8954/(httpAssets)/B7C992A51A9FC8BFC12583BB00637BB9/$file/CCW.GGE.1.2019.WP.1_R+E.pdf.

Salter, Mark B. 2008. "Securitization and Desecuritization: A Dramaturgical Analysis of the Canadian Air Transport Security Authority." *Journal of International Relations and Development* 11: 321–49.

Sauer, Frank. 2016. "Stopping 'Killer Robots': Why Now Is the Time to Ban Autonomous Weapons Systems." *Arms Control Association*, October. https://www.armscontrol.org/act/2016-09/features/stopping-'killer-robots'-why-now-time-ban-autonomous-weapons-systems.

Sauer, Tom, and Mathias Reveraert. 2018. "The Potential Stigmatizing Effect of the Treaty on the Prohibition of Nuclear Weapons." *The Nonproliferation Review* 25, no. 5–6: 437–55.

Schmitt, Michael N. 2013. "Autonomous Weapon Systems and International Humanitarian Law: A Reply to the Critics." *Harvard National Security Journal Feature*.

Schneiker, Andrea. 2016. *Humanitarian NGOs, (In)Security and Identity: Epistemic Communities and Security Governance*. New York: Routledge.

SCO [The Shanghai Cooperation Organisation]. n.d. *The Shanghai Cooperation Organisation*. Accessed October 3, 2019. http://eng.sectsco.org/about_sco/.

Sharkey, Noel E. 2012. "The Evitability of Autonomous Robot Warfare." *International Review of the Red Cross* 94, no. 886: 787–99.

————. 2017. "Why Robots Should not be Delegated with the Decision to Kill." *Connection Science* 29, no. 2: 177–86.

Shimko, Keith L. 2010. *The Iraq Wars and America's Military Revolution.* New York: Cambridge University Press.

Singer, Peter W. 2009. *Wired for War: The Robotics Revolution and Conflict in the Twenty-First Century.* New York: Penguin Books/Penguin Group.

Sloan, Elinor. 2002. *The Revolution in Military Affairs: Implications for Canada and NATO.* Montreal: McGill-Queen's University Press.

Smith, Ron, and Bernard Udis. 2003. "New Challenges to Arms Export Control." In *The Arms Trade, Security and Conflict,* edited by Paul Levine and Ron Smith, 94–110. London: Routledge.

Solovyeva, Anzhelika, and Nik Hynek. 2018. "Going Beyond the 'Killer Robots' Debate: Six Dilemmas Autonomous Weapon Systems Raise." *Central European Journal of International and Security Studies* 12, no. 3 (September): 166–208.

Sparrow, Robert. 2007. "Killer Robots." *Journal of Applied Philosophy* 24, no. 1: 62–77.

Stavrianakis, Anna. 2010. *Taking Aim at the Arms Trade: NGOS, Global Civil Society and the World Military Order.* New York: Zed Books.

Stevens, Tim. 2019. "Global Code: Power and the Weak Regulation of Cyberweapons." In *Regulating Global Security: Insights from Conventional and Unconventional Regimes,* edited by Nik Hynek, Vit Stritecky, and Ondrej Ditrych, 271–96. Cham: Palgrave Macmillan, Springer Nature.

Strange, Susan. 1994. *States and Markets.* Second edition. London: Pinter.

Tannenwald, Nina. 2016. "Normative Strategies for Disarmament." In *Global Nuclear Disarmament: Strategic, Political, and Regional Perspectives,* edited by Nik Hynek and Michal Smetana, 107–21. New York: Routledge.

TASS [Russian News Agency]. 2018a. *Russia's Okhotnik Attack Drone to Become Prototype of Sixth Generation Fighter—Source.* July 20. https://tass.com/defense/1014154.

————. 2018b. *Russia's Okhotnik Heavy Drone Makes First Ground Run.* November 23. https://tass.com/defense/1032118.

The Telegraph. 2017. "AI Is the Biggest Risk We Face as a Civilisation, Elon Musk Says." July 17. https://www.telegraph.co.uk/technology/2017/07/17/ai-biggest-risk-face-civilisation-elon-musk-says/.

UK [United Kingdom]. 2018. *Human Machine Touchpoints: The United Kingdom's Perspective on Human Control Over Weapon Development and Targeting Cycles.* CCW/GGE.2/2018/WP.1. Working Paper Submitted to Group of Governmental Experts of the High Contracting Parties to the Convention on Prohibitions or Restrictions on the Use of Certain Conventional Weapons Which May Be Deemed to Be Excessively Injurious or to Have Indiscriminate Effects. Geneva, August 8. https://www.unog.ch/80256EDD006B8954/(httpAssets)/050CF806D90934F5C12582E5002EB800/%24file/2018_GGE+LAWS_August_Working+Paper_UK.pdf.

Um, Jung-Sup. 2019. *Drones as Cyber-Physical Systems: Concepts and Applications for the Fourth Industrial Revolution.* Singapore: Springer.

UN [United Nations]. n.d. *The Convention on Certain Conventional Weapons.* Accessed October 1, 2019. https://www.unog.ch/80256EE600585943/(httpPages)/4F0DEF093B4860B4C1257180004B1B30.

UNGA [United Nations General Assembly]. 2018. *First Committee Weighs Potential Risks of New Technologies as Members Exchange Views on How to Control Lethal Autonomous Weapons, Cyberattacks.* GA/DIS/3611. UNGA First Committee, Seventy-Third Session, 19th Meeting, October 26, 2018. https://www.un.org/press/en/2018/ga-dis3611.doc.htm.

UNHRC [United Nations Human Rights Council]. n.d. *Welcome to the Human Rights Council: Promoting Better Human Rights and Standards.* Accessed October 23, 2019. https://www.ohchr.org/EN/HRBodies/HRC/Pages/AboutCouncil.aspx.

UNODA [United Nations Office for Disarmament Affairs]. 2014. *Convention on Certain Conventional Weapons.* Geneva: United Nations. https://unoda-web.s3-accelerate.amazonaws.com/wp-content/uploads/assets/publications/more/ccw/ccw-book-let.pdf.

UNSC [United Nations Security Council]. n.d. *Current Members: Permanent and Non-Permanent Members.* Accessed October 22, 2019. https://www.un.org/securitycouncil/content/current-members.

UNSG [United Nations Secretary-General]. n.d. *The Role of the Secretary-General.* Accessed October 15, 2019. https://www.un.org/sg/en/content/role-secretary-general.

USA [United States of America]. 2018. *Humanitarian Benefits of Emerging Technologies in the Area of Lethal Autonomous Weapon Systems.* CCW/GGE.1/2018/WP.4. Working Paper Submitted to Group of Governmental Experts of the High Contracting Parties to the Convention on Prohibitions or Restrictions on the Use of Certain Conventional Weapons Which May Be Deemed to Be Excessively Injurious or to Have Indiscriminate Effects. Geneva, March 28. https://www.unog.ch/80256EDD006B8954/(httpAssets)/7C177AE5BC10B588C125825F004B06BE/$file/CCW_GGE.1_2018_WP.4.pdf.

Vultee, Fred. 2011. "Securitization as a Media Frame: What Happens When the Media 'Speak Security.'" In *Understanding Securitisation Theory: How Security Problems Emerge and Dissolve,* edited by Thierry Balzacq, 77–93. New York: Routledge.

WA [Wassenaar Arrangement]. 2018. *Wassenaar Arrangement on Export Controls for Conventional Arms and Dual-Use Goods and Technologies.* Compiled by the Wassenaar Arrangement Secretariat December 2018. https://www.wassenaar.org/app/uploads/2019/consolidated/WA-DOC-18-PUB-001-Public-Docs-Vol-II-2018-List-of-DU-Goods-and-Technologies-and-Munitions-List-Dec-18.pdf.

Wagner, Markus. 2014. "The Dehumanization of International Humanitarian Law: Legal, Ethical, and Political Implications of Autonomous Weapon Systems." *Vanderbilt Journal of Transnational Law* 47, no. 5: 1371–424.

Walker, Jon. 2019. "Machine Learning in Manufacturing—Present and Future Use-Cases." *Emerj,* October 23. https://emerj.com/ai-sector-overviews/machine-learning-in-manufacturing/.

Walsh, James I. 2015. "Political Accountability and Autonomous Weapons." *Research and Politics* 2, no. 4: 1–6.

Wareham, Mary. 2017. *Letter to Aloysio Nunes, Minister of External Relations of Brazil.* April 26, https://www.stopkillerrobots.org/wp-content/uploads/2013/03/KRC_LtrBrazil_26Apr2017.pdf.

———. 2018a. *Letter to S. Brin, President of Alphabet Inc. and S. Pichai, Chief Executive Officer of Google Inc., Google.* March 13. https://www.stopkillerrobots.org/wp-content/uploads/2018/04/KRC_LtrGoogle_12March2018.pdf.

———. 2018b. *Letter to J. Bezos, Chief Executive Officer, President and Chairman of the Board of Directors, Amazon.* May 16. https://www.stopkillerrobots.org/wp-content/uploads/2018/05/5.16.2018_Letter-to-Amazon.pdf.

———. 2018c. *Letter to Florence Parly, Minister for the Armed Forces of France.* April 3. https://www.stopkillerrobots.org/wp-content/uploads/2018/04/KRC_LtrFrance_3April2018.pdf.

———. 2018d. *Letter to Kang Kyung-Wha, Minister of Foreign Affairs of Republic of Korea.* March 5. https://www.stopkillerrobots.org/wp-content/uploads/2018/03/3.5.2018-KRC-to-ROK_KAIST.pdf.

———. 2019. *Letter to Rt. Hon. Winston Peters, Deputy Prime Minister, Minister of Foreign Affairs, Minister for Disarmament and Arms Control of New Zealand.* April 4. https://www.stopkillerrobots.org/wp-content/uploads/2019/04/2019_NZ.pdf.

Zawieska, Karolina. 2017. "An Ethical Perspective on Autonomous Weapon Systems." In *Perspectives on Lethal Autonomous Weapon Systems,* UNODA Occasional Papers, no. 30: 49–56. New York: United Nations Publication.

Conclusion

Synthesis and Outline of the Logic

This book sought to grasp the logic of humanitarian arms control and disarmament. In pursuit of this, it scrutinized the general historical pattern of stigmatization and regulation/proscription of various weapons and weapons-related practices on humanitarian grounds. A series of empirical case studies was presented. In particular, the focus fell to international regimes featuring (elements of) humanitarian disarmament and/or humanitarian arms control. Because the utilized *power-analytical approach* not only allowed but also compelled us to review more complex constitutive forces behind these dynamics, we preferred not to term them "humanitarian regimes." Rather, with diverse accounts of security and their complex interplays in mind, we addressed the studied regimes more neutrally as "security regimes." What follows is a careful generalization of the findings, distilling the crucial characteristics, discourses, practices, and dynamics across the board. It builds upon cross-case (synchronic) and cross-period (diachronic) comparative analyses and comprehensively shows the degree of variation and homogeneity across the examined cases. It is on this basis that the logic of humanitarian arms control and disarmament is concurrently outlined, as well as graphically synthesized (see figure).

The *power-analytical approach* gave the proper analytical means and was utilized to distill this logic from within and across the selected case studies and to structure it here. For heuristic purposes, we prefer to start with an outline of the theoretical contribution of this book, which is twofold. It refines both the theorization of power in general terms and the theorization of international security regimes in particular. Cutting through the three waves of theorizing regimes within the discipline of IR—the neo-neoconvergence regime theory, the cognitivism and radical constructivist/poststructuralist understanding—we sought to strike a balance. It is for this reason that we utilized the conceptualization of "a fourfold taxonomy of power," the most sophisticated existing conceptualization of power available, offered by Barnett and Duvall (2005, 48). However, for organizing a comprehensive analysis of security regimes, we enhanced this intellectual framework by bringing onboard, inter alia, Barnett's (2011, 29) conceptualization of the forces of destruction, production, and protection, Strange's (1994, 24–32) conceptualization of the four components of structural power, Foucault's (1980, 196–97) dispositif-episteme dichotomy, and Deleuze and Guattari's (1983, 10–11) notion of "desiring production." Our metatheoretical orientation or theoretical eclecticism paved the way for a single intellectual framework interlinking all these strands and pieces of literature. Termed here as the *power-analytical approach*, it helped to organize regime analysis and order thinking. Compared to Barnett and Duvall's (2005) approach, the scope of the one proposed is broader (integration of further related literature and perspectives) and at the same time more focused (issue oriented rather than general). Moreover, the presented deep empirical inquiry into power operations in international weapons-related security regimes bears significant implications for the further refinement of Barnett and Duvall's (2005) power matrix. While we still consider it as an important integrative-analytical device for studying power configurations, our inquiry elucidated first, how the order of things and processes may be reverse; second, how the four types of power are not alike in terms of their initial explanatory value; and third, how the system of relations between/ among them is not subject to linear analysis. In particular, by virtue of going *from* broad, structural, and diffuse workings of power *to* specific interactions among actors (ranging from great powers to nonstate and business actors) rather than vice versa, we showed how everything starts with the workings of productive power. It was demonstrated how the constitutive power of the discourse works to either maintain or reverse structural power, and how this interaction utilizes the fruits of compulsory power to shape the contours of institutional power. The latter was often found to feature a reflection, or even product, of this "2+1" formula of contingent power interplay. Thus it has, to a large degree, a synthetic quality. Still more, we flagged and comprehensively showed how various types of power may be ontologically, and thus also analytically, inseparable. In particular, chapter 2 and chapter 4 showed how structural and compulsory powers may work in synergy, while chapter 3 depicted the joint operation of compulsory and institutional powers. Such a portrayal of *heterarchies and synergies of power configurations* provides not only an original approach to dissecting the notion of power in international politics but also a novel account of regime theorization. The contributions of this comprehensive study to regime theory can be best summarized under the rubrics of what Hasenclever, Mayer, and Rittberger (1997, 211) dissected as the "prospects for synthesis." This theory-only book concludes by the identification of four areas where no version of IR regime theory (including theirs) has been capable of making a strong contribution: power of legitimacy, narrative structures, identity-related binary separations, and conditions of possibility for emergence and transformations of historical orders. All four areas are made central and tackled by this book. We bring together insights from power- and interest-based approaches, as well as rationalist and cognitivist explanations of international regimes, for the most part disjointed in the existing literature (1997, 211–24). With this discerned gap unfilled to date, this niche is where the presented book is nested. This is what allows us to bring the current regime theorization much closer to the reality. It is particularly achieved by bridging the gap between the existing ideal typical regime explanations and the "messy" reality. Moreover, our unique approach to power configurations, not treated alike herein, allows us to evaluate the explanatory power of diverse factors to the prospects and robustness of international regimes. Though it may still be about searching for regularities in dispersion (Foucault 1972), the following paragraphs shed light on certain lessons concerning similarities and differences across the selected case studies.

The book systematically demonstrated how all of the examined security regimes came into being through the workings of *productive power*, in particular as certain "regimes of truth" (Foucault 1980, 131). Though each was particularly tailored to reflect case-specific and prevalent circumstances, all largely built upon the narratives of inhumanity, immorality, unethicality, and illegality to stigmatize the weapons in question. These narratives largely reflected concerns over "bodily harm," the key norm on which the discourse pivoted (Keck and Sikkink 1998, 27). Another closely related uniting feature that epitomized productive power across all the studied cases is the binary civilization-barbarian episteme. It had two major implications. First, it would allow anchoring of the moral, ethical, and religious superiority of the ingroup, that is, the civilized, and to marginalize the outgroup, that is, the uncivilized, along the same lines. This is the system of differentiation that would usually shape the contours of (mainly, though not exclusively, "transnational") "moral authority" (Hall 1997, 591). Second, it would facilitate the process of stigmatization by virtue of weapons viewed again through the prism of civilization. This is how weapons were framed as uncivilized, at best or, at worst, as a menace to the survival of civilization. The latter feature strongly manifested in the cases of nuclear weapons (chapter 5) and autonomous weapon systems (AWS) (chapter 6). In both cases, sci-fi imaginaries played a special and ostensibly strong constitutive role in this regard, a feature that was incidentally not prominent in the other studied cases. Another crucial commonality, or rather a pattern of spasmodic reinforcement, throughout all the presented case studies was the tradition of *legal grafting*, that is, processes of manipulation through which norms are organized into norm complexes. In particular, this implies a repeated practice of employing similar foundations of legal arguments and humanitarian language in framing successive security regimes. The convergence between International Humanitarian Law (IHL), later convergent also with International Human Rights Law (IHRL), and weapons law featured at the core of this process. Having taken a longue durée perspective, we demonstrated how all of the aforesaid coalesced into the *humanitarian-*

disarmament epistemic grid taking root in the nineteenth century and still shaping contemporary processes. The rise of (new) humanitarianism and the development of the notion of Western civilization, both traceable to the nineteenth century, were found to be of particular importance in this regard. The complex and nonlinear process of legal grafting also took root in the nineteenth century. As chapter 2 made clear, the nineteenth-century regime was grafted upon the antislavery norm, a norm remarkably unrelated in any direct way to the realm of weapons or the general principles of IHL. The following chapters detailed how contemporary regimes were similarly grafted upon the principles of the IHL, in particular those incorporated into the domain of weapons and warfare by the nineteenth-century regime, as well as newly upon the IHRL and the UN Charter. Notably, successive regimes were often grafted upon the success of preceding ones, especially the (further) institutional embeddedness of the core norms. Particularly strong linkages were detected between the cases of APLs and CMs (chapter 3), as well as between those of nuclear weapons and other, that is, chemical and biological, weapons of mass destruction (chapter 5).

Multiple commonalities among the studied cases, including between the nineteenth-century and contemporary processes, were also discerned in regard to the workings of *structural power*. In chapter 3, we introduced the notion of the *humanitarian transnational historical bloc* and discussed its rise and transformation in light of humanitarianism. Having referred to this concept also in subsequent chapters, we ultimately showed how the aforesaid humanitarian principles and the ideal of disarmament were advanced by specific categories of actors, often even the same ones across the studied cases. This bloc, with its multiple power heterarchies within, put together (I)NGOs and their various umbrellas, various elements of regional/global international organizations (IOs), epistemic communities of experts and professional associations, and the mass media. Across all the studied cases, they also closely collaborated with like-minded governments, often of (nonallied) smaller states and middle powers. The International Committee of the Red Cross (ICRC), the guarantor of IHL with its role cutting across the realms of NGOs, epistemic communities, and governments, stood among them too. This whole bloc of actors, in fact norm entrepreneurs, was always united by "humanity as an identity" (Agier 2010, 32). Its rise, together with related politics, mainly dates from the 1970s onward, as particularly associated with the spread of new constitutionalism. However, chapter 2 shed light on its nineteenth-century origins. What was found particularly remarkable that took root in the nineteenth century were early activist manifestations of (transnational) civil society, the special role of the ICRC, as well as the engagement of scientists and other actors with professional judgment. Through a detailed scrutiny of the transhistoricity of antinuclear advocacy, the case of one with the most and strikingly enduring nature, we additionally testified to the assumption of this bloc being "historical." We also considered how the notion of the humanitarian transnational historical bloc was challenged, though not displaced, as the other cases also testified to, by (nongovernmental) gun lobby advocacy in the case of small arms and light weapons (SALW) (chapter 4). Throughout history, humanitarian disarmament aspirations and campaigns would consistently meet powerful resistance foremost from the structurally favored states. This clash may be best described as the one between "identity politics" (Barnett and Weiss 2008, chap. 5), centered on desiring production of humanitarianism and humanitarization of politics, and great power politics. The nineteenth century was much about general military dominance and those structurally favored actors included the great, rising, and revisionist powers. Because technological advancements became increasingly associated with power (of weapons) at that time, military superiority or inferiority in weapons appeared to play a prominent role in defining the contours of structural military dominance. The rise of the economic within the political, as well as the acceleration in technologies of war, reinforced and broadened the horizons of this order toward the late twentieth century/early twenty-first century. Weapons-dependent governments, in a much broader sense, eventually emerged as the core of this *disarmament-resistant bloc*. This shift concurred with the consolidation of first-tier, second-tier, and third-tier states, chiefly driven by the pursuit of power, wealth, and victory in war, in the global system of (conventional) arms production and trade (Krause 1992, 97–98). This order and associated interests, for the most part contrary to disarmament ambitions, were most vividly showcased in the case of SALW (chapter 4). We also showed that it was mainly the major producers and users of antipersonnel landmines (APLs) and cluster munitions (CMs) that would oppose their prohibition (chapter 3). Taking into consideration how various weapons were associated with actual exercises of military power, we showed how the workings of *structural power* and *compulsory power* could be inherently intertwined. To account for such dynamics properly, we analyzed these power configurations jointly in chapter 2 and chapter 4. This is because the strategic environment associated with the nineteenth century and with SALW, respectively, served best to illustrate them. We graphically illustrated this nexus with an arrow connecting the loci of structural and compulsory power (see figure). Even though AWS are not yet fully operational, chapter 6 proved that the dynamics emerging around their development had already testified to the discerned trend. This is because the core of the opposition to their preventive prohibition already drew together the dominant producing states and many of the allied (particularly in terms of preestablished channels of arms trade) less technologically developed states. What is important is that we examined this contemporary *stratified* distribution of privileges on balance with the highly restrictive and exclusive system of arms diffusion within the colonial order of the nineteenth century. The latter featured a system of *binary* distribution of privileges, with the "haves" (mainly great/colonial powers) and "have-nots" (mainly colonies). To maintain their privilege, the powers codified this order in the Brussels Act (1890) (chapter 2). In that, this case most resembled the modern case of nuclear weapons, discussed in chapter 5. Nuclear powers similarly sought to secure their structural dominance within the binary structural nuclear order, with the "haves" (the nuclear club) and "have-nots" (the rest). It was reflected in the restrictive nonproliferation and nuclear commerce regime(s). However, apart from the possessors, opposition to disarmament in nuclear weapons also included their partners in nuclear deterrence. This brings us closer again to that broader notion of "weapons-dependent governments," still a more modern feature, as a way to define the disarmament-resistance bloc. However, the principal finding was that, despite this major transformation, most of the prominent powers of the nineteenth century eventually turned into those major weapons producers across all of the reviewed cases. A crucial concurrent discovery was that their structural dominance was also preserved. Except for the military means, their dominance became also newly maintained via institutional structures, as well as arms transfer (or arms guarantee, as in the case of nuclear weapons) dependencies on the part of the recepients. The former is discussed shortly within the confines of institutional power. Another related and noteworthy finding across all the studied cases was that *productive power*, in particular the constitutive power of the discourse, works to either maintain or reverse *structural power*. For example, the discourse of Western civilization worked to maintain the superiority of the West in the nineteenth century (chapter 2). In turn, the discourse of nuclear disarmament worked to reverse the binary and discriminatory ("haves" versus "have-nots") structural distribution of priviledges (chapter 5). This is the materiality of discourse, also graphically illustrated with an arrow linking these two power loci (see figure).

What facilitated such a broad-based structural embeddedness of weapons was also the rise of private/commercial actors as possessors of technological know-how in the contemporary global system of arms production and trade. We most extensively considered this trend in regard to APLs and CMs in chapter 3, with respect to SALW in chapter 4, and oriented toward AWS in chapter 6. As we systematically flagged, these actors driven by profit often sided with the disarmament-resistant bloc. It is helpful to refer to Strange's (1994, 24–32) conceptualization of the four components of structural power to summarize our findings. While the humanitarian bloc appeared prominent in knowledge production, the disarmament-resistant bloc preponderated in structural control over finance and material production in (military) technologies, including the possession of related know-how and—notably—the sphere of security. Another interesting observation pertinent to our inquiries into the workings of structural power deserves attention. While the current realities yet correspond to the global stratified system of arms production and trade that we featured throughout our study, the increasing privatization of (military) technology made us contemplate the sustainability of "tiers." Especially in light of contemporary technological realities, at least the emerging directions for further technological development, we could indeed speculate about the erosion of such tiers and associated barriers and potentially ubiquitous diffusion of military technologies. There is, for instance, the real potential for small AI-powered killer drones to be "mass produced" and "cost little more than a smartphone" (Tegmark 2017, 117). This will reflect the rise of "a frugal economy" (Radjou and Prabhu 2015, chap. 1) oriented toward "frugal," that is, "accessible, adaptable, affordable," innovation (Bhatti et al. 2018, 1–2). Another illustration of the potential for military technologies to diffuse beyond any current understandings of the stratified order is the developments in and concerns surrounding "3D printed firearms" (IANSA 2017).

The two other types of power operate through direct (*compulsory power*) and diffuse (*institutional power*) interactions of actors. This is in their workings where we found further common features across the studied cases. In regard to institutional power, these were related *institutional processes* of the nineteenth and late twentieth/early twenty-first century that bore significant resemblance among themselves. Norm entrepreneurs became increasingly embedded within the traditional deliberation and decision-making fora. As chapter 2 recorded, the door was opened— just a bit—for nonstate actors to influence intergovernmental negotiation processes as early as the nineteenth century. This happened under the rubrics of so-called open diplomacy. The following empirical chapters illustrated how their involvement dramatically increased toward the late twentieth/early twenty-first century as also an outcome of the spread of new constitutionalism. Not only were they given more space to lobby governments at home, but they were also granted observation and consultation roles within the global (UN) system of governance. Their institutional appeal was always supported and reinforced by like-minded governments, particularly Russia in the nineteenth century, and typically a group of middle powers and small states in contemporary processes. However, in part echoing the nineteenth century when states, in particular a cluster of the great powers, were the key decision makers, contemporary processes were similarly shaped by the general consensus rule and the five veto-bearing members of the UN Security Council. Blocking moves, typically but not exclusively from those key dominant players, often hampered progress on regimes and in most of the cases entailed compromises challenging their robustness. Such compromises could mainly be divided into those on *scope* (for example, the success of the laws of war on balance with the failure of disarmament or limitations on armaments and military budget in the nineteenth-century regime), *strength* (for example, the lack of mechanisms to ensure worldwide transparency and enforce general disarmament in the Non-Proliferation Treaty), and *membership* (for example, the adoption of the Treaty on the Prohibition of Nuclear Weapons with the nuclear powers left out). Further crucial illustrations of the latter could be the cases of APLs and CMs. These cases were of particular importance because they demonstrated how *institutional power* could operate jointly with, or even through, *compulsory power*. As we portrayed in chapter 3, the Ottawa and Oslo Processes showed how traditional deliberation and decision-making fora may be bypassed in favor of self-selecting countries uniting to establish single-issue and ad hoc security regimes. With an arrow directed from the locus of compulsory power toward the domain of institutional power, we graphically illustrated this process as an alternative procedural model (see figure). This was done to make clear that regime institutionalization does not necessarily occur within the traditional deliberation and decision-making fora but may potentially be transplanted from the outside.

Concerning the workings of *compulsory power* in its own courtyard, there were also similar dynamics detected across the studied cases. The key findings of Hall (1997), though related to the presovereign system of feudal Europe, may serve well to summarize our findings on this front too. We found compulsory power as a particular level of being, rather than doing, at which actors' authorities get translated into (coercive) resources for particular (coercive) strategies of direct influence. It is here where "moral authority" of norm entrepreneurs was "employed as a power resource to influence transnational outcomes" (1997, 591). Hall (1997, 594) also detected that moral authority "acquires utility as a power resource when it becomes socially embedded." In this light, we found it particularly useful to dissect the relevant workings of *productive power*, that is, the identification of underlying norms, and *structural power*, that is, the delineation of norm entrepreneurs, beforehand. Hall (1997, 594 and 596–97) was also right to stress that moral authority operates on balance with other "power resources," mainly state economic and political-military capabilities. Our comparative study uncovered an interesting paradox in this regard. Norm entrepreneurs usually lacked mechanisms of direct leverage over the disarmament-resistant bloc, including over the nonsignatories of particular regimes. However, their normative pressure—as a form of authority—was often powerful enough to compel many states and commercial actors in opposition to change their policies. This pressure mainly manifested as tabooization, naming and shaming, and peer pressure. The last was particularly generated by (further) states, especially middle powers, and actors of the commercial sector denouncing their association with stigmatized tools and practices. All of this also accounts for why regimes were often followed by those staying outside of them (for example, the tradition of nuclear nonuse or the adherence to the principle of meaningful human control in the case of AWS). This informal tradition became sedimented as a matter of "accountability" in light of "humanitarian ethics" and the reluctance by most of the involved actors to challenge their "humanitarian identity" (Barnett and Weiss 2008, chap. 5). Barnett and Finnemore (1999, 700) additionally noted that IOs, often "more than the reflection of state preferences," are also important actors in international politics. Their power, however, derives from their "rational-legal authority" and "control over expertise" (1999, 707). Our book reaffirmed this finding and systematically showed how various (elements of) IOs either pushed forward the humanitarian agenda (often the European Union) or hampered it (often the United Nations Security Council), or at least served as negotiation for the cause (often the United Nations General Assembly). Expert authority, "a major means by which knowledge translates into power" (Cross 2013, 138), in a much broader sense was also thoroughly examined in this book. This one was also found tricky. Actors with knowledge-based expertise were found on the side of norm entrepreneurs but also on that of the disarmament-resistance bloc. The International Committee of the Red Cross (ICRC) could best illustrate the former, while professional voices of support to nuclear deterrence or professional reviews of AWS military utility could well exemplify the latter. It is, however, remarkable that the most powerful IOs, in particularly the UNSC, would favor the disarmament-resistant bloc, while the humanitarian bloc would usually generate more of expert support. The intensity of the gradient shade graphically nuances both (see figure).

Despite multiple similarities, we concur with Barnett (Barnett and Duvall 2005) that the notions of "evolution" and "progress" are not identical and consider the former to better characterize the general process of "evolution" in international security regimes (Barnett 2009). This is because, as we systematically showed throughout the book, the general historic pattern of stigmatization and regulation/proscription of various weapons and weapons-related practices in light of humanitarianism did not follow a well-defined and consistent course. In general terms, Barnett (2011, 29) identified three longue durée periods to analyze the evolution of humanitarianism: nineteenth-century Imperial Humanitarianism, Cold War Neo-Humanitarianism, and post–Cold War Liberal Humanitarianism. In regard to weapons-related matters, however, Croft (1996, 34) highlighted that the Cold War could principally be epitomized by "strategic stability"–oriented arms control and disarmament. In agreement with his assumption, we repeatedly showcased how this era featured a period of interruption in humanitarianism-oriented arms control and disarmament, originating in the nineteenth century and reviving after the end of the Cold War. For instance, we marked how there were neglected antinuclear humanitarian sentiments in the 1950s–1960s (chapter 5), efforts by the ICRC to stigmatize APLs in the 1950s and especially the 1970s (chapter 3), and the Cold War attempts by Amnesty International and the

Stockholm International Peace Research Institute (SIPRI) to challenge SALW (chapter 4). Apart from such a gap generated by the Cold War, post–Cold War humanitarianism-oriented arms control and disarmament were also rather selective and contingent. In the realm of conventional weapons, the 1990s' successful proscription of APLs facilitated a broader-based stigmatization of SALW. With more ambitious aspirations appearing inadequate in regard to the entire category of SALW, the focus shifted toward prohibition of CMs (2008), also via their alignment with APLs under the umbrella of explosive remnants of war (ERW), as well as on transfers in the domain of SALW and eventually the Arms Trade Treaty (2013). In light of recent technological advances, the focus of humanitarian efforts with respect to conventional weapons was reoriented toward a ban on AWS. Generally in parallel, but often in turns, with all these processes, there proceeded the tabooization of nuclear weapons, with major bursts in the 1980s and after the end of the Cold War, especially at the turn of the twenty-first century, as well as in culmination with the Treaty on the Prohibition of Nuclear Weapons (2017). What we found that aggravated this generally muddled pattern of development were divergences in the quality of security regulation across the studied cases. First, regulatory/prohibitive efforts could be ex post such as, for example, in the cases of APLs and CMs (chapter 3) or SALW (chapter 4), as well as ex ante such as in the case of AWS (chapter 6). Second, both weapons and weapons-related practices could be subject to regulation/prohibition. In regard to practices, for example, the discharge of projectiles and explosives from balloons was prohibited in the nineteenth century (chapter 2), while practices of international marking, record keeping, and tracing were brought up to regulation in the domain of SALW, in particular by virtue of the 2005 International Tracing Instrument (chapter 4). Finally and most importantly, regulatory/prohibitive efforts du jour could evolve, but not necessarily so, into security regimes. It was a matter of cognitive (re)framing, on balance between humanity and strategic considerations, that weapons-related security regimes would (not) come into being at particular points of time. This is where and how all the aforesaid and graphically illustrated dynamics (see figure) played out into various security regimes in practice. This is also where and how humanitarian disarmament aspirations usually met resistance, with implications for certain, if any, outcomes related to humanitarian arms control and disarmament. In "power" terms, this epitomizes the interplay between *productive power* and *structural power* (often in deep nexus with *compulsory power*), with implications for *institutional power*, in particular the *qualities of regimes*. We graphically illustrated this complex interplay with dashed arrows (see figure). Importantly, this logic was found fitting to both ex post and ex ante regulatory/prohibitive endeavors.

If or when they occurred, security regimes usually shaped up in various ways, a further crucial point of divergence among the studied cases of security regulation. Three major dichotomies were found to be of particular importance in defining regimes, namely those between *prohibition* (preventive ban or disarmament) and *regulation*, between particular *weapons* and broader weapon *(sub)categories*, as well as between *simple* (issue-oriented) and *complex* (combining aspects of prohibition/regulation of weapons/weapons-related practices) regimes. The question of a structural "window of opportunity" was found pivotal to cut through the thicket of these notions and order thinking with respect to weapons-related security regimes (Risse-Kappen 1994, 204 and 207). It implies a constellation of structural forces that open the space for norm entrepreneurs to advance humanitarian disarmament or that, at least, allow for certain forms of humanitarian arms control. Building on our findings, we can decompose this complex notion into what we term the questions of *strategic centrality* and *strategic concurrence* for heuristic purposes. It is useful to start with the former for some initial orientation between and among the discerned dichotomies. Based on our comparative case study, we regard *strategic centrality* as the structural indispensability of certain arms at certain points of time, as defined by the prevalent strategic environment, including associated political-economic models/rationalities, amity/enmity patterns, and the availability of technological alternatives. Most importantly, we consider strategic centrality to be subject to (re)interpretation. As this book demonstrated, *prohibition* (preventive ban or disarmament) was only possible upon the reconsideration and suppression of strategic centrality. It is in this light, for example, that the Cold War efforts by the ICRC to stigmatize APLs failed, while a ban and subsequent *disarmament* in this realm became possible in the 1990s. The core condition that enabled this shift was the dramatic change in the strategic environment after the end of the Cold War, in particular the departure from a symmetric interstate confrontation and the overall degradation of APLs' strategic centrality. In light of the threshold for their use being elevated by the humanitarian discourse, CMs lost their strategic centrality largely due to the availability of technological alternatives at the turn of twenty-first century (chapter 3). Though this term is of greater value for grasping other cases, as referred to shortly, it is reasonable to introduce it at this point. Both of the aforementioned cases feature instances of *strategic concurrence*. It implies that, although based on different reasoning and typically in opposition, strategic motives may to various extents reconcile with the postulates of humanity. By default, it could be assumed that weapons or weapons-related practices, never (or not yet) positioned as strategically central, could also be subject to prohibition. Though not dissected for related processes in this book, prohibition of blinding lasers could then serve as a good illustration of a successful *preventive ban* of weapons still "in the prototype phase of development" and never deployed to the battlefield (Akerson 2013, 70). Again going beyond the scope of the presented study, we can also assume that a difference between particular *weapons* and broader *weapons (sub)categories* matters little when their strategic significance gets downplayed in favor of prohibition regimes. This is because we are aware of, for instance, bans issued upon the broader subcategories, that is, chemical and biological weapons, under the umbrella of weapons of mass destruction. However, this book systematically demonstrated that this difference matters for understanding the logic under which strategic centrality and regimes may coexist. In particular, it showed how *complex* regimes would most likely be associated with broader *weapons (sub)categories*, distinguished by their *strategic centrality*. Most importantly, the contours of *strategic concurrence* would be paramount to enabling and shaping such regimes. Such "complex" regimes would at best entail aspects of *piecemeal disarmament* but would for the most part be centered upon *regulation* of weapons/weapons-related practices.

For instance, the nineteenth-century regime built upon a broader terrain of conventional technological advancements increasingly associated with the power (of weapons) and military superiority. Chances for broad-based humanitarian disarmament were negligible in the prevalent strategic environment, with arms races and strategic competition among the major and rising/revisionist powers gaining momentum. However, certain strategic conditions opened space for a humanitarian regime. Most importantly, these included the sedimented military inferiority of Russia and the use of a noble argument to slow down technologically leading countries, as well as the general need to civilize industrialized warfare as a legitimate instrument of foreign policy. Such an interplay between strategic centrality and strategic concurrence paved the way for a few compromises, though mostly concerning matters of little or no military utility or strategic significance. Having encompassed, inter alia, a ban on expanding bullets, a ban on the launch of projectiles/explosives from balloons, as well as the codification of certain laws of war conduct, this regime may be considered complex (chapter 2). Another case illustrative of similar dynamics is the experience with security regulation of SALW. It in part echoed the nineteenth-century situation in that it concerned a category of weapons, rather a subcategory of conventional weapons in this case, associated with actual exercises of military power. However, unlike the colonial order and restriction to sell arms to the colonies (Brussels Act 1890), the strategic centrality of SALW was much broader because it became embedded globally. As described earlier, a major shift in the dominant political-economic model accounted for this. In addition, the strategic centrality of SALW got reinforced with the codification of the right of national self-defense in case of an armed attack (UN Charter 1945). It is reasonable to recall for comparative purposes that their strategic centrality was complemented by civil gun culture and extensive commercial trade in SALW. This structural force, having indeed done a lot to shape the prospects of SALW regulation, featured a unique phenomenon in the realm of weapons and weapons control. All combined, humanitarian disarmament in SALW would be virtually impossible. This was even reflected by a nontraditional form of humanitarian activism in the case of SALW, that is, the central focus of norm entrepreneurs eventually falling not to these weapons as such but to their flows. However, the drastic change in the strategic environment produced by the end of the Cold War drove security regulation of SALW. The balance shifting from interstate to intrastate conflicts and the resurgence of terrorism were of particular importance in this regard. It is for this reason, in particular the lack of favorable strategic forces, that the Cold War attempts by Amnesty International and SIPRI to challenge SALW failed. As a compromise between the strategic centrality of SALW and strategic concurrence for some sort of regulation, a complex regime emerged. It was aimed at prohibiting illegal transfers/trade and illegal end-use, thus (preventatively) disarming prospective illegal end-users, as well as regulating practices of marking, record keeping, and tracing in this light. In terms of disarmament, this regime was also complemented by programs of Disarmament, Demobilization, and Reintegration (DDR) in conflict-ridden environments (chapter 4). Another case that may support this line of reasoning is that of security regulation of nuclear weapons. The Treaty on the Prohibition of Nuclear Weapons (2017) seemingly moved it closer to the cases of legal proscription of the other subcategories of WMD, namely chemical and biological weapons. However, we consider the case of nuclear weapons a much more complex regime and integrate it into this discussion. This is particularly, though not exclusively, in light of the reluctance on the part of the nuclear powers to abide by this convention. Strategic centrality of nuclear weapons long lay with (a)symmetrical deterrence practices and the maintenance of the world order. The lack of technological alternatives to their unique deterrent effect was crucial in this regard. They were found to be of particular importance to their possessors, including for the reasons of state or regime survival, internal or external prestige, and power or superiority. However, various episodes of nuclear brinkmanship, extensive modernization programs, the rising/upcoming nuclear powers, as well as nuclear aspirations on the part of terrorists paved the way for a complex security regime in the domain. Inter alia, it put together prohibition of certain practices of nuclear weapons testing, prohibition of nuclear weapons in certain regions (nuclear-weapons-free zones), as well as regulation of nuclear commerce. Importantly though, on balance between strategic centrality and strategic concurrence, its nonproliferation quality, thus (preventive) disarmament of prospective nuclear powers, gained a much stronger foothold than that of general disarmament. Based on our findings from these three complex regimes, it is interesting to remark that the notion of "piecemeal" disarmament may denote prohibition of particular, singled-out types of weapons (*piecemeal opted disarmament*) and/or prohibition of the flow or access of weapons to particular, singled-out geographic or abstract zones (*piecemeal spatial disarmament*). For instance, the nineteenth-century ban on "dum-dum" bullets featured an instance of piecemeal opted disarmament, the nuclear nonproliferation regime clearly depicted piecemeal *geographic-spatial* disarmament, and prohibition of SALW transfers to illegal end-users vividly illustrated piecemeal *abstract-spatial* disarmament.

This book also incorporated a current case of nonregime surrounded by regulatory politics. It was performed in order to consider conditions under which regimes do not come into being. Because it was only a single case of this sort reviewed herein and because it particularly concerned preventive measures, there is little space for generalization on this front. However, on balance with the other thoroughly scrutinized cases and the basics concerning the preventive prohibition of blinding lasers, the examined case still provided valuable insights into the problematic. Attempts to fully grasp the interplay between humanity and strategic considerations in regard to weapons subject to preventive prohibition may indeed entail certain ambiguities. However, while "still experimental" blinding laser weapons (Akerson 2013, 70) were likely less susceptible to structural forces and strategic dependences, they were preventatively banned as a clear reflection of the deeply embedded norm of bodily harm, even bodily integrity. This is because the Protocol on Blinding Laser Weapons (1995), replicating other successful cases of humanitarian disarmament, targeted a specific weapon with a well-defined harmful effect: "weapons designed to cause permanent blindness" (Sivakumaran 2012, 399). As we showed in chapter 6, the case of AWS shrouded in greater ambiguities could not, at least for now, take the same path. In contrast to blinding laser weapons, current definitions of AWS position them at the crossroads of weapons, methods of warfare, and warriors, along with their potential harmful effects never having been clearly delineated.

The utility of the power-analytical approach for studying the selected cases of international weapons-related security regimes is twofold. First, it allowed us to avoid ontological selectiveness, a flaw common in the existing literature. This implies that the presented book did not decide which parties "count" as actors. Rather than focusing on particular actors and their actions—be they humanitarian activists or great powers—it observed the entire spectrum. Second, this book remedied the fallacy of agent-based explanation. It showed how important it is not only to study actors in action, but also to seriously consider the complexity of structural forces enabling, shaping, or constraining their existence, form, and operation. Simply said, this book sought and was given the analytical means to observe the reality as it was, in all its complex manifestations. Its unique power-analytical approach and related lines of reasoning may serve as a benchmark for studying other security regimes, including those without (explicit) humanitarian aspirations, as well as regimes in general IR. Be-

PRODUCTIVE POWER	STRUCTURAL POWER	
Humanitarian - Disarmament Epistemic Grid	**Humanitarian Transnational Historical Bloc** *of*	**Disarmament-Resistant Bloc** *of*
• norm of bodily harm => weapons as immoral, unethical, inhuman, illegal, and •	*norm entrepreneurs* • like-minded governments (esp. middle powers)	binary order *19th C.* — military powers vs the rest nuclear club vs the rest
uncivilized	• (I)NGOs • epistemic communities	*20th-21st C.* — nuclear deterrence partners tiered order weapons-dependent governments
• standard of civilization => binary civilization-barbarian episteme	• ICRC • (elements of) IOs • media	sovereignty and weapons culture/identity + *civil gun culture and NGO gun lobby (SALW)* economics of arms production and trade
• tradition of legal grafting (principal role of IHL/IHRL)	*humanity as identity*	**first-tier states** + *role of commercial sector* special political position (UNSC/P5)
materiality of discourse / identity politics **ideal of humanitarian disarmament**	(re)constitution of positionality	structural dominance by great powers *great power politics*
INSTITUTIONAL POWER	cognitive (re)framing	resistance vs window of opportunity • strategic centrality • strategic concurrence
Institutional Processes	knowledge production	control over security, technological know-how, finance and material production
increasing access and influence of non-state actors **institutional dominance**	**COMPULSORY POWER**	
key decision-makers: states — great powers *19th C.*	*authority as power resource for coercive strategies (to achieve/promote interests)*	weapons associated with actual exercises of military power
states — UNSC veto-bearing *consensus rule* member-states *20th-21st C.*	**Humanitarian Transnational ——→ Disarmament-Resistant Bloc** *lack of mechanisms*	
BLOCKING MOVES	**Historical Bloc** *of direct leverage*	
	IOs *rational-legal authority*	
Regime Qualities: • regimes/non-regimes • ex post/ex ante • prohibition/regulation of	*taboorization* *moral authority* *naming and shaming* *peer pressure*	*economic and political-military capabilities*
• weapons/weapons-related practices • simple/complex regimes	**epistemic communities** *knowledge-based expertise*	
• compromises on scope/strength/membership (incl. inclusiveness and mechanisms of enforcement, verification, transparency)	*alternative procedural model*	*(informal) adherence as accountability and humanitarian identity*

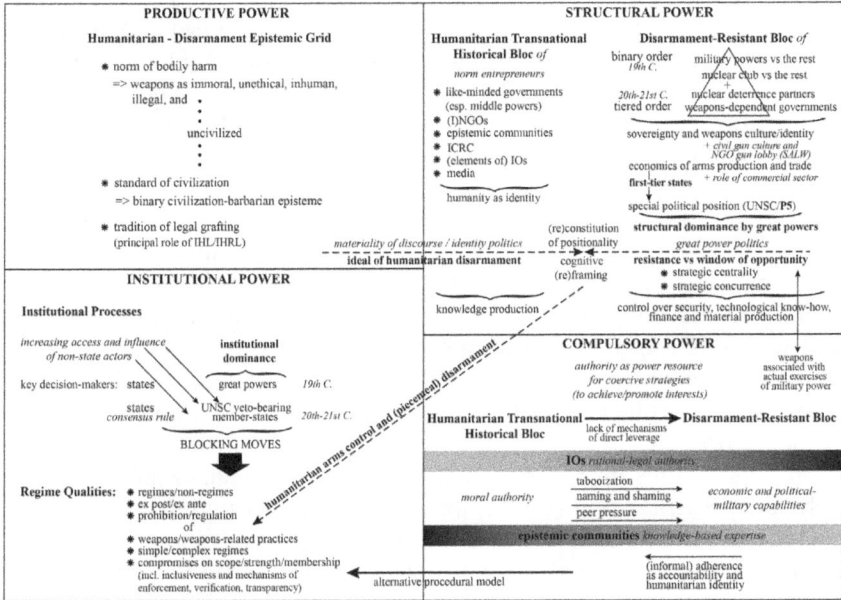

The Logic of Humanitarian Arms Control and Disarmament. *Source*: Author's own based on the typology by Barnett and Duvall 2005, p. 48.

cause the focus of the book was on dissecting the logic of humanitarian arms control and disarmament, the utilized approach could be of use for a more extensive and balanced scrutiny of other weapons regimes with strong humanitarian qualities (for example, the bans on laser blinding, chemical and biological weapons, and the emerging regime on cyberweapons). Broadening the horizons, our approach to analyzing humanitarianism and human security in more general terms may serve well for scrutinizing humanitarian/human security regimes (for example, the global refugee regime, the global internally displaced persons protection regime, the EU asylum regime, and even atrocities regimes). Another important suggestion for further research on this front is power analysis of the Convention on the Rights of Persons with Disabilities. This case would reverse the principal logic of the presented analysis by showing how the movement from weapons regimes to human security (and human rights) may also be possible. The Convention on Cluster Munitions has taken victim assistance a step further by inextricably linking the issue of CM victims in the weapons treaty to their—and their families'—human rights and dignity. It has furthered the determination to cover "the special needs of vulnerable groups" and linked this to the Convention on the Rights of Persons with Disabilities (CRPD). The latter convention, which entered into force in 2008, has established a complex legal regime at the interface between humanitarian law, which was the basic legal reference for the weapons regimes analyzed in the preceding chapters, and human rights law. It is between the CMC and CRPD where operations of power managed—legally, politically, and economically—to merge human security and human rights for the first time. This is why we believe this case would be paramount to show the mutual—and unprecedented—dependency of humanitarian security regimes and human rights regimes on each other. Because this book extensively showed how the power-analytical approach may be applied to examine various interpretations and configurations of security, the utilized framework is also useful for analyzing security regimes outside of the realm of weapons and weapons control (for example, the global and regional regimes for counter-terrorism). As the presented study also systematically scrutinized various economic/financial interests and modi operandi for related regime processes, the developed line of reasoning may be of use for analyzing restrictions on the movement of goods, capital, or labor. In this light, the presented power analysis is qualified for studying regimes with even deeper intertwined security and economic aspects (for example, UN economic sanctions regimes, the Kimberley Process, and WTO food trade regime). Going beyond, the utilized approach is also of use for a novel—and unprecedented—examination of monetary, financial, and trade regimes (for example, the global GATT/WTO trade regime, the global IMF/World Bank finance regime, the Bretton Woods System, and the Organization of Petroleum Exporting Countries commodity/oil trade regime). This is because, having generally showed how different power configurations interplay to produce regimes with different qualities, we made it readily applicable far beyond security-laden, and even broader humanitarian/human security, regimes. In this light, we may consider it directly applicable to studying, inter alia, regime complexes (for example, the global warming carbon regime and the Uruguay Round), regulatory regimes (for example, the global regime for trade in endangered species), or prohibitive regimes (for example, the Vienna Convention for the Protection of the Ozone Layer and the Montreal Protocol on Substances that Deplete the Ozone Layer) in other and any domains. In addition, having scrutinized a nonregime (potentially an emerging regime) on AWS, we also showed how the power-analytical approach can be utilized to comprehend the dynamics associated with emerging regimes (for example, global governance for and protection of environmental refugees) and nonregimes (Dimitrov et al. 2007, 238–48) (for example, forest management, coral reef management, international economic governance on competition policy, and regulation of tactical nuclear weapons). As the proposed examples evidenced, we discerned the security, economic, and environmental domains as strong prospective beneficiaries of power-analytical regime analysis. However, it was done to illustrate the broad cross-domain applicability of the utilized approach rather than limit it to those listed.

REFERENCES

Agier, Michel. 2010. "Humanity as an Identity and Its Political Effects: A Note on Camps and Humanitarian Government." *Humanity* (Fall): 29–45.

Akerson, David. 2013. "The Illegality of Offensive Lethal Autonomy." In *International Humanitarian Law and the Changing Technology of War*, edited by Dan Saxon, 65–98. Boston: Martinus Nijhoff Publishers.

Barnett, Michael. 2009. "Evolution without Progress? Humanitarianism in a World of Hurt." *International Organization* 63 (Fall): 621–63.

———. 2011. *Empire of Humanity: A History of Humanitarianism*. Ithaca, NY: Cornell University Press.

Barnett, Michael, and Raymond Duvall. 2005. "Power in International Politics." *International Organization* 59 (Winter): 39–75.

Barnett, Michael N., and Martha Finnemore. 1999. "The Politics, Power, and Pathologies of International Organizations." *International Organization* 53, no. 4 (Autumn): 699–732.

Barnett, Michael, and Thomas G. Weiss. 2008. *Humanitarianism in Question: Politics, Power, Ethics*. Ithaca, NY: Cornell University Press.

Bhatti, Yasser, Radha Ramaswami Basu, David Barron, and Marc J. Ventresca. 2018. *Frugal Innovation: Models, Means, Methods*. Cambridge: Cambridge University Press.

Croft, Stuart. 1996. *Strategies of Arms Control: A History and Typology*. Manchester: Manchester University Press.

Cross, Mai'a K. Davis. 2013. "Rethinking Epistemic Communities Twenty Years Later." *Review of International Studies* 39: 137–60.

Deleuze, G., and F. Guattari. 1983. *Anti-Oedipus: Capitalism and Schizophrenia*. Minneapolis: University of Minnesota Press.

Dimitrov, Radoslav S., Detlef F. Sprinz, Gerald M. DiGiusto, and Alexander Kelle. 2007. "International Nonregimes: A Research Agenda." *International Studies Review* 9: 230–58.

Foucault, Michel. 1972. *The Archaeology of Knowledge*. New York: Pantheon Books.

———. 1980. *Power/Knowledge: Selected Interviews and Other Writings 1972–1977*. Brighton: Harvester Press.

Hall, Rodney Bruce. 1997. "Moral Authority as a Power Resource." *International Organization* 51, no. 4 (Autumn): 591–622.

Hasenclever, Andreas, Peter Mayer, and Volker Rittberger. 1997. *Theories of International Regimes*. Cambridge: Cambridge University Press.

IANSA [International Action Network on Small Arms]. 2017. *3D Printed Firearms: A History of Their Creation, Distribution and Efforts at Restriction*, authored by Gwilym Roberts Harry. Briefing Paper. https://92054894-4da4-47e4-9276-4b6cfef27021.filesusr.com/ugd/bb4a5b_f34298c623da4167b27f1d5b69e846ab.pdf.

Keck, Margaret E., and Kathryn Sikkink. 1998. *Activists beyond Borders: Advocacy Networks in International Politics*. Ithaca, NY: Cornell University Press.

Krause, Keith. 1992. *Arms and the State: Patterns of Military Production and Trade*. Cambridge: Cambridge University Press.

Radjou, Navi, and Jaideep Prabhu. 2015. *Frugal Innovation: How to do Better with Less*. London: Profile Books.

Risse-Kappen, Thomas. 1994. "Ideas Do not Float Freely: Transnational Coalitions, Domestic Structures, and the End of the Cold War." *International Organization* 48, no. 2 (Spring): 185–214.

Sivakumaran, Sandesh. 2012. *The Law of Non-International Armed Conflict*. Oxford: Oxford University Press.

Strange, Susan. 1994. *States and Markets*. Second edition. London: Pinter.

Tegmark, Max. 2017. *Life 3.0: Being Human in the Age of Artificial Intelligence*. New York: Alfred A. Knopf.

Index

ABM. *See* Anti-Ballistic Missile Treaty
abstract-spatial disarmament, 202
activism, 50–52, 202–205
actors: Berlin Statement for, 174;
   compulsory power for, 32;
   definitions of, 202–205; for
   government, 15–16; institutional
   power for, 30; interaction and, 28;
   moral authority of, 53; new
   humanitarianism for, 45; NGOs as,
   110; ontological pluralization and,
   23; politico-juridically independent,
   30; structural power for, 29. *See also*
   non-state actors
advocacy groups, 110–111, 169–170
AEC. *See* Atomic Energy Commission
Africa, 49, 111–114, 143–145
ahistorical approach, 22
AI. *See* Artificial Intelligence
Amnesty International, 200–202
Analyses of Security Regimes (ASR),
   2–3
Angell, Norman, 50–52
Annan, Kofi, 86
Anti-Ballistic Missile Treaty (ABM),
   127–128, 142
antinuclear humanitarian
   transhistorical bloc, 10, 147
antipersonnel landmines (APLs), 4–6;
   in ATT, 9, 100; CMC and, 72–73,
   85–86; CMs and, 8, 65–66, 70–72,
   76–82, 83–84, 88–90, 90–92, 140,
   171–172, 191–195, 198; conventions
   for, 66–70, 104–105; for military,
   163–165; NGOs against, 108–109;
   Ottawa process for, 11, 175
Arms and the State (Krause), 3
arms control. *See specific topics*
Arms Trade Treaty (ATT), 6, 117; APLs
   in, 9, 100; for Europe, 115; for UN,

116
Artificial Intelligence (AI), 159–160;
   AWS and, 6; risks of, 163; for
   weapons, 168. *See also* Killer Robots
ASR. *See* Analyses of Security Regimes
Atomic Energy Commission (AEC),
   127
ATT. *See* Arms Trade Treaty
Attwood, David, 84–85
Australia, 79
Austria, 172
Austro-Prussian War, 48
authority: of IOs, 111–112; moral, 53,
   84–85; of OSCE, 174
autonomous weapons systems (AWS),
   6, 159–160, 161; future of, 202;
   institutionalization of, 171–172; for
   IOs, 170–171; in media, 167; nuclear
   weapons and, 196–197; regulation
   of, 175–176; SALW and, 194–195,
   198; for security regulation,
   162–166, 168–170; stakeholders of,
   166–167; for stratified global arms
   business, 192–194; tabooization of,
   172–174. *See also* Killer Robots
Axworthy, Lloyd, 85–86

Ban Ki-moon, 110–111
Barton, Clara, 50–52
BASIC. *See* British-American Security
   Information Council
Battlestar Galactica (TV show), 172–174
Berlin Statement, 174
Biological Weapons Convention, 66,
   71–72
biopolitics, 44–45
Boston Dynamics, 168
bracket metatheory thesis, 24
British-American Security Information
   Council (BASIC), 108–109

About the Authors

Nik Hynek is a professor specializing in security studies and affiliated with Metropolitan University Prague and Charles University in Prague. He received his research doctorate from the University of Bradford and was previously affiliated with SIWPS at Columbia University, LSE, ANU, Carleton University, and Ritsumeikan University. He leads the inter-scientific Charles University Research Centre of Excellence "Periculum" (UNCE).

Anzhelika Solovyeva is a lecturer specializing in strategic studies at the Institute of Political Studies, Faculty of Social Sciences at Charles University in Prague. She works as a doctoral researcher at the Charles University Research Centre of Excellence "Periculum" (UNCE). Her forthcoming monograph (with Nik Hynek) is *Militarising Artificial Intelligence: Theory, Technology and Regulation*.